ART IN ANIME

ALSO BY DANI CAVALLARO AND FROM MCFARLAND

CLAMP in Context: A Critical Study of the Manga and Anime (2012)

The Fairy Tale and Anime: Traditional Themes, Images and Symbols at Play on Screen (2011)

The World of Angela Carter: A Critical Investigation (2011)

Anime and the Art of Adaptation: Eight Famous Works from Page to Screen (2010)

Anime and the Visual Novel: Narrative Structure, Design and Play at the Crossroads of Animation and Computer Games (2010)

Magic as Metaphor in Anime: A Critical Study (2010)

The Mind of Italo Calvino: A Critical Exploration of His Thought and Writings (2010)

Anime and Memory: Aesthetic, Cultural and Thematic Perspectives (2009)

The Art of Studio Gainax: Experimentation, Style and Innovation at the Leading Edge of Anime (2009)

Anime Intersections: Tradition and Innovation in Theme and Technique (2007)

The Animé Art of Hayao Miyazaki (2006)

The Cinema of Mamoru Oshii: Fantasy, Technology and Politics (2006)

Art in Anime

The Creative Quest as Theme and Metaphor

Dani Cavallaro

McFarland & Company, Inc., Publishers
Jefferson, North Carolina, and London

LIBRARY OF CONGRESS CATALOGUING-IN-PUBLICATION DATA

Cavallaro, Dani.
    Art in anime : the creative quest as theme and
metaphor / Dani Cavallaro.
        p.   cm.
    Includes bibliographical references and index.

    ISBN 978-0-7864-6561-3
    softcover : acid free paper ∞

    1. Animated films — Japan — Themes, motives.   2. Art
and motion pictures — Japan.   3. Creation (Literary, artistic,
etc.) in motion pictures.   I. Title.
NC1766.J3C385 2012
791.43′340952 — dc23   2011047935

BRITISH LIBRARY CATALOGUING DATA ARE AVAILABLE

© 2012 Dani Cavallaro. All rights reserved

*No part of this book may be reproduced or transmitted in any form
or by any means, electronic or mechanical, including photocopying
or recording, or by any information storage and retrieval system,
without permission in writing from the publisher.*

Front cover design by David K. Landis (Shake It Loose
Graphics)

Manufactured in the United States of America

*McFarland & Company, Inc., Publishers
    Box 611, Jefferson, North Carolina 28640
        www.mcfarlandpub.com*

To Paddy, with love and gratitude

Contents

Preface 1

1 — Cultural Perspectives 5
2 — The Search for a Language 58
3 — Mythopoeia 110
4 — Performance and Visuality 156

Filmography 217
Appendix: Japanese Art Periods Timeline 224
Bibliography 225
Index 231

Imagination will often carry us to worlds that never were. But without it we go nowhere. — Carl Sagan

Preface

The quality that we call beauty ... must always grow from the realities of life.—
Junichirou Tanizaki

The critical study of anime's relationship with art constitutes a twofold enterprise. On the one hand, it explores anime's representation of characters pursuing diverse artistic activities and cognate aesthetic visions. This aspect of the discussion focuses closely on the concepts of creativity, talent, expressivity and experimentation, and on the dialectical interplay of personal dreams and public expectations. On the other hand, the analysis engages with anime's own artistry, proposing that those characters' endeavors provide metaphors for the aims and objectives pursued by anime itself as an ever-evolving art form. The thematic deployment of arty personae fuels anime's self-reflexive proclivities, enabling it to articulate an elaborate metacommentary on its own technical procedures.

As a vital component of the animated image, art straddles numerous genres and the shows here explored accordingly belong to categories as varied as romance, comedy, slice of life drama, science fiction, bildungsroman and school drama. Characters with artistic propensities have inhabited anime for a long time. However, anime's dual involvement with art in the terms delineated above is a relatively recent phenomenon. This has most likely been triggered by the intensification of the form's theoretical, philosophical and, most crucially, self-referential tendencies over the past decade. The chosen titles are therefore drawn mainly from that period. Some of these are foregrounded as principal case studies, whereas others are treated as ancillary or background materials.

The book comprises four chapters. The first chapter, "Cultural Perspectives," examines anime's concurrently thematic and technical engagement with the concept of art, promoting a comprehensive and multibranching approach to this concept as a fundamental definer of both the treatment of art in anime and of the conception of art embedded in Japanese culture at large. The discussion encompasses an assessment of four key aspects of Japanese culture and art: their hybrid identity, their resolutely anti-mimetic proclivities, their conceptual underpinnings in salient Eastern philosophies, and their material expression in the guise of specific objects and symbols.

The second chapter, "The Search for a Language," focuses on the ways in which diverse individuals strive to externalize their talent, creativity and expressivity by recourse to particular artistic discourses. It is through the progressive discovery and appropriation of a body of tools, techniques and rules — and, no less importantly, of the desire to propose new ones by challenging convention — that artistic endeavor transcends the stagnant pond of mere training and imitation.

With the third chapter, "Mythopoeia," the analysis turns to the significance of the creative practices dramatized and embodied by anime as means of ideating novel mythologies which articulate simultaneously both contemporary encodings of emerging (and even controversial) cultural meanings, and revivals of time-honored narratives and underlying belief systems. Mythologies, in this perspective, stand out at once as conservative repositories of tradition and as experimental sites of interrogation and resistance. This does not mean that everything contemporary automatically militates in favor of positive change, and everything traditional in favor of stuffy conformism: in fact, thought-provoking theses might emanate from an imaginative reassessment of the old no less than from cutting-edge manipulations of the new. Moreover, invoking tradition does not necessarily amount to visual or stylistic citation. In fact, as the internationally acclaimed architect Kenzo Tange maintains, we often find that "the role of tradition is that of a catalyst, which furthers a chemical reaction, but is no longer detectable in the end result. Tradition can, to be sure, participate in a creation, but it can no longer be creative itself" (in Lim, p. 31).

The fourth chapter, "Performance and Visuality," concentrates on the dialectical interplay of these two concepts. It proceeds from the premise that Japanese culture is intensely visual and that all levels of its social and economic structure, accordingly, are saturated with images. The ascendancy of visuality is confirmed by the privileged place accorded by Japanese art to a wide range of both ancient and new-fangled patterns, emblems, symbols and stylized figures. In contemporary Japan, the abiding vivacity of the country's visual sensibility at the globalized and traditional ends of the representational spectrum is incarnated by the overpowering amount of graphic data bombarding the sensorium in Tokyo's shopping quarters, on the one hand, and the gentler but likewise awesome flow of long-established imagery regaling the visitor's eye in Kyoto, on the other. However one might choose to define anime itself, one cannot fail to pay heed to its reliance on distinctive visual codes and conventions which render its products recognizable as such despite the stunning diversity of possible styles evinced by the form over the decades. Anime, in this respect, represents a relatively modern manifestation of what is actually an age-old preference evident in the pictorial nature of Japan's writing systems, and particularly *kanji*, as not only a conceptual system of signification but also an eminently corporeal reality.

Concomitantly, Japanese culture is eager to underscore the performative qualities of all artistic practices and of all the materials these employ as bodily presences in their own right alongside — and often over and above — their communicative and expressive capabilities. This position is especially crucial in the case of a medium which, like anime, is designed for performance. What several of the anime here studied, specifically, seek to emphasize is the performative energy not solely of their actors but also of the graphic, chromatic and auditory elements of the image. For instance, their handling of line indicates that this is not considered just as a vehicle but rather as a performer of autonomous standing endowed with life and even sentience. The overall quality of a production is ultimately no less dependent on the power of its lines than on its narrative or dramatic content — just as in the era of classical Japanese poetry, the paper on which a poem was written was deemed no less instrumental in the communication of its literary worth than its words.

Even though this study utilizes anime as its focal medium, it suggests that its key arguments and hypotheses carry cross-cultural resonance. Therefore, they are potentially of interest not solely to anime fans but also to anyone willing to address the relationship between animation per se and the phenomenon of image-making at large. In order to exemplify this proposition, the book incorporates succinct allusions to animators originating in areas other than anime. These include the pioneering silhouette animator Lotte Reiniger (Chapter 2), puppet animators Jiří Trnka and Kihachirou Kawamoto (Chapter 3), and the acclaimed screen wizards Yuri Norstein and Sylvain Chomet (Chapter 4).

Chapter 1

CULTURAL PERSPECTIVES

In writing about traditional Asian aesthetics, the conventions of Western discourse — order, logical progression, symmetry — impose upon the subject an aspect that does not belong to it. Among other ideas, Eastern aesthetics suggests that ordered structure contrives, that logical exposition falsifies, and that linear, consecutive argument eventually limits. — Donald Richie

The Object of Study

Inspired by the writings of Jacques Derrida, this study operates on the assumption that the sheer presence of the *grapheme* — as written character, as drawn mark or simply as a scratch, provided that it is intentionally created — signals the existence of the sign-making drive and hence of culture (Derrida 1981; 1998). Signs produce cultures as there is no known or imaginable culture without signs. This contention is here extended to propose that no sign can be produced in the absence of a creative urge, however inchoate or embryonic. In this regard, creativity is no less vital a definer of culture than the making of signs: creativity produces culture by triggering semiosis. Thus, if culture is a product of signs and signs, in turn, are a product of creativeness, no genuine culture is feasible — either as a concept or as a social reality — without the desire to create.

"Art," in the framework of this study, is conceived of in the broadest imaginable sense of the word, in full consonance with Japanese aesthetics, and therefore evaluated with reference to practices as disparate as drawing, painting, calligraphy, sculpture, pottery, drama, fiction writing, photography, film, music, gardening, ornamental horticulture, floral design, gastronomy, dance, acrobatics, fashion design, architecture and interior design — always reserving room for additional disciplines. One of the fundamental aesthetic principles underpinning this book, therefore, is the idea that any human activity entailing creative production constitutes "art." This stance renders conventional distinctions of the Western ilk between artistic and artisanal engagement quite spurious. Even practices as seemingly supplementary as ornamentation, in fact, can hold vital significance as manifestations of creativeness and imagination. The vital importance of ornamentation in Japanese art is illustrated, for example, by the role which indigenous architecture accords to the *nageshi*, the horizontal bracing component of a building, on the basis not merely of its practical function but also of its ability to create beautiful patterns by intersecting with corners and pillars and thus standing out as an aesthetic entity of autonomous caliber. Similarly, the deep eave overhang is employed both for its exterior visual impact and to dim the atmosphere of interiors by encouraging the propagation of diffused and mellow lighting.

If the idea that any creative activity deserves to be called art is axial to this book, likewise significant is the concomitant aesthetic tenet whereby all art is considered material: i.e., a process of direct involvement with corporeal substances grounded in nature. The physical act of creation and the sheer labor which this involves are more significant than the finished artifact. The everyday actions which surround the creative activity at all times and often motivate the production of particular objects carry greater value than the objects housed within the fortress of the museological establishment. Hence, any claim to the ethereally transcendental character of artistic genius is no less irrelevant to this context than the arts/crafts binary. In light of Japan's Shintoist beliefs, this position also implies that anything material ought to be understood as (at least latently) animate. Both the comprehensive conception of art and the regard for the material dimension are sustained by an intimate and generous relationship with nature — and, most importantly, with the *ki*, the spirit intrinsic in all entities.

In its capacious purview of the concept of art and attendant emphasis on the material dimension, contemporary Japanese art still reveals the influence of the *Mingei* (Folk Crafts) Movement promoted in the 1920s by the philosopher Muneyoshi Yanagi. Triggered by the alienating and atomizing impact of industrialization on traditional notions of culture and identity, the *Mingei* blends Western and Eastern perspectives in a typically Japanese syncretic move. As Rupert Faulkner explains, "Yanagi's thought combines two main elements. One derives from the social and moral concerns expressed in the writings of William Morris and other thinkers whose views contributed to the British Arts and Crafts movement in the late nineteenth century. The other, an essentially mystical attitude towards perception and aesthetic appraisal, derives from Yanagi's experience of various forms of oriental philosophy" (Faulkner, p. 160). In its pursuit of both of these conceptual strands, the *Mingei*'s prime objective is the union of practical beauty and the timeless appeal of everyday artisanal design.

A particularly interesting facet of the artistic landscape here addressed is music. Accordingly, the significance of this art is consistently underscored throughout the three chapters to follow. Music clearly plays a major role as a topos and structural foundation in several of the chosen productions, and particularly in the titles elected as pivotal case studies. However, this is not the only reason for according it a prominent place. No less importantly, this study seeks to emphasize how music has repeatedly colluded with other arts throughout history — and not solely those performing arts in which it is literally deployed as a constituent (e.g., drama, dance, opera). In fact, music has also engaged in an ongoing dialogue with the visual arts by providing them with a virtually endless repertoire of themes and symbols, and by drawing inspiration in turn from their compositional and chromatic techniques as the basis of its own experiments. At the same time, painters have endeavored to translate musical forms and rhythms into visual signs, while composers have sought to articulate visual motifs in their creations. Relatedly, there are numerous instances both of visual works inspired by musical compositions and of musical works inspired by pictures. This is obviously not the place to indulge in an exhaustive taxonomy of such works — even assuming that such a task were realistically feasible. Even a handful of examples of musical-visual influences occurring in both directions is, however, sufficient to indicate the thematic and chronological breadth of the phenomenon.

The ample clan of visual works based on music include Henri Fantin-Latour's fantasy and mythological paintings, inspired by Wagner, Berlioz, Brahms and Schumann; Gustav Klimt's *Beethoven's Frieze*, a monumental fresco aiming to capture the spirit of the composer's music and specifically of his Ninth Symphony in D minor; Georges Braque's Cubist works, which make explicit reference to Bach by means of words or images (e.g., *Aria de Bach*); Marc Chagall's painting for the ceiling of the Opéra Garnier in Paris, stimulated by Mozart's *Magic Flute*, Berlioz's symphony *Roméo et Juliette*, Wagner's *Tristan und Isolde*, Debussy's *Pelléas et Mélisande*, Ravel's *Daphnis et Chloé*, Stravinsky's *Fire Bird*, Tchaikovsky's *Swan Lake*, Adam's *Giselle* and Mussorgsky's *Boris Godunov*. The likewise copious array of musical works based on visual artifacts includes Franz Liszt's piano piece *Lo Sposalizio*, based on Raphael's painting *The Betrothal of the Virgin*; Sergei Rachmaninov's symphonic poem *Island of the Dead*, a musical rendition of Arnold Böcklin's painting *Die Toteninsel*; Modeste Mussorgsky's *Pictures at an Exhibition*, a suite in ten movements portraying an imaginary tour of an art exhibition prompted by the public display of works from the collection of his late friend Viktor Hartmann; Enrique Granados' *Goyescas*, Op. 11, subtitled *Los majos enamorados* (*The Gallants in Love*), a piano suite inspired by the paintings of Francisco Goya.

The interplay of music and the visual arts is further attested to by their use of shared concepts and terminology (e.g., note, harmony, color, tone, contrast, gradation, scale). As will be argued at several junctures throughout this book, musical-visual relations constitute a key aspect of anime's explorations of creativity. This is a logical corollary of the intrinsic nature of the medium of anime itself as an eminently visual form whose ability to create the illusion of movement depends on sonoric no less than dynamic effects — as demonstrated not only by the musical scores per se but also by the development of increasingly refined lip-syncing and dubbing techniques. The synergy between music and the visual arts acquires unrivaled significance in the context of anime concerned specifically with the representation of diverse creative activities (and germane aesthetic perspectives) insofar as it is here afforded a unique opportunity for vivid and palpable dramatization. This allows it to transcend the level of exclusively theoretical abstraction, and hence reach wider and more diversified audiences. Therefore, if the synergy of music and the visual arts is greatly pertinent to the medium of anime at large, this phenomenon can be deemed most relevant to anime engaged with art both as a theme and as the basis of self-referential reflection.

The productions here examined assiduously show that the visual arts harbor an acoustic dimension as the shapes, hues and patterns of motion of which their images consist work together to emit sensory vibrations akin to waves of sound. Simultaneously, they throw into relief the visual dimension of music as an art reliant on both textual imagery (at the level of notation) and dramatic imagery (at the level of embodied enactment). In the process, the anime remind us that throughout history, art forms and media which we now tend to regard as discrete have in fact coalesced in variable constellations in accordance with context-bound social expectations and ideological requirements. The boundaries which today we perceive to be separating different arts are themselves cultural constructs associated with specific times and places, not universal givens or immutable essences. The very etymology of the word "music" confirms this proposition, since the Greek word *mousike* originally designated any "art of the Muses" and not only the field we have come to think of as music — i.e., a fundamentally auditory artistic phenomenon. In articulating these messages, the chosen anime cumulatively convey a vision of artistic multifacetedness which aptly mirrors Japanese art's motley constitution and its attendant penchant for compositeness and bricolage. With this vision, they communicate a tantalizing interpretation of the concept of creativity itself as described by Simon Shaw-Miller: "rather than thinking of purity at all, it might be better to see hybridity as the more natural state for art, because purity is a historical contingency, whereas hybridity is part of the flux of creativity itself: the putting of things together" (Shaw-Miller, p. 27).

The perception of color and the perception of sound have been intimately interconnected since ancient times. Given the semiotic preeminence of color in anime's language system, this particular aspect of the synergy between music and the visual arts constitutes an especially fascinating object of study in the present context. Theoretical speculations concerning the existence of essential affinities between the chromatic and the sonoric domains can be traced back to classical antiquity. As John Gage explains, "some Greek theorists considered 'colour' (*chroia*) to be a quality of sound itself, together with pitch and duration; it may have been thought akin to what we now describe as timbre. What most impressed the Greeks, it seems, was the capacity of colour, like sound, to be articulated in a series of regularly changing stages whose differences were perceptible in an equally regular way.... By Plato's time the description of melody as 'coloured' had become part of a professional jargon.... Conversely, the musical terms 'tone' and 'harmony' soon became integrated into the critical vocabulary of colour in visual art" (Gage, p. 227). Aristotle's writings bear witness to the popularity of these ideas, proposing that bright and dark hues find direct parallels in clear and hushed sounds. Concurrently, the philosopher maintains that "it is possible that colours may stand in relation to each other in the same manner as concords in music, for the colours which are (to each other) in proportion corresponding with musical concords are those which appear to be most agreeable" (cited in Goethe, p. 418). Furthermore, the Greeks were careful to differentiate the effects likely to be evoked by the diatonic scale as opposed to the chromatic scale on emotive and moral grounds. While the former tended to be associated with a sense of constancy and firmness, the latter was seen to carry connotations of instability and flightiness.

Since ancient times, the theoretical issues entailed by the interdisciplinary encounter of disparate arts, and especially of music and the visual arts, is intimately bound up with the phenomenon of synaesthesia, the simultaneous perception of parallel aesthetic systems whereby colors can be perceived as melodies and sounds, in turn, can be visualized as endowed with chromatic attributes. This concept will be revisited later in this chapter with reference to Charles Baudelaire and his interpretation of the interrelated concepts of metaphor, imagination and musicality. One of the most ancient portrayals of the synaesthetic nature of color-sound relations can be witnessed in Plato's myth of Er in Book X of the *Republic*, where each of the eight classical planets is ascribed a particular color and matched with a tone sung by a siren. Insofar as the eight tones sung by the sirens combine to give rise to a single harmony, the synaesthetic fusion of color and sound is here invested with the capacity to ensure the ultimate equilibrium of the cosmos at large. This concept will be again alluded to in the analyses of the anime *Touka Gettan* (Chapter 3) and *Nodame Cantabile* (Chapter 4).

Wassily Kandinsky (whose theories will shortly be returned to) intriguingly compares synaesthesia to "an echo or reverberation," whereby a sense impression communicates itself from one sense organ to another, "such as occurs sometimes in musical instruments which, without being touched, sound in harmony with some instruments struck at the moment." Commenting on the types of cross-sensory events entailed by synaesthesia, the artist observes: "many colours have been described as rough or sticky, others as smooth and uniform, so that one feels inclined to stroke them.... Some colours appear soft (rose madder), others hard (cobalt green, blue-green oxide), so that even fresh from the tube they seem to be dry. The expression 'scented colours' is frequently met with. And finally the sound of colours is so definite that it would be hard to find anyone who would try to express bright yellow in the bass notes, or dark lake in the treble" (Kandinsky 1977, p. 25). In addition, Kandinsky draws attention to the affinity between certain hues and the distinctive timbre of diverse musical instruments. "Violet," for instance, is described as having "an air of something sickly, something extinguished about it" which makes its "deeper tones" germane to those of the "lower woodwind (e.g., the bassoon)" (cited in Vergo, p. 175). "Dark red," as Peter Vergo observes, was associated with "the sound of the cello in its lower register, and yellow and blue with the lower tones of the violin" (Vergo, p. 175).

A key moment in the history of the synergy between sound and color is indubitably the sixteenth century, when colors came to be associated more intimately than ever before with sonoric properties while painters were increasingly compared to musicians in their ability to evoke those attributes. The achievement of a delightful chromatic balance in the pictorial sphere was thus considered analogous to the pleasurable execution of a song. Groundbreaking developments in the field of optics during the following century gave new impetus to the pursuit of adventurous color-sound syntheses. Concomitantly, as Gage emphasizes, "the extended and more coherent colour-scales of the Baroque made it possible to devise more complete correspondences with musical scales," with the result that "combinations of colours" could be held to "have harmonic relationships with each other" (Gage, p. 232). In the early modern period, the most influential interpretation of the relationship between color and sound emanates from Isaac Newton's *Opticks* (1704), where it is proposed that the seven colors of the spectrum and the seven notes in a diatonic scale are closely related.

The analogy between color and sound promulgated by Johann Wolfgang von Goethe with his *Farbenlehre* (*Theory of Colours*) of 1810 resonates even more powerfully with the aesthetic vision offered by the medium of anime insofar as the dedication to natural phenomena which this form inherits from its parent culture finds a felicitous correlative in the enticing water imagery employed by the German author to animate his own message. "Colour and sound," argues Goethe, "do not admit of being directly compared together but both are referable to a higher formula.... They are like two rivers which have taken their source in one and the same mountain, but subsequently pursue their way under totally different regions" (Goethe, pp. 298–299). Moreover, even though Goethe's *Theory of Colours* may be scientifically questionable, it is of immense relevance to artists insofar as it accords considerable importance to the subjective nature of the reception and processing of colors. Thus, whereas Newton had approached color as a fundamentally physical problem, Goethe argues that the sensations of color entering the human brain are also created by personal perception. Romantic art, in particular, was greatly inspired by Goethe's emphasis on the subjectivity of experience, which implicitly acknowledges the part played by imagination and speculation in the shaping of empirical reality. The interdisciplinary interpretation of art proposed by several of the anime under scrutiny recalls the Romantic take on of the multidimensionality of art, and attendant promotion of an integrated creative gesture.

In more recent times, the quest for an art capable of synthesizing and interrelating disparate disciplines and spheres of creativity finds some of its most influential proponents of all times in the artists associated with the avant-garde circle of Der Blaue Reiter ("The Blue Rider"), and especially Franz Marc, Kandinsky and Paul Klee. The positions emerging from this context are here worthy of detailed consideration given their underlying pertinence to the dynamics of the medium of animation itself. Especially notable, in this respect, is the suggestion that the notes, shades and vibrations radiated by melodies and color arrangements share spiritual and affective powers. In animation, the musical powers of sounds and chroma alike sustain the orchestration of motion, and hence the conception of that illusion of movement—and life—by which the art is essentially defined. Colors have the potential to radiate like waves in music. Inspired by the musical experiments of Arnold Schoenberg, Marc rejects conventional notions of harmony and thus achieves the equivalent of dissonance in his treatment of color in painting. Of more immediate pertinence to this discussion are Kandinsky's writings. Seeking to disengage painting from the strictures of representationalism in order to enable artists to express their inner lives and visions in non-material guises, Kandinsky champions a type of painting which is capable of incorporating the lessons of music into its most fundamental procedures. "Colour is the keyboard, the eyes are the hammers, the soul is the piano with many strings," Kandinsky famously proclaims. "The artist is the hand which plays, touching one key or another, to cause vibrations in the soul" (Kandinsky 1977, p. 25). As argued later, Japanese art is guided by markedly non-mimetic propensities, and is thus capable of engendering an atmosphere of evocative spirituality which, even when it is inhabited by recognizable forms from nature, strives toward abstract abstraction.

In his writings on the relationship between music and the visual arts, Klee proposes that "both art forms are defined by time" (Klee, p. 640). Time is also the very principle governing the creation and functioning of the art of animation itself. This contention is memorably conveyed by Richard Williams' seminal volume *The Animator's Survival Kit* as follows: "our work is taking place in *time*. We've taken our 'stills' and leapt into another dimension" (Williams, p. 11). Norman McLaren, relatedly, proposes a direct correspondence between music and animation: "music is organized in terms of small phrases, bigger phrases, sentences, whole movements and so on. To my mind, animation is the same kind of thing" (cited in McWilliams, p. 29). In the specific case of anime, the temporal dimension holds distinctive significance due to the form's reliance on a kind of so-called "limited" animation whereby the generation of the illusion of movement — and hence of a temporal process — depends more on the deft employment of appropriate camera moves than on the actual number of frames included. One of the animator's chief objectives is to emulate the impression of change over time without having to rely on too many drawings. The fascination with creative gestures capable of crossing dimensional and spatial barriers is likewise central to Klee's vision. Since the world has no finite reality, the artist should feel free to interpret it in the most playful and uninhibited manner — hence the ludic feel of so many of the artist's pictorial and graphic fantasies. Whereas Klee opts for play and humor as the tools best suited to the celebration of art's world-building power, Kandinsky's cosmic vision conveys the same fundamental message in more dramatic tones (arguably congruous with the artist's liking for Wagner). "Painting," according to Kandinsky, is nothing less than "a thunderous collision of differing worlds; a clash whose outcome is the creation of a new world which we call a work of art. Technically, each piece comes into being just like the earth was made — from catastrophes which can produce, out of the cacophony of instruments, a symphony, which is called the music of the spheres. The creation of a work of art is the creation of a world" (Kandinsky 1955, p. 25).

Some of Klee's most enterprising chromatic experiments, conducted through the medium of watercolor, are particularly relevant to anime (such as *Honey and Clover*, *Nodame Cantabile* and *Kimikiss Pure Rouge*, to cite just some of the major titles) in which this same technique is prevalent. In describing his methodology in the context of his *Diaries*, the artist states: "I studied the tonal values found in nature by adding layer upon layer of a thin black watercolour wash. Each layer has to be thoroughly dry. This produces a mathematically proportioned light to dark ratio" (Klee, p. 840). The artist would

1—Cultural Perspectives

then combine the tone-values thus obtained with shades of color, utilizing the rules of musical notation as his guidelines. He thus found that "translating the shadowy image ... into colour means that ... each tone-value corresponds to a single colour. That is to say, do not add white to lighten or black to darken the colours, but use one single colour for one layer. The following layer gets another colour" (p. 879). By working with single colors, Klee felt that he could enable each of them to communicate its presence as pure sound.

In the specific context of anime, the use of layers of watercolor paint is a logical corollary of the nature of animation at large as an assemblage of stacked visual strata. In simplified terms, the affinity between Klee's method and animation can be summed up as follows: just as the various images representing single characters are bound to change as they are superimposed over other sets of drawings representing their settings, so the colors imbuing each layer of watercolor paint are bound to change as they come into incremental contact with other hues. As a compositional method, layering has acquired unprecedented resonance in the domain of contemporary anime thanks to the evolution of technologies obviously unavailable in Klee's days. In computer-assisted anime production, drawings are usually scanned into the computer, digitally inked and painted, superimposed over appropriate backgrounds and finally computer-animated. The movements of discrete portions of a character's body are drawn and scanned in separately, as are the backgrounds and any moving objects within them.

While most anime studios favor 2D graphics as a distinctive marker of their medium's aesthetics, the digital programs available today enable them to generate highly effective 3D solids and 3D optical effects, such as shadows, reflections and refractions, when required. Tools of this kind are utilized, for example, in the design and animation of numerous frames representing musical instruments and the relevant body parts associated with their playing in *La Corda d'Oro* and *Nodame Cantabile*. However, it is important to recognize that 2D graphics themselves have the capacity both to convey the impression of depth by pasting the separate layers onto the virtual canvas in a certain order, and to evoke particular lighting effects by endowing those layers with different chromatic gradients, levels of opacity, transparence or translucence. Digital layering enables anime to play with single colors in novel ways, and thus develop ever-changing strategies to release their sonoric essences. The medium's overriding, yet tastefully understated, goal, in this respect, is the accomplishment of a polyphony wherein distinct fields of color, by being allowed to coalesce in both intentional and aleatory fashions, may initiate a concurrently acoustic and visual experience of harmony.

It is also worth noting, at this point, that Klee's black watercolor paintings often bring to mind the art of *sumi-e* (ink painting) and its uniquely evocative employment of an entirely monochrome palette. The poetic portrayal of this art offered in the website *Prairiewoods* is especially apposite in this context: "all civilizations leave an imprint of their lives: figures on rock, stone, or paper.... *Sumi-e* embraces the history of language, memory, and the desire to leave behind a trace ... *Sumi-e*, like any art form, is about a sense of transitions, about transformations. The objective of *sumi-e* is not to recreate a subject to look perfectly like the original, but to capture its essence — that is, to express its essence. This is achieved not with more but with less. Therefore, useless details are omitted and every brush stroke contains meaning and purpose. There is no dabbling or going back to make corrections. The strokes themselves, then, are said to serve as a good metaphor for life itself. That is, there is no moment except for this moment" ("The Spirit of Sumi-e: An Introduction to East Asian Brush Painting"). The very essence of *sumi-e* can be seen to reverberate through anime's multifarious explorations of creativity. (This quintessentially Japanese art form will be revisited in the course of this discussion.) Another important parallel between music and the visual arts underscored by Klee, of which anime indubitably partakes, is their shared commitment to the value of rhythm as the basis of movement in time. The critical significance held by this principle in the art of animation at large can hardly be overestimated. Even more pertinent to the specific field of anime, given the preponderance of two-dimensional visuals in this form, is Klee's concurrent emphasis on the power of line. As Hajo Dütching explains, the "analysis of line" provides the foundation of the artist's "theory of form." According to Klee, "there are 'active, medial and passive lines' as well as positive and negative planar elements resulting from them ... the free play of interplaying lines is able to produce the most varied forms of expression ranging from tranquility to turbulence" (Dütching, p. 33).

Not only is the imaginative manipulation of the elemental concept of the line pivotal to anime's graphic construction: its capacity to generate affective tensions between the most disparate states also echoes an aesthetic preference embedded in Japanese art itself for time immemorial. This is inspired by one of the most fundamental tenets of Buddhist and Shinto philosophy, which John Reeve describes as an interplay of "serenity and turbulence, spirituality and slaughter" (Reeve, p. 22). Mitsukuni Yoshida, relatedly, observes: "even the most glorious life will end in darkness and death; holiness and profanity, splendour and gloom form the dual basis of man's culture" (Yoshida 1980, p. 22). On both planes, one perceives an unaffected desire to approach reality as a process of unrelenting flux — as impermanence (*mujou*) — and therefore as continually embroiled in multifarious cycles of birth, death and rebirth. Images of the Indian guru Daruma, said to have introduced Zen Buddhism, supply a cogent example of the tendency to bring together conflicting affects, presenting the venerable figure as comparable at once to a "death-dealing knife" and to a "life-giving blow" (thirteenth-century Chinese poem cited in Reeve, p. 27). This antibinary attitude is replicated by the artistic handling of the line itself, which enables it to communicate simultaneously a soothing sense of composure and a galvanizing surge of dynamism. Elegant lines, ingeniously juxtaposed with swathes of bold hues, have time and again colluded in the exploration of audacious approaches to composition and perspective.

Concurrently, graphic composition frequently resorts to powerful diagonals in order to imbue otherwise static locations with vitality and energy. In both traditional Japanese art and anime, the geometric lines used to dynamize the inanimate elements of space are often additionally enlivened by their combination with imaginary lines defined by character interaction as a network of intersecting gestural and verbal exchanges — or merely wordless glances. In the process, cadenced impressions of kinesis and stasis fluidly alternate, and the spectator's eye is prompted to travel not only across the space of the frame but also beyond it. Nevertheless, the visuals' punctilious attention to details ensures that there is always sufficient material for the eye to rest upon, and hence prevents their rushed consumption. On countless occasions, the sense of space is more effectively evoked by recourse to subtle linear intimations of motion than through a blunt differentiation between figure and ground. No less effective is the handling of converging or even clashing lines to suggest scenarios of strife and turmoil and so intensify the impression of menace. At its most intense, this technique serves to convey the feeling that the threat is about to break through the surface of the picture — or through the screen itself — to invade the viewer's private space, transforming the visual plane into a door incautiously left ajar for darkness to creep in.

One of the main areas of Japanese art in which a musical sensibility makes itself felt most distinctively consists of its approach to the visual as a search for chromatic harmonies. Color is here regarded as a sign system underlying both the visual arts and music. In its perception of color, Japanese culture asserts its twin sense of rhythm and balance most distinctively, revealing an unmatched sensitivity to the impact of the minutest nuances of chroma on the evocation of different moods. Japan's conception and rendition of color was initially influenced by Chinese philosophy and art. An especially influential role was played, in this matter, by the theory of the Five Elements or Five Movements (*Wu Xing*), and by Chinese artists' own translation of that theory into chromatic symbols. As Yoshida explains, contemporary Japanese culture still honors the elemental hues inherited from ancient China, "blue, red, yellow, white and black," and their association with the primary substances of "wood, fire, earth, metal and water" of which the entire universe is held to consist by the followers of *Wu Xing*. However, Japan's own chromatic ethos has been independently shaped by a profound fascination with "the beauty of the intermediate shades that lie between the five colours," and an attendant appreciation of "the aesthetic value of the harmonious mixture that results when they are combined with one another." Contributing vitally to "the emergence of a feeling for elegance and grace," this sensibility finds inception with "the ladies of the Heian period ... who were the first to discover and develop an appreciation of the beauty of these blended colours" (Yoshida 1980, p. 19).

Heian culture was indubitably blighted by lack of political foresight and, as Ivan Morris emphasizes, by "an imbalance of energies poured into intellectual and artistic pursuits" at the expense of more pragmatic concerns (Morris, p. 6). This mentality was conducive to decadent mores, self-indulgence and, eventually, to the erosion of Heian culture. It is nonetheless undeniable that the era's achievements in all the arts are quite unique, and indeed constitute so important a chapter in Japanese cultural history as to make the country's artistic heritage unthinkable in the absence of the bountiful harvest they yielded. Moreover, the Heian period's simultaneous "delight in the aesthetic joys of the world" and apprehension of the "vanity of human pleasures" (p. 13) lies at the root of modern Japanese aesthetics and, by extension, of Japan's artistic influence on other cultures. The collusion of radiance and darkness, an aesthetic predilection inaugurated by the Heian treatment of color, still plays a vital part in contemporary Japanese culture, being especially suited to the expression of a world picture in which the celebration of pleasure and beauty is at all times inextricable from a sincere acknowledgment of their vaporousness.

In Heian culture, the fascination with harmonious chromatic gradations and blends manifested itself most spectacularly in the realm of sartorial fashion as an axial facet of social existence and gender-coded embodiment. Often relying on hues that do not have precise equivalents in any Western language — and of which not even contemporary Japanese people would necessarily know the names — the Heian age cultivated a vestimentary sensibility in which the art of juxtaposing different shades in both the manufacture and the donning of costumes held unrivaled significance. The particular cult of beauty enshrined in this attitude found its supreme expression in the *juunihitoe* (literally, "twelve-layer robe"), an elaborate kind of kimono which first came into fashion in the tenth century and rapidly established itself as the crux of female courtly fashion. The orchestration of the *juunihitoe*'s layers and the harmonization of its hues in particular sequences constituted twin skills in a complex art in its own right, abiding by at least two hundred rules. Of special notice, in the current context, is the tendency to identify the various colors by means of poetic designations inspired directly by the seasonal cycles. As the essay "Kimono History" explains, "certain colors" were "associated with November to February" and were known as "*ume-gasane* or 'shades of the plum blossom.' Such kimonos were white on the outside and red on the inside. For March and April there was a combination called 'shades of wisteria,' a kimono with lavender outside and a blue lining. Winter and Spring had their own set with an outer garment of yellow and orange. The colors were set to mirror the seasons and their moods, showing just how closely the Japanese were attuned to the world of nature around them" ("Kimono History: The Heian Era"). While its symphonic complexity may seem sufficient to explain the *juunihitoe*'s enduring charisma, no less resonant is the silent music of plurichromatic waves radiated by its interacting layers — a melody which invites the imagination to visualize its power to imbue even the duskiest of ancient rooms with dancing iridescent light.

Relatedly, the commitment to harmonious orchestration underpins the language and art of smell. Heian attitudes to olfaction indicate that this sense, often treated as the Cinderella of the sensorium in the West due to its markedly close connection with the body and its functions, in fact represents an aesthetically sophisticated and culturally esteemed expressive vehicle. Women's garments were studiously imbued with delicate incense blends intended to express the wearers' individuality by means of their metonymic association with particular fragrances. Therefore, while aristocratic ladies and female members of the royal retinue were not permitted to exhibit their faces in public, they could assert their unique presence through the olfactory trails which they left in their wake — an inevitable corollary of the tendency to wear (and even sleep in) the same garments for often protracted periods of time. According to Aileen Gatten, the sense of smell is still accorded considerable significance in contemporary Japanese culture. This is borne out the practice of the incense ceremony, or *Genji-kou*: a ritualized parlor game combining "the matching of rare sensations" with "easy sociability." This practice harks back to Heian culture and to its establishment of the art of smell as a vital building-block of aristocratic etiquette which demanded as much training and dedication as the cultivation of calligraphic, poetic and musical talents. Just as the colors used in the arrangement of the *juunihitoe*'s layers correspond figuratively to different times of the year, so the encoding of the art of olfaction revolves around six fundamental fragrances, each of which is equated to a particular season. "Plum Blossom is linked with spring, Lotus Leaf with summer, Chamberlain with the autumn wind, and Black with deepest winter" (Gatten, p. 37). In the arts of both sartorial fashion and olfactory appreciation, therefore, musical effects are conjured up through the graceful handling of sign systems which, though unrelated to the auditory dimension in any literal sense, are capable of releasing symbolic melodies of timeless appeal.

While it is useful to appreciate the relevance of music, by metaphorical analogy, even to anime which do not employ this art as their thematic focus, it is also important to acknowledge the pervasive presence across anime of certain artistic practices of eminently social significance — most notably, architecture, interior design, fashion design and gastronomy. Even when these arts do not explicitly constitute an anime's focal object of presentation or analysis, insofar as thematic emphasis falls in fact on quite a distinct field (such as painting or gardening), they can often be seen to be instrumental in the genesis of a story's world and mood. Thus, they leave their mark not only on anime where the creative voyages of aspiring architects or designers are vibrantly dramatized, but also on anime keen to situate their personae in particular cultural and historical milieux by reference to specific spatial, structural and ornamental attributes or preferences. Those arts' ubiquitous impact results from their power to capture with intense levels of both visibility and concreteness the broader phenomena of aesthetic, ideological and economic change affecting a society. The processes through which buildings, furnishings, garments and dishes are created and through which a culture's tastes, styles and desires are concomitantly shaped speak volumes about the unfolding dynamics of an entire cultural imaginary. Therefore, an anime's interpretation of those arts, interstitial though it might be, can also shed light on its stance toward other artistic fields and related aesthetic perspectives, while supplying useful insights into the historical markers of the periods in which it is set, the types of community which it seeks to bring into relief, and its position on status, age, wealth and gender relations. Above all else, those arts stand out as axial to the construction of meanings and identities (collective and personal alike), and thus to the articulation of elaborate semiotic vocabularies of far-reaching resonance.

Cultural Hybridization

Addressed as a holistic ensemble, anime's engagement with disparate arts echoes the vision pursued by the Japanese Agency for Cultural Affairs, *Bunka-cho*: a special branch of the Ministry of Education established for the purpose of promoting not only indigenous arts and culture but also ongoing cross-cultural interaction. This approach emphasizes that culture cannot be situated in a sealed space and that cultural identities cannot unproblematically coincide with national borders or geographical boundaries. As Commissioner for Cultural Affairs Seiichi Kondo explains, the organization's mission pivots on three essential concepts: the interdependence of "the past, present, and future"; the paramount importance of "creation and development"; the commitment to "preservation and dissemination" (Kondo). These ideas are symbolically encapsulated by the Agency's logo, a set of three interlacing oval rings inspired by the Japanese character for "art," *bun* (文), colored in the traditional hue of cinnabar red. In seeking to capture the essence of the Agency's agenda, the *Bunkacho*'s logo concurrently reflects certain fundamental proclivities which have distinguished Japan's artistic practices and aesthetic sensibility for centuries. Insofar as these ideas underpin the productions here examined, and are therefore likely to elucidate the cumulative frame of reference adopted in this study, they deserve detailed consideration at this juncture.

The image projected by Japanese culture corroborates Chris Barker's hypothesis that the tendency, well embedded in classical cultural studies, to refer to culture as a "whole way of life ... glosses over too many problems," and is therefore powerless to capture the actual complexity and multiaccentuality of the concept. The assumption that culture is wedded to a clearly defined location is particularly spurious, in this matter, since it tends to fuel fundamentally nationalistic values. Japanese culture, in fact, encapsulates to a paradigmatic degree Barker's suggestion that "culture is more profitably thought of in terms of 'fields,' 'flows,' 'knots' involving the continual hybridization of meaningful practices or performances in global space.... To talk about culture as flow, as hybrid, as global, as constellations of temporary coherence ... is to celebrate difference and diversity" (Barker, pp. 66–67). Most importantly, the collusion of past, present and future — allied to a sustained dialogue between creation and development, and between preservation and dissemination — can be said to constitute the foundations of the syncretic approach which typically imbues Japanese art with unique vitality. This outlook does not pursue a homogeneous cultural pattern as its chief objective but rather fosters an ingenious eclecticism in frankly acknowledging the ubiquity in its midst of dualities and divergences. This stance manifests itself as a persistent synthesis of indigenous and global trends, Eastern and Western vogues, tradition and innovation. The aggregational approach, as noted, is central to the philosophy of the *Mingei* movement, and hence to a major influence on modern Japanese art. Of special pertinence to a phenomenon as emphatically global as anime is the Japanese tendency to blend native elements with external influences, as a result of which local traditions simultaneously adapt to, and distinguish themselves from, foreign imports.

Non-native styles are enthusiastically adopted, assimilated and integrated, yet frequently reinterpreted and restyled in ways which serve to impart them with a distinctively Japanese flavor. For example, even during periods of intense Chinese influence on all aspects of Japan's political system and cultural productivity, such as the period spanning the late seventh century to early eighth century, indigenous art exhibited an exhilarating aversion to the mechanical imitation of Chinese styles and techniques. Archeological research shows that this is especially true of areas, such as ceramic manufacture, in which Japan's reputation as a cradle of unparalleled genius and industry began to develop in its very prehistory. A key chapter in Japanese art's self-emancipation from Chinese models in the specifically visual field coincides with the Heian era. At this juncture, Chinese-style painting (*kara-e*) progressively gives way to a distinctively indigenous style (*yamato-e*) in which themes and settings of Chinese derivation are superseded by subjects of overtly native orientation, notably in the rendition of the natural world throughout the seasons, and of renowned Japanese locations dear to the artists' hearts. As Tsuneko S. Sadao and Stephanie Wada point out, "the transformation of culture and art" marking this phase of Japanese history went hand in hand with a "new desire to make a clear distinction between Japanese and Chinese style" which had a special impact on "narrative painting and calligraphy. In a secular context, both of these art forms were closely connected to developments in literature." Both forms, moreover, were pointedly drawn to "episodes from romantic prose stories like lady Murasaki's *The Tale of Genji*" (Sadao and Wada, p. 92).

The horizontal picture scroll (*emakimono* or *emaki*) which evolved in Japan between the eleventh and the sixteenth centuries was particularly suited to narrative unfolding, foreshadowing recent developments of an eminently cinematic stamp and, most notably, the art of animation itself. It is also at this point in history that a special visual sensibility begins to emerge of which traces can still be detected in modern Japanese illustration, advertising, manga and anime. Anime, in particular, is still indebted today to the formal predilection, ushered in by that epochal cultural climate, for techniques capable of evoking a certain mood by primarily compositional means. In much anime, as in the *Genji*-based type of court painting discussed by Sadao and Wada, the environment plays a lead role in defining the tone and rhythms of a specific ambience — so much so that that the dramatic input of individual actors temporarily recedes into the background and no leeway is therefore allowed for gratuitous histrionics. Thus, in both anime and the narrative pictures of the Heian period, we often find that "the atmosphere or emotion of the scene" emanates not so much from the "characters" as from the "composition." In such contexts, "strongly angled lines of architectural elements" prove incomparably efficacious in the evocation of "tension," while "a wind-tossed cluster of foliage" can be proficiently deployed in order to allude to "the grief of a man whose beloved is about to die" (p. 94).

As Reeve argues, "compared with most countries, traditional culture is still remarkably intact and respected in 21st-century Japan — its craft skills, theatre and music, temples and rituals. One reason for its survival is the Japanese ability to fuse the new and the old, the innate and the imported" (Reeve,

p. 8). Thus, while Japanese culture is characterized by a potent element of continuity, the infiltration of local ("innate") traditions by foreign ("imported") voices should never be underestimated. This contention is corroborated by the section on manga, anime and games of the publication *Creative Japan*, issued in 2007 by the Japanese Ministry of Foreign Affairs (MOFA): "it is sometimes said that the Japanese culture of manga, anime and games is simply a continuation of a tradition beginning with religious illustrated scrolls such as the *Choju Jinbutsu Giga* (Scrolls of Frolicking Animals and Humans) drawn in the 12th century and the *ukiyo-e* (woodblock prints) of the Edo period. However, the immediate roots of Japanese pop culture can be traced to the importation of overseas comics and animation after the period of modernisation in the late 19th century onwards, and particularly the period of industrialisation of the anime and manga industry under the influence of the USA after World War II. This fact shows that cultures which transcend borders, languages and religions are the embodiment of a universal trend born out of contact with foreign cultures, much as globally influential impressionist art gained great inspiration from Japanese *ukiyo-e*" (MOFA). An alternative take on this point will shortly be considered with reference to the volume *Japanese Animation from Painted Scrolls to Pokémon*.

It is crucial to appreciate, as the article emphasizes, that the relationship between Japanese culture and Western arts is not a unilateral process but rather a mutually enriching dialogue. As Natalie Avella observes, "many academics and art historians" go so far as to maintain that "Western modernism would not have happened were it not for the Japanese influence." However, Japanese art did not only exert a profound influence on nineteenth-century Western painters as diverse as Édouard Manet, Claude Monet, Henri de Toulouse-Lautrec, Vincent Van Gogh, James Abbott McNeill Whistler and Pierre Bonnard (among several more): it also served as a major source of inspiration for Art Nouveau, especially in the representation of forms and motifs drawn from nature. No less importantly, as Gian Carlo Calza points out, "architects like Bruno Taut, Richard Neutra, Mies van der Rohe, Frank Lloyd Wright, Le Corbusier and Walter Gropius adapted and reinterpreted concepts of space, such as organicity, modularity and fusion with nature, that are characteristic of the Japanese architectural tradition" (Calza, p. 11).

It is also worth noting, incidentally, that in the realm of painting, Whistler's art is relevant to this context by virtue of its hybridization not only of Western and Eastern motifs but also of visual and sonoric codes. This is attested to by the painter's attribution of aesthetic primacy to the principle of tonal harmony, and predilection for titles capable of furthering his vision with notable symbolic conciseness: "symphonies" (usually daylight depictions of beautiful women) "arrangements" (for the most part portraits executed in darker tones), "nocturnes" (dusky seascapes or riverscapes) or simply "harmonies." Whistler's nocturnes are especially worthy of notice in their interpretation of musical-visual relations. Distinguished by a deliberately imprecise and sketchy style, these paintings echo the character of the musical nocturne: a form generally unfettered by rigid rules, as indicated by several of Chopin's famous compositions of this kind, and hence evocative of a string of spontaneous reflections more than of premeditated performance. Whistler himself has commented thus on the choice of musical designations for his paintings: "why should I not call my works 'symphonies,' 'arrangements,' 'harmonies' and 'nocturnes'? ... The picture should have its own merit, and not depend upon dramatic, or legendary, or local interest.... Art should be independent of all claptrap — should stand alone, and appeal to the artistic sense of eye or ear, without confounding this with emotions entirely foreign to it, as devotion, pity, love, patriotism and the like. All these have no kind of concern with it; and that is why I insist on calling my works 'arrangements' and 'harmonies'" (Whistler, pp. 126–128).

In this respect, Whistler's perspective closely recalls the Japanese propensity to foreground imprecision and ambiguity as crucial attributes of all art. This affinity is no mere coincidence: in fact, it is a logical corollary of Whistler's attraction to Japanese art and aesthetics as something deeper than a desire to pander to the fashionable *japonisme* of his day and actually embrace their seminal precepts. As Richard Dorment explains, "through the art of Japan Whistler sought both to avoid the superficialities of academic neo-classicism, and to re-assert the true classical tradition: the search for balance and the relentless simplification of form." In order to pursue this adventurously assimilative project, the painter endeavored to integrate "the fundamental Japanese principles of simplicity of design and economy of expression into his art" (Dorment, p. 85). Ironically, Japanese art is here posited as intimately akin to classical art despite its apparent departure from so many of the criteria which Western culture has conventionally associated with antiquity. Whistler's vision will be revisited in Chapter 4 vis-à-vis music's own efforts to cultivate an aesthetic of vagueness.

In addition, Japanese art was at one point responsible for spawning singlehandedly the far-reaching vogue known as *japonaiserie*. Whereas the term *japonisme*, held to have been coined by the art critic and collector Philippe Burty, describes the assimilation of Japanese motifs by Western artists, *japonaiserie* designates the faddish passion for all manner of artifacts issuing from Japan triggered by the advent on the cultural scene of Japanese objects of various kinds in the 1860s. This was enabled by the public display of such objects at the Great Exhibitions, staged in all of the principal European cities of that epoch, which had been rendered possible, in the first place, by the inauguration of novel trade routes with Japan in 1853. The same period witnessed the impact of Japanese art on the developing industries of advertising and graphic design, which rapidly led to the emergence of a brand-new art form, poster art. As Avella explains, "Toulouse-Lautrec and Jules Chéret were the first practitioners of what we know as 'graphic design' today. Both used the *japoniste* elements of solid-color background, cut-off figures, and unusual viewpoints" (Avella, p. 11). Although they were deemed quite shocking at the time, these and other traits of poster art are sights with which any Western person who has had any contact with visual publicity is now entirely familiar. No less significantly, they are also defining attributes of the art of anime, contributing decisively to its picturesque qualities, tactile appeal and knack of establishing intimate visual communication with the viewer. The aesthetics of poster art can also be detected in the stylistic paradox whereby anime cultivates a sparse graphic vocabulary eschewing superfluous detail, yet does not demur from exaggeration — notably in its approach to mass and proportion — or even extravagance — in the handling of hues and evocative geometry in particular. In poster art and anime alike, one encounters a tantalizing fusion of allusive vagueness and visceral density.

The appetite for hybridization typical of Japanese culture has not only resulted in its enthusiastic incorporation of foreign ideas. In fact, it has also consistently manifested itself as an inclination to revisit local trends from the past and impart them with fresh connotations and a markedly contemporary feel. The introduction to *Creative Japan* corroborates this point, lucidly conveying the vision of the Agency of Cultural Affairs as follows: "we see our contemporary culture not only as absorbing elements from other cultures but also as interpreting them from a unique perspective, then re-shaping them into a new style and fusing them with something completely different. It is a culture in which the old and the new co-exist, one that appeals to the general population and that anyone can enjoy" (MOFA). Recent decades have witnessed an increasing tendency to rekindle some time-honored indigenous styles in numerous areas of design. According to Sarah Lonsdale, this trend is largely a corollary of economic and political anxieties generated by the failure of Japan's "bubble years of the 1980s," and concomitant acknowledgment of the pressure to conceive of alternative options "driven primarily by cost consciousness" (Lonsdale, p. 6). This is not to say that the revival of traditional vogues is univocally tantamount to the imperative to be thrifty. In effect, it attests to a sensibly and sensitively refined approach to design, and hence to artistic production generally. This attitude refuses to prioritize eccentric consumption as its ultimate goal and aims instead at the development of habitats and lifestyles congruous with today's starker realities.

In assessing the prismatic character of Japan's arts and culture, it is indeed critical to refrain from simplistic explanations of an entirely materialistic ilk. This point is underscored by Kondo in relation to the *Bunkacho*'s mission. "All humans aspire to a fulfilling life," the Commissioner asserts. "This state of mind can be created only when we feel a clear sense of identity and belonging at the same time. It is culture and the arts that enable us to achieve these objectives. Unfortunately, however, today's world is heavily preoccupied with military and economic power. Although security and prosperity are important *means* to create the necessary conditions for a fulfilling life, they are not adequate. They even seem to have become *objectives* themselves. It is time to remind ourselves that culture and arts have important roles to play in achieving our ultimate objectives in life" (Kondo). In the seemingly mundane but by no means negligible context of interior design, the contemporary propensity to revive the past not simply out of antiquarian respect but also to investigate and appreciate its relevance to the present is pithily illustrated by Junichirou Tanizaki in his both atmospheric and thought-provoking essay *In Praise of Shadows*. The "recent vogue for electric lamps in the style of the old standing lanterns," for instance, can be seen as an outcome of "a new awareness of the softness and warmth of paper" which attests to a "recognition that this material is far better suited than glass to the Japanese house" (Tanizaki, p. 13). The cultural specificity of paper as a distinctively indigenous material is confirmed, according to the illustrious writer, by the fact that "Western paper turns away the light, while our paper seems to take it in" (p. 17). It is therefore perfectly suited to the perpetuation of the culture of shadows, examined later in greater detail, which Tanizaki posits as a prime marker of Japan's aesthetic sensibility. The magnetic pull of past styles will be revisited in the course of this discussion.

In the evolution of the art of anime itself, Japan's deep-rooted propensity to appropriate foreign elements and reconceptualize them to suit its own particular world view is paradigmatically borne out by its utilization of an art imported from China in the tenth century: illuminated scroll painting. There is copious evidence, meticulously collected by Brigitte Koyama-Richard in the aforementioned *Japanese Animation From Painted Scrolls to Pokémon*, that illuminated scrolls are the ancestors of contemporary anime. These graphic works of an eminently narrative stamp were originally devoted to the representation of all manner of "religious, literary, or historical scenes," as well as to the ideation of "a fantastical bestiary," and to the adaptation of "morality tales or stories designed for children" (Koyama-Richards, p. 12). Most importantly, from a structural angle, the scrolls evince compositional modalities of a cinematic nature, harboring in embryonic form some of the technical qualities typically associated with anime. The original Chinese style was indeed modified on Japanese soil through the introduction of novel constituents of indigenous conception, such as "real-life facial expressions, blocks of color as in celluloid (cels), parallel movement, effects of zoom, the portrayal of characters linked to action" (p. 13). Besides, anime's inveterate penchant for multiperspectivalism in the presentation of both its stories and its personae finds a precursor in the ancient scroll's tendency to recount a narrative from plural viewpoints.

Multiperspectivalism, it is worth noting, also plays a notable part in various manifestations of garden design, another traditional art of pivotal significance to Japan's heritage. This quality is especially prominent in the modestly proportioned pond gardens, designed primarily for strolling, which came into prominence in the Kamakura period, by and large replacing the ample boating gardens favored by the aristocracy throughout the Asuka, Nara and Heian eras. While the latter already afforded multiple perspectives for viewers as their boats glided along, the strolling gardens made multiperspectivalism an absolute priority. Employing a pond with a central island (*nakajima*) surrounded by hilly paths as its protagonist, the strolling garden was designed so as to guarantee that its visitors could sample a whole range of views as they sauntered around the pond. As Katsuhiko Mizuno explains, the chief principle underlying the construction of strolling gardens was precisely to provide an aesthetic environment in which visitors would be able "to enjoy pleasing scenes from wherever they happened to be in the garden. Accordingly, the gardens featured a variety of ingenious artifices to ensure delightful views from different angles, including artificial hills to climb and waterfalls to complement the surrounding scenery" (Mizuno, p. 2). The aesthetic juggling of multiple perspectives is similarly instrumental in the enjoyment of scenic viewing gardens of the kind designed in both the Kamakura and the Muromachi periods. At first meant to be viewed essentially from within the home, these gardens gradually evolved in accordance with design principles which enhanced their viewability from diverse external angles by people ambling about on verandas. In the Edo period, the fascination with multiperspectivalism in garden making led to the ideation of "round windows with sliding paper doors behind them, especially designed for teahouses," which facilitated the evocation of markedly cinematic, or even specifically animational, effects. "When the doors were open," Mizuno explains, "a circular segment of the garden could be seen from inside the teahouse, and the window served as a kind of picture frame.... The scenery viewed through the windows changed depending on how wide the doors were open" (p. 30).

With the development of new art forms, techniques and methodologies over the centuries, the substratum provided by traditional artifacts such as Japan's ancient scrolls has evolved into a veritable coral reef of incrementally accruing strata. What anime, at its best, enables us to experience is just such an intricately layered structure of gem-encrusted worlds as its implicit inspirational bedrock. When anime elects artistic endeavor as its theme, its implication in a long history of graphic and aesthetic developments gains additional fascination, inviting us to draw parallels between its thematic and its technical dimensions. In the process, Japanese culture stands out a mobile galaxy of interlocking practices which resonate at once with both indigenous and international influences, both age-old principles and experimentative drives. Thus, it could be said to epitomize the composite cultural scenario posited by Barker as a reality in the face of which "we are required to oscillate between the concept of culture as in-place and the notion of flows within a field of no-place" (Barker, p. 85).

In the domain of contemporary architecture, an apt example of Japan's hybrid sensibility is supplied by the works of Tadao Ando and Kezuyo Sejima (to cite just two of the most prominent names in the field). With these artists, solid walls and concrete structures — characteristics of modern architecture of chiefly Western derivation — are amalgamated with basic elements of traditional Japanese buildings and construction methods. What is thereby accomplished is a unique balance of concurrently formal and conceptual flexibility. It is also noteworthy, in this matter, that Japanese architecture itself has progressively hybridized its Western counterpart since the modernist era by instilling its time-honored commitment to the horizontal axis into the predominantly vertical formations favored by the West. In the visual arts, hybridity finds a vibrant champion in Heisuke Kitakawa (a.k.a. PCP), a contemporary artist who moved to the United States at the age of 10, there to spend the first two years of his school education in total silence before proceeding to learn the English language and obtain a master of arts in illustration from California State University. Having returned to Japan at the age of 26, Kitakawa has developed a style in which lightheartedness and tenebrosity uncannily coalesce. As Laura Fumiko Keehn observes, Kitakawa's "work is a far cry from the tangy world of Japanimation, but nevertheless leaves a distinctly 'cute' aftertaste. Like his piece 'hungry ghosts got in my way, get away,' which features ominous doe-eyed blobs (the hungry ghosts), the PCP cocktail is sweet with a poisonous kick" (Keehn [a]). This mixed visual repertoire reflects the artist's ambivalent perception, itself rooted in Japanese lore, of his otherworldly creatures' inherent multifacetedness. "These ghosts are pretty scary," Kitakawa declares. "They will chew you up. They are so lonely that they want to make anyone and everyone to be part of them. But the good thing about becoming a ghost is that they are so simple minded, they don't have to worry about miscommunication" (cited in Keehn [a]).

The most famous expression of the spirit of hybridity in contemporary Japan is the work of Takashi Murakami, the founder of the postmodern movement Superflat—i.e., a style inspired by various aspects of Japan's popular culture and traditional arts and, in particular, by their preference for flattened, explicitly two-dimensional forms. Murakami's works typically emit charming notes but lurking behind his colorfully pretty designs, one frequently intuits some deeply disorienting messages. The artist himself has commented thus on this characteristic duplicity: "I always emphasize that the power of the dark side exists even in cuteness and in the thoughts of peace-addicted people" (cited in Keehn [b]). As a prime instance of Japanese art's penchant for hybridity, Superflat warns us that we are bound to misunderstand the prismatic products of indigenous culture if we presume to evaluate them with reference to monolithic aesthetic or ethical models. The flatness of Superflat and its sources should not be automatically interpreted as coterminous with shallowness. As Michael Darling emphasizes, "'Superflat' is far from unnuanced or superficial and has cracked open the discourse about contemporary Japanese culture and society.... Like a Japanese transformer toy, it has the capacity to move and bend to engage a wide range of issues: from proposing formal historical connections between classic Japanese art and the anime cartoons of today to a Pop Art–like cross-examination of high and low to a social critique of contemporary mores and motivations" (Darling, p. 77).

The Play with Form

For several centuries, the supreme goal of Western art was the perfection of techniques enabling a flat surface to divest itself of the impression of flatness in the service of ideals of depth and three-dimensionality—concepts which were deemed coterminous with technical, intellectual and moral profundity. Two-dimensionality, by contrast, has been pivotal to Japanese art for time immemorial—one of its most recent manifestations, as noted above, being the experimental art of Murakami and his followers. In the context of Japan, two-dimensionality has consistently yielded works so superbly refined as to defy the stereotypical assumption underpinning pre-modernist Western art that the absence of depth connotes ignorance of the lessons of perspectivalism, and is therefore tantamount to lack of realism on the compositional plane, and to primitiveness on the broadly cultural plane. Japanese art simultaneously defies the principles of classic realism, with its mimetic or representational imperatives, by vigilantly fostering an aesthetic of presentation that does not shy away from the opportunity to expose the artifact's artificiality with utter frankness.

Perception and intuition are valued over logic and rationality, and the activity of creative construction is granted precedence over the final product itself. In the process, variable constellations are spawned by the collusion of several dialectically interrelated pairs: figure and pattern, rhythm and substance, abstraction and embodiment, form and matter, stylization and naturalism. These are recurrently distinguished by an emphatic use of firmly sketched silhouettes, essential forms and fluid lines, bold and uniform colors, blank airy spaces, and an adventurous take on both composition and perspective. Such stylistic traits share precious little with the priorities advanced by classic realism, yet radiate their own distinctive brand of realism, and have influenced deeply several Western painters eager to release their visions from the shackles of strict representationalism. Notable names include the aforementioned Impressionist and Postimpressionist artists, as well as Edgar Degas, Paul Gaugin, Paul Cezanne and Pablo Picasso.

As Charles Dawson points out, Japanese visual culture generally eschews mimetic accuracy insofar as it does not include techniques such as "modelling and chiaroscuro," which can help the artist "pretend that the paper he works on is anything else but flat." In fact, the artist typically "takes no trouble to deceive the eye with contours." Yet, "while he never imitates, he is a wonderful realist. With marvellous energy and power he seizes the very essence of what he wishes to portray, grips it intensely and allows nothing of its vivid and lifelike qualities to escape him" (Dawson, p. 96). Avella reinforces this proposition by arguing that "Japanese design ... does not present the viewer with an accurate representation of form or object" since "colors are exaggerated or eliminated; an object is reduced to its barest elements; any superfluous element is discounted." Nevertheless, it delivers stunningly credible and affecting images by capitalizing on suggestion rather than explicit statement, on implication rather than explicitness. This tendency is typically attested to by "a tendency to work in similes and vague nuances" (Avella, p. 15). In this regard, the underlying goal of Japan's visual arts could be said to be the engagement with latent essential realities that elude rational scrutiny and depiction, seeking to articulate their mystery through tastefully measured allusions and supple tropes. As Yoshida contends, in developing its own distinctive approach to the handling of space, Japanese art has also cultivated a "peculiar form of symmetry" which does not pivot, in the way Western symmetry of classical derivation tends to do, "on precise geometrical values." In fact, it endeavors to "achieve a balance based on inner meaning rather than shape: in a pair of folding screens, the left-hand screen might represent autumn by a maple tree and the right-hand screen, spring, by a cherry tree. To Japanese eyes such a composition seems symmetrical and well balanced, in spite of the fact that cherry trees and maples are not at all symmetrical as shapes" (Yoshida 1980, p. 18).

Saying that Japanese art is traditionally disinclined toward the tenets of perspectivalism, classic realism and hellenic notions of symmetry is not, however, tantamount to arguing that Japan has been entirely insensitive or resistant to Western art or its technical underpinnings. In the Edo period, in particular, the Japanese were able to familiarize themselves with linear perspective through Chinese translations of Western treatises on the subject, and to apply its lessons in the execution of some famous woodblock prints representing highly detailed townscapes. Japanese art was also exposed to Chinese artifacts inspired by stereoscopic views of Western origin in which both perspectivalism and chiaroscuro play a key part. Often regarded by the Japanese as amusing ornamentation rather than high art, such works were frequently meant to be viewed by recourse to varyingly complex optical contraptions. It is also worth noting, in this context, that the passion for optical play endemic in Europe from the sixteenth century onward also impacted on Japanese culture in the guise of shadow games, while spinning lanterns found a local correlative in the lanterns traditionally hanging outside shops or employed in children's play. Furthermore, Japanese culture was eager to import the Western magic lantern and to adopt this device in the staging of hugely popular performances. These were generally known as *utsushi-e* and allowed people of various classes and ages to encounter images, tales and even actual facts which they had never seen or heard of before through any other means. Hence, they served a social function not exclusively as versatile vehicles for the production and enjoyment of illusion but also as practical education and communication instruments. As Koyama-Richard explains, *utsushi-e* differed from their Western predecessors insofar as they did not rely on "fixed" visuals but rather employed a "movable" lantern. Hence, they were able to assert their distinctive technical excellence as autonomous products transcending the status of mere imitations. At the same time, they sought to surpass the relative clumsiness of Western machinery by producing "lanterns made from paulownia wood ... lit by lamps of rapeseed oil" (Koyama-Richard, p. 52).

The Western fascination with automata likewise finds a stunning correlative in the exquisite *karakuri ningyou* created in the Edo period: mechanical dolls and puppets intended for a variety of entertainment purposes and often invested, in keeping with indigenous culture's animistic proclivities, with an aura of aliveness usually unknown to their Western counterparts. The dolls portrayed in the anime *Touka Gettan* (2007) epitomize this position. It has frequently been noted that the experience of seeing entities which one knows to be inert suddenly come to life can be quite disorientating or even downright distressing (depending on the context in which the experience occurs and on the beholder's personal baggage). Robyn Ferrell neatly conveys this idea in his essay on the uncanny: "the doll that comes to life, the friendly robot and the dog that makes a fellow adventurer are not frightening but desirable; the revival of a childhood wish, suggests Freud. But the sly turn of a doll's head, the imperceptible flicker of a statue's stone eyelids, the animal whose expression is for a moment almost human, these can be uncanny.... It is a type of moment rather than a class of objects; an effect of a process of perceiving rather than an image perceived" (Ferrell, p. 132). In the pursuit of this kind of argument, three-dimensional objects such as puppets, dolls, mannequins, statues and automata are normally invoked as prime generators of eerie sensations in their viewers. What is seldom, if at all, addressed, however, is the potentially disquieting impact of two-dimensional drawn creations. According to Maureen Furniss, this kind of animation is less likely to produce such an unsettling effect because it is more explicitly "marked as being fabricated, rather than something of the 'real world'" (Furniss, p. 165). It could nonetheless be argued that the spectator's recognition of the entity's artificiality is not necessarily, let alone automatically, conducive to a comforting sense of distance enabling him or her to categorize the viewed object as a separate species with no more than a metaphorical relation to humanity. In fact, a two-dimensional drawn entity capable of coming across as alive and conscious might be deemed even more disconcerting than a sculptural artifact — in other words, an object one could logically expect to be quite lifelike due to its three-dimensionality and textural qualities.

Therefore, while seeing an animated puppet spring to life on the screen is undoubtedly perplexing, such a sensation should not come as too much of a surprise. Conversely, witnessing the degree to which a drawing of an overtly constructed (or even deliberately distorted) nature is capable of exuding vitality, alertness and interactive power despite its unrealism compels us to ponder the latent aliveness not only of anthropomorphic entities but also of incontrovertibly non-human forms. Relatedly, while the uncanny feelings induced by a puppet can be kept at bay by the decision to regard such an object as an extension of humanity, the animated drawing does not readily lend itself to such a move of figurative transposition. In fact, it remains resolutely non-human. The recognition that it is endowed with human-like capacities and affects must therefore lead us to acknowledge that what we have hitherto considered quintessentially human is not a sacrosanct prerogative and might actually be possessed by other species. The type of fleetingly disturbing "moment" cited by Ferrell in corroboration of his thesis is, ultimately, more likely to visit the blatantly non-human than the amicably humanoid or humanesque. Anything, in this context, is intrinsically alive.

Central to Japan's cultural inheritance across the arts is the reverential attitude to materials traditionally exhibited by their practitioners. As Calza contends, "the appreciation of materiality" is "reflected in a vast range of expressive forms in which what is emphasized is their inherent qualities rather than their ability to embody ideas" (Calza, p. 9). Taking the innate properties of each material as the set of principles directing all formal and compositional decisions, Japanese craftsmen and artists of all kinds prioritize the lessons imparted by nature over the anthropocentric and anthropomorphic priorities often favored in the West. Thus, the intrinsic qualities of stones, shrubs and water will tell the garden landscaper how best to organize them into an aesthetically harmonious whole. As Yuriko Saito maintains, quoting the eleventh-century treatise *Book on Garden Making*, "the scenic effect of a landscape" is best achieved "by observing one principle of design: 'obeying ... the request' of an object." Thus, "the gardener 'should first install one main stone, and then place other stones, in necessary numbers, in such a way as to satisfy the request ... of the main stone.' ... The whole art ... requires the artist to work closely with, rather than in spite of or irrespective of, the material's natural endowments" (Saito, p. 86).

The crucial importance of paper, as a further example, is stressed by Haruo Shirane, whose discussion of traditional Japanese poetry proposes that the aesthetic value of a piece often surpassed in importance the quality of the content, while the materials employed in the process of composition were considered similarly vital. "A poor poem with excellent calligraphy," the critic avers, "was probably preferable to a good poem with poor calligraphy" and the "type, color, and size of the paper" upon which it was executed also carried critical weight. Additionally, a writer could "add a sketch, attach a flower or leaf, or add incense or perfume to the poetry sheet" (Shirane, p. 224) as a way of maximizing the medium's inherent appeal through the inspired incorporation of a personal touch of style. Analogously, the inherent properties not only of paper but also of wood and numerous vegetable fibers determine the shapes and sizes most appropriate for a particular wrapper or container, guiding the package designer as autonomous animate agents. These materials are not handled with exclusively economic and pragmatic priorities in mind but are actually allowed to decide, by means of their innate attributes, the overall constitution of the package. Another indigenous material traditionally accorded a privileged status over the centuries is bamboo: a wood whose proverbial combination of toughness and flexibility has come to provide the template for an ethical ideal of self-perfection based on the simultaneous cultivation of those complementary qualities.

In the realm of gastronomy, the chef's orchestration of a dish tends to be governed by the unique flavors, colors, fragrances and consistence levels of disparate food items, its overall objective being the enhancement of their gustatory and visual potential. According to Kenji Ekuan, the processing, amalgamation and juxtaposition of different ingredients is informed by the desire to allow their essential strengths to manifest themselves unimpeded.

The arrangement of the traditional Japanese lunchbox (*bento*), for instance, is directed by one major goal: to garner "normal, familiar, everyday things from nature, according to season" and augment "their inherent appeal" in order "bring each to full life" (Ekuan, p. 6). Fish will therefore be rendered "more fishlike" and rice "more ricelike" (p. 77). By displaying contrasting flavors, colors and textures, all of the items in a *bento* contribute to the creation of a synaesthetic harmony in which visual, aromatic and gustatory impressions alluringly coalesce. It is also worth noting that the *bento* encapsulates a critical aspect of Japanese art insofar as it depends for both its aesthetic impact and its enjoyment on the fleeting moment. Indeed, it is capable of acquiring a new configuration and basic composition every time it is laid out: each new day inaugurates fresh possibilities without ever repeating the previous day's performance down to the minutest detail. Therefore, like the art of flower arrangement (*ikebana*), the art of lunchbox preparation conceives of beauty as a quality which does not proceed from eternity and immutability but rather from transience and continual transformation. Anime such as *Yakitate!! Japan* (2004–2006), *Antique Bakery* (2008) and *Yumeiro Pâtissière* (2009), where the gastronomic arts are accorded pride of place, exemplify these views with uplifting energy.

According to Lonsdale, Japan's traditional "reverence of materials" finds emblematic expression in the domain of sartorial fashion, typically manifesting itself in the "selection, treatment and manipulation of fabric." These practices seek to harmonize "functionality with beauty" and ensure that "textiles ... are highly tactile in nature" and hence able to feel "just as exquisite to the touch as they are to the eye" (Lonsdale, p. 36). At the same time, the fabric employed in the execution of a garment and the form achieved by the final product are indistinguishable. The Japanese regard for an art's raw materials is underpinned by a disarmingly modest stance to the creative act — an attitude clearly conveyed by Yohji Yamamoto's comments on his creative labor. "In the final analysis," the stylist observes, "nothing is actually being created. Faced with fabric that is obviously going to be more beautiful the less one plays around with it, we designers are like swimmers wallowing in a tsunami or raging torrent. It's fabric. Beautiful as it is, we want to handle it, push it" (cited in Fukai 2010b, p. 18). Humbly subservient to the inherent beauty and plastic requirements of his materials, the artist is nonetheless tantalized by their power to such an extent that their manipulation feels like an inevitable outcome: "it's like a current, it draws us in. But I didn't make anything, really. Not this time" (p. 25). The artifact, in this perspective, is the result not of a human being's masterful control of nature's bounties but rather of a refreshingly collaborative effort between the enticing fabric and the designer's eager hand.

Concomitantly, the emphasis on the corporeal dimension underpinning Japanese art's stance toward materials extends to respect for its tools, as evinced by the custom whereby a tool which has outlived its usefulness is ritually thanked for its services and then buried. In Kyoto, for example, proper funerals are held for needles no longer considered serviceable. This attitude entails that the sense of beauty is inextricable from an object's function (*yo*): a term, according to Sori Yanagi, which "embraces the mental or spiritual dimension of human life" (Yanagi, Sori, p. 32) alongside the corporeal element. *Material* and *materialistic* are here implicitly posited as starkly divergent concepts. In valuing their materials, their tools, and the functional properties of their creations, Japanese artists eschew the classicist ideal according to which artistic production should be viewed as an act which stems primarily from the mind. Nonetheless, they do not reduce the artifact to the status of a starkly physical entity insofar as they also foster consistently its psychological implications. The emphasis placed by Japanese art on the material properties of its objects finds a potent correlative in Shinto's reverence toward each and every facet of the natural realm as the receptacle of spiritual powers. Moreover, the celebration of the corporeal dimension of art is fostered by the teachings of Zen Buddhism, where great emphasis is laid on the concrete dimension of all life and on the coalescence of intellectual and sensuous pleasures.

As a lynchpin of Japanese aesthetics, the desire to foreground a material's inherent properties has also characteristically shaped Japan's approach to artistic training. As Lonsdale observes, "the traditional way of learning a craft has always been one of emulation: an apprentice observing a master, learning through osmosis as the student becomes familiar with the materials. Perfection for the master was traditionally more about enhancing the natural beauty of a material rather than asserting the individual ego" (Lonsdale, p. 147). This proposition is paradigmatically illustrated by the formative experience of one of the most widely recognized Japanese artists of recent decades, the architect Ando. As Sunamita Lim observes, "this introspective architect mastered the traditional art of Japanese wood designing and building first…. In the time-honored tradition of studying from the masters, he learned the precision techniques required in building with wood joinery, sans hardware" (Lim, p. 20).

The preceding observations corroborate the contention, advanced earlier in the opening segment of this discussion, that in Japanese culture, and hence in anime concerned with artistic endeavor, creativity is an eminently bodily phenomenon. It is only logical that the materials through which it expresses itself should accordingly be valued as physical realities. It is here worth pausing to reflect on the nature of indigenous writing as a system which, given its pictographic roots, is itself instrumental in affirming the material dimension of existence. Pictograms are relatively straightforward representations of objects in the actual world executed in a stylized fashion. Ideograms also strike their roots in empirical referents but these external entities are less instantly identifiable in ideograms than they are in pictograms. *Kanji* (and, by extension, the *hiragana* and *katakana* syllabaries emanating from them) participate in both signifying modalities, at times displaying intimate connections with real objects and at others deploying extreme, even rarefied, methods of stylization. Either way, the characters emphasize the physical foundations of language by preserving the corporeal essence of words in their visible shapes. Naturally, words do not solely describe material entities. No less often, in fact, they designate impalpable and inchoate thoughts, feelings, sensations, fantasies and dreams. Nevertheless, even in such instances, *kanji* and their graphic offspring assert themselves as concrete images that emblematically suggest those experiences without becoming altogether incorporeal themselves.

The status enjoyed by Japanese calligraphy (*shodou*) as a pictorial art in its own right is itself rendered possible, above all else, by the nature of native writing as a multilayered body of signs of pictographic derivation. Hence, calligraphy foregrounds the concreteness of language even when it denotes abstract concepts, and thus underscores the material roots of narrative and drama alike in all their manifestations, as well as of other media likewise reliant on language in the broad sense of the term. This specific semiotic ethos underscores the performative nature of textuality — i.e., the power of words to function not merely as sounds but also as gestures and actions — by allowing writing to stand as a dynamic tool unhindered by the limitations of a static sheet or leaf.

Like practically all written languages, pictograms and ideograms depend on the principle of metaphor: the ideation of relationships between material and conceptual entities. In the West, this accomplishment has conventionally been credited to the human mind's knack of logical abstraction and cognate tendency to disengage thought from its physical setting. Yet, as Ezra Pound trenchantly argues in "The Chinese Character as a Medium for Poetry," the model at the basis of metaphoric association is actually provided by nature: "primitive metaphors do not spring from arbitrary *subjective* processes. They are possible only because they follow objective lines of relations in Nature herself. Relations are more real and more important than the things which they relate.... Nature furnishes her own clues. Had the world not been full of homologies, sympathies, and identities, thought would have been starved and language chained to the obvious" (Pound 1936). Pound's own lyrics, moreover, often emulate Japanese aesthetics in their search for compactness and for the evocation of intellectual and emotive complexity through the briefest of forms. Such compositions come across as ideogrammatic in themselves to the extent that they capture abstract concepts and affects through visually condensed signs. A musical correlative of this poetic vision can be found in Igor Stravinsky's *Three Japanese Lyrics* insofar as in these pieces, as Richard Taruskin comments, "the verbal and musical stresses ... cancel each other out, leaving a dynamically uninflected, stressless line, the musical equivalent of the flat surface ... of Japanese paintings and prints" (Taruskin, p. 840).

Pound's propositions regarding the natural realm's inherent relationality is memorably enshrined in Baudelaire's "Correspondances" and its unique visual semiosis:

> La Nature est un temple où de vivants piliers
> Laissent parfois sortir de confuses paroles;
> L'homme y passe à travers des forêts de symboles
> Qui l'observent avec des regards familiers.
> Comme de longs échos qui de loin se confondent
> Dans une ténébreuse et profonde unité,
> Vaste comme la nuit et comme la clarté,
> Les parfums, les couleurs et les sons se répondent
> [Baudelaire 1961].
>
> [*Nature is a temple where living pillars*
> *Let sometimes come forth garbled words.*
> *Man walks through these forests of symbols*
> *That observe him with knowing eyes.*
> *Like prolonged echoes blending in the distance*
> *In a dark and deep harmony,*
> *As vast as night and light,*
> *Perfumes, colours and sounds converse with one another*
> [Author's translation].

Baudelaire himself, moreover, emphasizes the principle of metaphoricity as the wellspring of creativity, insofar as its originator is the imagination itself—namely, the "Queen of the Faculties." It is from this power, argues Baudelaire, that humanity first acquired "the moral meaning of colour, of contour, of sound and of scent. In the beginning of the world it created analogy and metaphor" (Baudelaire 1965b, p. 156). A key aspect of the imagination as ideated by Baudelaire consists of "musicality"—a concept of pivotal significance to the overall argument pursued in this study since it signals the intimate coalescence of acoustic and visual values by equating color and line to tone and rhythm.

The relevant passage is so deeply relevant to the present discussion as to deserve comprehensive citation: "harmony is the basis of the theory of colour. Melody is a unity within colour, or overall colour. Melody calls for a cadence; it is a whole, in which every effect contributes to the general effect. Thus colour leaves a deep and lasting impression on the mind.... The right way to know if a picture is melodious is to look at it from far enough away to make it impossible to understand its subject or to distinguish its lines. If it is melodious, it already has a meaning and has already taken its place in your store of memories" (Baudelaire 1965a, p. 50). As Peter Vergo observes, Baudelaire's contention stems from the conviction that "if a picture is well composed, its overall structure will be imbued with a particular logic capable of being apprehended without reference to any element of representation, just as we apprehend the 'abstract' significance of purely musical forms such as the rondo, the passacaglia or the fugue" (Vergo, p. 71). Baudelaire's perspective, therefore, resolutely emancipates the imagination from the strictures of mimesis by subordinating representational accuracy to a creatively holistic experience grounded in the aforementioned principle of synaesthesia. Two or more of the senses are thus allowed to cooperate in perception, making it possible, for example, to hear harmonies as though they were physically endowed with colors. As argued at a later stage in this discussion, Japanese aesthetics evinces a marked preference for allusiveness and vagueness. These qualities find an apt correlative in Baudelaire's vision of the melodious artifact as an entity which reveals its essence most potently when it surrenders high definition.

The importance of the natural environment as a fundamental agency in Japanese culture is substantiated by the virtual ubiquity of symbols more or less explicitly inspired by its flora and fauna in disparate arts of both traditional and innovative varieties. According to Reeve, a profound respect for nature in all its forms indeed constitutes one of the most fundamental attributes of Japanese culture at large. In the realm of art, this has progressively contributed to the development of a varied "symbolic vocabulary from nature" which makes itself felt in all sorts of indigenous artifacts. Paradigmatic examples are representations of animals and plants believed either to carry mystical connotations or to embody demonic creatures in disguise. "For the artist," the critic comments, "the challenge is to convey the essence of the seasons or the creature" (Reeve, pp. 38–39). As Donald Richie maintains, the key lesson derived by Japanese art from the natural world is the paramount value of "simplicity"— a value tersely communicated by the fact that "there is nothing merely ornate about nature: every branch, twig, or leaf counts" (Richie, p. 19).

Some of the most striking manifestations of natural symbolism in Japanese art can be found in the domain of garden design. While several types of indigenous garden aim to emulate nature closely, seeking to replicate its rhythms in miniaturized form by artificial means, others rely on conceptual stylization. For instance, it is not unusual for the designer to evoke a natural waterfall by creating a dry waterfall (*karetaki*) which emblematically captures its model's essence though the deft arrangement of rocks and placement of sand or pebbles in their vicinity to symbolize moving water. The preference for stylization asserts itself most resonantly in the dry landscape gardens established in the Muromachi period in conjunction with the rise of Zen Buddhism:

a revolutionary development in which stones, rocks and trees can be adopted with astounding flexibility and inventiveness in the abstract evocation of mountains, rivers, oceans and all manner of natural phenomena associated with those primordial forms.

Inspired by dry Zen gardens, the *roji* (tea gardens) introduced in the Momoyama era and destined to flourish in the Edo period take stylization to unique levels of aesthetic refinement as veritable distillations of a quintessentially Japanese design sensibility. It is also common for garden designers to employ particular facets of the natural world as metonymic avatars of its spiritual energies. Some of the recurring ingredients in this approach are pine trees symbolic of eternal life; stones and sand cones reputed to host powerful spirits; rock arrangements alluding to the Buddhist trinity consisting of Buddha and two supporting Bodhisattvas (*sanzon-iwagumi*); bridges whose crossing is symbolic of the transition to an ideal world; and islands representing one or more of the three ideal islands emblematic of the Buddhist concept of paradise (*horai*, the island of eternal life, *tsuru shima*, crane island, and *kame shima*, turtle island).

Just as the relationships and interactions forged by nature have concrete underpinnings, so do the metaphorical linkages ideated by written systems of signification. Sadly, that concreteness has been insistently marginalized (or even suppressed) by Western thought in its systematic elevation of disembodied concepts over anything even vaguely corporeal. According to Pound, this entails that "languages today are thin and cold because we think less and less into them. We are forced, for the sake of quickness and sharpness, to file down each word to its narrowest edge of meaning.... We are content to accept the vulgar misuse of the moment. A late stage of decay is arrested and embalmed in the dictionary" (Pound 1936). Stressing the autonomous aesthetic worth of pictographic and ideogrammatic matrices of textuality, Japan's writing system asserts the enduring materiality of language in a kaleidoscopic dance of graphic possibilities.

Aesthetics

The preference for hybrid combinations of cultural motifs, influences and styles traditionally evinced by Japan's arts and culture entails a healthy aversion to dualism. Tanizaki advances this world view in *In Praise of Shadows*, proposing that light cannot be grasped without darkness — that light, ironically, does not dissolve darkness but is, in fact, illuminated by it. This contention is validated, in the context of Japanese art, by the treatment of materials whose essence and beauty can only be adequately recognized with the assistance of obscurity. "Lacquerware decorated in gold," for example, "should be left in the dark," only partially touched by "a faint light." It is by dwelling discreetly in the shadows that the substance enables the emergence of a "dream world built by that strange light of candle and lamp, that wavering light bearing the pulse of the night," and indeed laying "a pattern on the surface of the night itself" (Tanizaki, p. 24). In the architectural domain, the unique power of shadows as an infinitely varied source of beauty asserts itself most markedly, permitting invisible energies of ghostly distinction to work their "magic." The cultural willingness to accommodate "lack of clarity" as an appealing— rather than intimidating—reality ushers in a world imbued with "a quality of mystery and depth superior to that of any wall painting or ornament" (p. 33).

It is in the Japanese conception of spectrality that the "propensity to seek beauty in darkness" is paradigmatically captured: "Japanese ghosts," Tanizaki explains, "have traditionally had no feet; Western ghosts have feet, but are transparent. As even this trifle suggests, pitch darkness has always occupied our fantasies, while in the West even ghosts are as clear as glass" (p 47). Self-immersion in a dusky environment is a natural proclivity in the culture portrayed by Tanizaki, in much the same way as the incidence of supernatural phenomena on the here-and-now is regarded as a relatively natural event and not as a hazardous infringement of sacrosanct boundaries. The indigenous approach to the interplay of tenebrosity and spectrality is poetically consolidated by the writer's depiction of old buildings in which the very "color" of darkness could be perceived in the "suspension of ashen particles" pervading the rooms. "It must have been simple," Tanizaki avers, "for specters to appear in a 'visible darkness,' where always something seemed to be flickering and shimmering, a darkness that on occasion held greater terrors than darkness out-of-doors. This was the darkness in which ghosts and monsters were active" (p. 53).

The passion for shadows celebrated by Tanizaki finds an intriguing correlative, according to Susannah Frankel, in the realm of fashion design. The garments and fabrics first launched by Rei Kawakubo of Comme des Garçons and Yamamoto in the early 1980s exemplify this proposition in their use of an "unassuming, harmonious shade" of black redolent of "Japanese ink painting." The "expressive use of a black palette," argues Frankel, shares the aesthetic principles upheld by Tanizaki in his description of shadows as the "essence" of Japan's aesthetic thinking (Frankel 2010a, p. 41). In establishing subtle correspondences between Tanizaki's study, modern couture and monochrome *sumi-e*, this vision engenders an artistic polyphony of forms and media of uniquely evocative vigor. Most importantly, both *In Praise of Shadows* and the design strategies of the kind described by Frankel eschew the binary opposition between light and darkness underpinning many of Western philosophy's cherished dualities by proposing that clarity of form is not necessarily a product of luminosity but may well ensue, in fact, from a sensitive handling of somber palettes and moods.

This antidualistic stance finds a direct correlative in the teachings of Shinto, where the divine and the earthly are by no means as rigorously contrasted as they are in mainstream Western creeds. While in the Judaeo-Christian world picture, the deity is regarded as external to both time and space, in Shinto, spiritual forces (*kami*) are held to fill the entire universe — mountains and trees, rivers and waterfalls, rocks and stones, as well as human beings and other animals. Moreover, whereas the Judaeo-Christian tradition maintains that a more peaceful and harmonious world can only be accomplished by a transcendental entity, in Shinto, the idea that the spiritual principle is omnipresent implies that any being, in principle, harbors the potential to shape reality. For the Shinto shaman engaged in the performance of thaumaturgic practices, a daunting challenge is posed by the dizzying diversity and profusion of *kami* throughout the universe. Indeed, *kami* "come in all varieties, from elemental spirits to the ghosts of ancestors to strange and wonderful animals. They are so numerous that they are commonly referred to as the 'Eight Million Kami.' Some are kindly and helpful, while others are mischievous or selfish. Shinto *kannushi* [priests] use many ritual tools in their magic, including *haraigushi*, a wand covered in paper streamers used to purify an area, and *ofuda*, paper prayer strips used for good luck or to deal with malicious spirits" ("The Shinto Tradition," p. 41).

While the principles of diversity and multifariousness are obviously central to Japan's conception of the *kami*, they can be seen to play no less vital a part in Japanese art insofar as its creations assiduously capitalize on the integration of balance and chaos, tranquillity and discord. The representation of motion — so vital to animation in all its guises — characteristically gains from the application of this lesson to creative production, often leading to the evocation of an atmosphere of peacefulness and harmony (*wa*) through imbalance, conflict or even tumult. The inherent animateness of even ostensibly inert entities is thus emphasized. Simultaneously, such a strategy enables the artist to bring out the specifically kinetic qualities of space, encouraging the eye to travel beyond the frame of a painting or the tangible boundaries of a sculpture.

Japan's antibinary stance also manifests itself prominently in the context of native architecture in the guise of a deep-seated aversion to the separation between the inside and the outside. This is deftly conveyed by the tendency to establish ongoing and mutually enriching exchanges between a building and its environment — typically by recourse to ethereal space dividers such as *shouji*, paper-covered sliding doors or windows, and *fusuma*, interior sliding partitions. Artificial and natural forms are thereby treated as gracefully interdependent parties in the evocation of an atmosphere of unmatched airiness and openness. This facet of Japanese architecture carries psychological implications insofar as it reflects closely what the Jungian scholar Hayao Kawai describes as one of the principal attributes of the Japanese mentality. This consists of "the absence of a clear distinction between exterior and interior world, conscious and unconscious.... In short for [the] Japanese the wall between this world and the other world is ... a surprisingly thin one. That the membrane between inner and outer or this and that world is paper-thin like a *fusuma* ... or *shoji* ... reflects the nature of the Japanese ego" (Kawai, p. 103).

The dialectical exchange between inside and outside is also notable in the type of garden, normally described as *Shakkei* (literally, "borrowed scenery"), in which the garden's layout enables natural forms beyond its boundaries, such as streams, seas and mountains, to interact with the manmade visual ensemble to great dynamic effect. The dialogical spirit inherent in the interaction of inside and outside as a pathway to harmony finds diverse expressions in Japanese art. At times, ironically, it operates according to the principle of apparent discord. Using again the context of traditional gardens as an example, it is noteworthy that a sense of peace can be strikingly emphasized not through the imposition of hieratic silence onto the scene but rather, as Mizuno explains, through sounds produced by various kinds of "*tensui* or *sozu*, a simple bamboo tool designed to create sounds whenever water passes through it." One such device, the *shishi-odoshi* (i.e., "deer scarer" or "deer chaser") deploys a bamboo pipe through which water flows, balanced like a seesaw on a wooden support. When the pipe is full, it moves downward to empty the water out and, by moving back again, it hits a rock causing an echoing noise. The "intermittent reverberation," Mizuno states, "acts as a refreshing counterpoint to the tranquility of the gardens" (Mizuno, p. 24).

Japanese aesthetic thinking is inextricable from a keen sensitivity to the inexorable passing of time. This expresses itself in a range of concepts which seek to throw into relief, with variable degrees of emphasis, both the impermanence of beauty and, by imaginative extension, the ephemerality of the human condition and the notion of aliveness itself. This idea is beautifully conveyed by Yoko Woodson in his essay "On Idleness": "the fact of impermanence now becomes a spiritual and an aesthetic value, producing in a sensitive person the possibility of a sense of beauty deriving from an inevitable self-awareness concerning one's own evanescence" (Woodson, p. 85). Of particular significance, in this respect, is the concept of *mono no aware*, or the "sadness of things": namely, the pathos associated with sensitivity to the transience of beauty and pleasure. As the entry for "Japanese Aesthetics" in the *Stanford Encyclopedia of Philosophy* explains, "the feeling of *aware* is typically triggered by the plaintive calls of birds or other animals." Acoustic effects of this nature are frequently brought into play by the art of anime in order to evoke all manner of sensations, emotions and memories, alongside the often unfulfillable yearnings which those psychic events are notoriously prone to spawn. As the principle of *mono no aware* is extended to the "affective dimensions of existence in general" ("Japanese Aesthetics"), one often discovers that it is through apparently inanimate objects — and not solely through the representation of human motion and its outcomes — that pathos is most potently conveyed.

In garden making, the principle of *mono no aware* is poetically encapsulated by the use of sand emblematic of various water effects in dry landscape gardens of the Zen-inspired variety, where the inseparability of beauty from transience reaches an authentic apotheosis. As Mizuno observes, "temple priests rake the sand into the form of big and small waves, tiny ripples, running water and scrollwork. Thanks to their design skills and painstaking, meticulous efforts, the temple gardens are transformed into delightful but ephemeral works of art" (Mizuno, p. 18). Time and again, anime throws into relief the agency of inert and static forms drawn from both the natural realm and interior design (such as rocks, stones, shells, screens and other common household articles) to communicate dynamism in the most economical fashion, and thus express the latent vitality of the apparently lifeless.

If *mono no aware* points to inevitable transience, the concept of *yugen*, conversely, alludes to the baffling timelessness of cosmic infinity. As David Pascal observes, *yugen* "is not the presence of, but the hint, the glow, of the eternal, the incorruptible." The idea of ineffable beauty is intrinsic to *yugen* and serves to underscore the ultimate unfathomability of the world we inhabit as a dimension we can never presume to master and can only strive to approximate through imagination and sympathetic identification. Temporality is also pivotal to the aesthetic tenet of *wabi*: a celebration of the incomparable beauty of the aged and the imperfect which seeks to honor the spiritual power harbored by materially flawed objects as opposed to pristine and unadulterated entities. *Wabi* proposes that greater beauty and grace can be ultimately descried in the frayed tatters of a culture's humble everyday creations than in its hermetically sealed and glamorized monuments. The concept of *sabi* likewise praises "pleasure in that which is old, faded, lonely ... a love of imperfection. *Sabi* differs from *aware* in that one does not lament for the fallen blossom, but loves it, and from *yugen* in that the flower does not (or rather need not) suggest greater eternities" (Pascal). According to the *Stanford Encyclopedia*, the poetic mood of *sabi* is typified by the haiku of the seventeenth-century poet Matsuo Bashou — for example: "Solitary now — / Standing amidst the blossoms / Is a cypress tree." As the article points out, the spirit of *sabi* is characteristically captured not by "the colorful beauty of the blossoms" but by "the more subdued gracefulness of the cypress" ("Japanese Aesthetics").

The principles of *wabi* and *sabi* are often handled in tandem as *wabi-sabi* to designate a generous acceptance of ephemerality allied to the elevation of the defective and the limited. These ideas are grounded in the Buddhist belief that emptiness — and, by implication, all lacunary states — should not to be regarded as flaws but rather as fertile soil ideal for imaginative and creative development. The existence of gaps is seen to stimulate thought insofar as it urges the mind and body to go on inventing new ways of filling them, albeit provisionally, while any bounded vision of completeness is bound to deaden both imagination and creativity. An image of the moon or of the sun partly obscured by clouds or fog is more enticing, in the logic of *sabi-wabi*, than an unimpeded view. This aesthetic preference for the approximate and the incomplete is echoed by contemporary popular culture, as demonstrated by the tendency, pervasive in anime, to work with "faces half-sketched" and "backgrounds half-done" and to leave "things critical to the story never explained" (Pascal).

As Andrew Juniper proposes, when an artistic practice is specifically influenced by the teachings of Zen, and therefore mirrors the lifestyle of its monks, *wabi-sabi* plays a crucial role. Its chief objective, in this case, is "to try and express, in a physical form, their love of life balanced against the sense of serene sadness that is life's inevitable passing." In so doing, it promulgates "the precepts of simplicity, humility, restraint, naturalness, joy, and melancholy as well as the defining element of impermanence" and thus prompts us to "rediscover the intimate beauty to be found in the smallest details of nature's artistry" (Juniper, p. ix). This preference is poignantly borne out by indigenous designers who spare no toil in executing to the highest of standards even the tiniest or seemingly most insignificant of objects. Just as leading a simple life is not, in itself, simple but actually requires discipline, at least to begin with, so creating an artifact capable of exuding an aura of utter simplicity if often a laborious task. T. S. Eliot pithily captures this state of affairs in "Little Gidding," describing "a condition of complete simplicity" as an achievement "costing not less than everything" (Eliot).

According to Yoshida, simplicity is often married to the principle of "modularity, by which a desired shape is achieved by the combination of simpler unit forms." For instance, the limited space wherein the tea ceremony unfolds is "regulated by the use of *tatami* mats of fixed size for flooring" upon which people rely "as a guide to systematise their physical actions" in the course of the event (Yoshida 1980, p. 21). The ethos of *wabi-sabi* also reverberates in one of the stylistic preferences which have enabled modern Japanese fashion to achieve a unique image on an international scale: that is, its take on the principle and practice of ornamentation. Eschewing the preference for rigidly sculpted lines, endemic in Western haute couture, major Japanese designers such as Kawakubo and Yamamoto have adopted what Akiko Fukai aptly terms "an entirely new decorative language" in which prominence is given to "holes, rips, frays and tears" that appear to be "emerging from the stuff of the fabric itself" and capture precisely "the beauty of things imperfect, impermanent and incomplete," as well as "things modest and simple," upheld by the aesthetic of *wabi-sabi* (Fukai 2010a, p. 9).

The idea that a flawed object can be aesthetically pleasing is no doubt anathema to Western traditions governed by hellenic parameters. Yet, it has inhabited Japanese culture for centuries, finding one of its most notable incarnations in the tea ceremony (*chanoyu*), where an unsurpassed atmosphere of solemnity is achieved by recourse to stark minimalism. Similarly, the affluent classes of the Edo period favored sartorial styles capable of communicating the wearer's worth not through blatant luxury and glamor but rather through the evocation of an ironical image of shabby sophistication. Japanese culture's deep-seated aversion to binary oppositions makes itself felt once again in this attitude to apparel. As Soetsu Yanagi emphasizes, the principle of *wabi-sabi* is intimately connected with the idea of *shibui*—the kind of beauty typically associated with the tea ceremony. This is a quality supposed never to display itself transparently but rather to abide unobtrusively within an object as a source of inner luminosity, and to manifest itself gradually as the beholder interacts with the object and studies it patiently over time. Although the word *shibui* can be translated into English as "solemn," "muted" and "discreet," it also carries potent connotations of simplicity, modesty, humility and introspective serenity. According to Yanagi, *shibui* is primarily "not a beauty displayed before the viewer by its creator; creation here means, rather, making a piece that will lead the viewer to draw beauty out for himself. In this sense, *shibui* beauty ... is beauty that makes an artist of the viewer" (Yanagi, Soetsu, pp. 123–124). As Lim observes, *shibui* is capable of operating at once on "both inner and outer planes" (Lim, p. 41), thus challenging the binary oppositions between introspection and expression, spiritual experience and bodily activity.

Another crucial aspect of Japanese aesthetics lies with its marked preference for approximation, adumbration and inconclusiveness. This propensity finds material expression in myriad artifacts eager to communicate in allusive form the inscrutable dimension of the creative experience as instrumental in the generation of beauty. According to Nancy G. Hume, "when looking at autumn mountains through mist, the view may be indistinct yet have great depth. Although few autumn leaves may be visible through the mist, the view is alluring. The limitless vista created in imagination far surpasses anything one can see more clearly" (Hume, pp. 253–254). Another relevant portrayal of the unique charm of ineffability and vagueness is offered by the thirteenth-century writer Kamo no Choumei: "it is like an autumn evening under a colorless expanse of silent sky. Somehow, as if for some reason that we should be able to recall, tears well up uncontrollably" (quoted in "Japanese Aesthetics").

One additional aesthetic tenet worthy of consideration in the present context is that of *kire* ("cut") or *kire tsuzuki* ("cut continuity" or "cut continuation"). This idea is underpinned by the Zen teaching according to which to see the world with eyes unclouded by acquisitive longings and ambitions, it is vital not to look to the future so single-mindedly as to neglect or ignore the here-and-now. The materialistic values fueled by consumer culture enjoin us to focus insistently on the future, fallaciously inducing us to believe that technological and economic progress are coterminous with individual enhancement. In fact, they merely serve to make us obsessively goal-oriented, precluding attentive consideration of the present and thus attenuating any chances of self-understanding. It is in order to counteract inventively the addiction to future objectives and tangible outcomes that Japanese culture has fostered the practice of arts which are devoid of either pragmatic aims or obvious aesthetic appeal, and are in fact undertaken solely for the purpose of bringing the mind and senses into closer, more mindful contact with themselves. As Calza maintains, the tea ceremony exemplifies this approach insofar as "it requires the practitioner to be versed in the many arts that converge in it; and, above all, to be aware of the human value of what he or she is doing and not necessarily attached to results" (Calza, pp. 15–16). The *chanuyo* is also averse to the inculcation of rigid lessons. Thriving on the Zen passion for paradox, it adheres to punctiliously formalized rules and yet opposes indoctrination in the belief that dogmatism is no less insidious and confining than reckless desire: "no more and no less than all Zen disciplines, the art of tea must therefore be practised with devotion, but also with detachment" (p. 16).

A life of luxury, in this world view, is a life stripped of superfluous encumbrances. Pivotal to its attainment is the willingness to cut oneself off from the pursuit of prospective achievements, and focus instead on the passing moment as the only truly available reality. The value of ephemerality is aphoristically invoked by the indigenous saying "*ichi-go ichi-e*," which translates literally as "one time, one meeting," and is therefore often used to express the idea that every experience is unique, unanchorable and unrepeatable. By consciously embracing a condition of rootlessness, the self might become capable of living in harmony with the impermanence of the universe at large — to attain a sense of fullness by emptying itself, and to distance itself from its actions enough to become a witness without sinking into total apathy. At the same time, in positing movement as an offshoot of the sequential ordering of distinct, though adjacent, scenes (a defining characteristic of the art of animation itself as a frame-by-frame construct), *kire* and *kire tsuzuki* emphasize the episodic character of human life in its entirety. Zen's emphasis on the here-and-now finds one of its most interesting artistic expressions in Japanese calligraphy. Since the brush strokes, once they have been traced, cannot be altered, the calligrapher only has one chance to create in the space of any one writing surface. The presentness of the writing is simply unrepeatable, and the creation itself must be seen to reflect nothing other than a fleeting moment in time. *Hitsuzendo*, the Zen "way of the brush," places great emphasis on the calligrapher's freedom, encouraging the hand and brush to move freely over the page to express the immediate vitality of experience instead of curbing their movements in the name of strict compositional rules aimed at the attainment of well-proportioned and aesthetically pleasing outcomes.

The notions of *kire* and *kire tsuzuki* also intimate that it is possible to value the beauty of each single element of a large ensemble of interacting objects without losing sight of the magic of the overall configuration. Italo Calvino explores this idea to splendid effect in the portion of his novel *If on a Winter's Night a Traveler* entitled "On the Carpet of Leaves Illuminated by the Moon," which is set in a traditional Japanese milieu. Observing the legion ginkgo leaves which fall relentlessly from the boughs and come to rest on the lawn below, the narrator ponders the possibility of identifying "the sensation of each single ginkgo leaf from the sensation of all the others." His host and mentor Mr. Okeda assures him that this is plausible. The secret is to focus on an individual leaf first and then gradually move on to reconstruct the wider scenario: "If from the ginkgo tree a single little yellow leaf falls and rests on the lawn, the sensation felt in looking at it is that of a single yellow leaf. If two leaves descend from the tree, the eye follows the twirling of the two leaves as they move closer, then separate in the air, like two butterflies chasing each other, then glide finally to the grass, one here, one there. And so with three, with four, even with five; as the number of leaves spinning in the air increases further, the sensations corresponding to each of them are summed up, creating a general sensation like that of a silent rain" (Calvino, p. 194). This process entails simultaneously the ability to separate each of the individual parts from the whole to which it belongs — which involves a cut or series of consecutive cuts — and the capacity to appreciate the interrelatedness of the various parts by concentrating on the overall rhythm of continuity which connects them into a flow.

Leaves, its should be noted, play an important role in Japanese philosophy at large (alongside blossom and other aspects of the vegetable kingdom). This idea is famously exemplified by the Zen anecdote in which a priest in charge of the garden adjoining a renowned temple scrupulously rakes up and arranges the dry autumn leaves in preparation for the impending visit of eminent guests. When the priest asks his master if the result of his efforts is to his liking, the older man praises him but also declares that there is room for improvement. He then unleashes a fresh cascade of leaves by shaking a tree trunk, and prompts his disciple to dispose them in the pattern formed by the initial layer prior to his tidying intervention. The parable communicates the proposition that the true beauty of the natural world can only be recognized as long as one refrains from the urge to domesticate it in accordance with anthropocentric priorities so as to achieve a sensitive understanding of the design criteria according to which nature itself disposes and displays its materials.

In recent years, the most conspicuous aesthetic principle readily associated with Japan by popular culture the world over has been undoubtedly the concept of *kawaii*. Considered synonymous with everything childlike, tender, lovable, charming and, above all else, cute, *kawaii* is generally regarded in the West as a preeminently contemporary phenomenon. In fact, as Fukai points out, "the peculiarly Japanese aesthetic of *kawaii* was articulated as early as the eleventh century by the author of *The Pillow Book*, Sei Shounagon, when she wrote: 'All small things are adorable'" (Fukai 2010b, p. 25). Undeniably, the partnership of the small and the beautiful is pivotal to disparate areas of Japan's creative endeavor. According to Lim, this propensity is typified by the indigenous proclivity to capitalize on "creative ways for doing more with less" (Lim, p. 14). Moreover, the taste for pretty decorative objects is deeply embedded in Japanese aesthetics. According to cultural analyst Tomoyuki Sugiyama, "cute" is indeed a fundamental facet of "Japan's harmony-loving culture." For instance, the tendency to collect figurines and other diminutive ornaments as mementoes — so very typical of the contemporary take on *kawaii*—"can be traced back 400 years to the Edo period, when tiny carved 'netsuke' charms were wildly popular" ("Japan smitten by love of cute"). *Netsuke*—literally, "root-fix"— were originally designed to serve an entirely practical purpose as toggles by which various items could be attached to the belt and hence make it possible to carry them around in the absence of pockets from the customary indigenous robe. *Netsuke* still stand out as uniquely intriguing artifacts, their frequent infusion of humorous, grotesque and risqué motifs in the otherwise fairly naturalistic representation of deities, ordinary humans and animals imparts these objects with lasting freshness.

Nowadays, the appetite for cute characters, accessories and gadgets is borne out by all sorts of people regardless of age, gender or class. At the same time, it is instrumental in the creation and consolidation of corporate identities with a friendly face, so to speak. On the one hand, as Diana Lee emphasizes, the cult of cuteness could be seen to originate in a culturally ingrained "need to be liked" and "accepted in society." This is quite consonant with the Japanese conception of politeness as a means of achieving societal and familial concord. On the other hand, it could be seen as a playful way of evading the responsibilities and duties linked with an "austere life in work, family and social responsibility," and thus of resisting the more "traditional values of Japanese lifestyle" (Lee). According to Sharon Kinsella, such an attitude results from social alienation, and signals a longing to take comfort from the establishment of "relationships" with "cute objects" in the absence of real connections with "people" (Kinsella, p. 228). On a more positive note, *kawaii* can be seen to be intimately and fruitfully related to indigenous philosophy insofar as it echoes an essentially Buddhist perspective in its inclination to foster the concepts of "weakness" and "inability" as qualities deserving recognition and even commendation (Lee). It is also plausible, in this regard, to see *kawaii*'s celebration of the beauty of childlike simplicity and playful freedom as a corollary of the teachings of Zen. In the spirit of *kawaii*, as in Zen, those ideals are inextricably intertwined with a non-teleological approach to reality. In the domain of art, this implies that artifacts are accorded a right to stand as autonomous — and elatingly ephemeral — entities instead of being expected to derive their raison d'être from an external validator, such as a digest of moral precepts or an artistic canon.

Relatedly, artificial though they are, the images unleashed by the *kawaii* vogue typically exude an aura of spontaneity: an idea which, in the context of Zen philosophy, is virtually indistinguishable from "freedom" (*jiyuu*). The latter does not amount, as it often does in Western philosophy, to the unrestrained assertion of subjective desires but rather to a force capable of arising out of nothing of its own accord since the individual itself is fundamentally "nothing." Both organic and inorganic entities, in this ontological perspective, share one essential characteristic: rootlessness. To depict life as it truly is, one must first of all acknowledge its lack of any definite foundations. The venerable native art of floral arrangement, "*ikebana*," encapsulates this position insofar as it is precisely by cutting the living flower from its roots in the earth that the designer discloses its genuine nature as an ephemeral being. As Makoto Ueda maintains, *ikebana*'s "ultimate aim" is "to represent nature in its innermost essence" (Ueda, p. 86). The word itself, after all, actually translates as "make flowers live" (from "*ikeru*" = "to live" + "*hana*" = "flower").

In assessing the enduring legacy of traditional philosophies in contemporary aesthetics, it is also noteworthy that some old concepts still in use today have progressively altered to satisfy the requirements of new contexts and audiences. For example, the notion of *fuuryuu*, originally denotative of polished manners, is still in use as a signifier of chic stylishness and creative ingenuity. *Shibui*, a traditional indicator of subtle and unostentatious beauty, is still often used in ordinary parlance, normally to refer to tastefully subdued hues and simple forms. Also common are the terms *jimi*, which strictly speaking defines understated good taste or modest simplicity but frequently comes to connote marginal drabness, and its antonym *hade*, a marker of showiness and flamboyance. A cognate pair of antithetical principles consists of *ga* (decorum, elegance) and *zoku* (coarseness, vulgarity). Germane aesthetic ideas encompass the concepts of artless simplicity (*soboku*), gracefulness (*reiyou* or *yuu*), propriety (*ga*), and unadorned charm (*karumi*) grounded in an appreciation of even the most prosaic of forms (*hosomi*). One of the most interesting terms is *iki*—an ideal which still represents an object of debate among both contemporary aestheticians and lay people due to its multiaccentuality and versatility. Originally used as the marker of a stylish, sophisticated and fundamentally bourgeois type of beauty with subtle tinges of eroticism, *iki* could also be used to describe the type of wealthy individual who appears nonchalant about wealth or appreciates sensual delight but is not enslaved to carnal appetites. It could also fittingly describe artworks characterized by the inventive handling of muted shades in preference to stark hues or writing in which sexuality is poignantly portrayed, yet never allowed to yield an overbearing sense of sensuous intoxication. Nowadays, however, *iki* is deployed primarily to describe a "cool" attitude.

Art and Its Objects

The final segment of this preliminary analysis recapitulates a few key aspects of Japanese art and aesthetics addressed in the preceding segments with exemplary reference to the domains of interior design, architecture and fashion. These encompass: the devotion to ornamentation; the cultivation of eminently corporeal vocabularies; the regard for nature and its materials in diverse creative practices; the integration of the old and the new, on the one hand, and the native and the imported on the other; the assertion of a frankly non-mimetic and self-reflexive approach to creation.

As noted, emblematic ornamentation constitutes one of the most distinctive and immediately recognizable attributes of Japanese design. Equally important is the commitment to compositional procedures which will enable the artist to match the geometric or organic properties of the decorative elements to the shapes of the objects they complement. For example, a pattern containing a wave or a whirlpool used to adorn a porcelain bowl might take advantage of the curve of the vessel itself in order suggest the kinetic qualities of the water theme. Similarly, the rotund contours of persimmon or lotus petals might be enhanced by their application to the domed portion of a lidded jar. Even the most conceptual of forms is thereby imbued with a vibrant sense of aliveness. The stylized figures represented in prehistoric clay sculptures were already enlivened by the infusion of animal or quasi-anthropomorphic traits into minimalistically cylindrical pots. More recent instances of ornamental pottery, and matching textiles, evoke an intense impression of latent animateness through their efficient balance of chromatic and linear components. This is equally true of the designs used in the decoration of writing-boxes of the Edo period in which black lacquer and eggshell come together to produce interlocking shapes reminiscent of M. C. Escher's optical pictures.

In assessing Japanese art's take on its objects, it is also vital to appreciate the cultural specificity of various indigenous words pertaining specifically to the root of the term aesthetics, i.e., *aesthesis*, or sense experience. Indeed, the Japanese language features a wide range of words which refer to concepts not necessarily available in other languages. An appropriate illustrative example is supplied by the art of gastronomy. In this specific field, as Richie observes, we find that "in addition to those enumerated in the West (sour, sweet, etc.), the Japanese distinguish a number of tastes they believe to be uniquely sensible to themselves. These include *awai* (delicacy), *umami* (deliciousness), and *shibui* (astringency) ... *Nigai* is used for 'bitter' and *egui* for 'acridity.' English does not differentiate between acridity and bitterness" (Richie, p. 23). A comparable degree of specificity distinguishes the realm of gestural language, and especially the ritualized motions brought to bear on the treatment, manipulation and molding of particular materials. A notable case in point is offered by the repertoire of gestures according to which paper is processed and folded so as to maximize its distinctive aesthetic appeal. Paper, it is worth stressing, stands out as a privileged material which native design still eagerly employs in numerous areas even as it endeavors to modify and perfect its products through the introduction of novel substances. Many of the actions performed by contemporary manufacturers in the meticulous conception of paper-based items designed for a variety of wrapping and packaging purposes strike their roots in time-honored practices. The same is true of the motions which still accompany the handling of other traditional materials classically utilized in the studious and loving execution of all manner of indigenous artifacts. Even though items produced by recourse to Western substances like plastic make regular appearances in contemporary Japanese culture, special attention is still devoted to the creation of objects of traditional derivation.

The manufacture of all sorts of time-honored articles involves ancient techniques, such as metalwork, mother-of-pearl inlay, glazed and unglazed stoneware, bamboo craft, straw basketry, cypress and cedar products based on the art of wood-bending (*magemono*), mulberry paper panels and, most memorably perhaps, the quintessentially Japanese treasure known as lacquerware. Reliant on the native *urushi* (i.e., "lacquer tree"), the crafting of lacquer originates in prehistoric times. As Reeve explains, it was initially deployed "as a way of waterproofing wooden objects such as bowls and protecting fragile objects like combs." However, these entirely pragmatic priorities were rapidly superseded by artistic aspirations as it became evident that the technique lent itself to the evocation of unique impressions. For example, "by applying many layers" of resinous *urushi* sap (usually colored black or red), "it is possible to cut through them to create sculptural effects." Furthermore, the use of "gold foil or gold dust (*makie*, 'sprinkled pictures') and mother-of-pearl" could lead to a stunning sense of multidimensionality (Reeve, p. 54).

The art of anime consistently references a wide range of traditional Japanese items (and underlying crafts) with varying degrees of emphasis in the depiction of both its outdoor and its indoor settings. These encompass *chochin*, paper lanterns with both commercial and ritual functions, and *shimenawa*, sacred straw ropes linked with the Shinto tradition to which paper streamers (*gohei*) are characteristically attached for ceremonial purposes. (The art of *origami* is held to have found inception in this practice.) Also in evidence are the *furoshiki*, a square piece of cloth used as an extremely adaptable and eco-friendly carrier, *washi* (handmade paper), *mizuhiki* (decorative paper cords), *noshi* (folds of white and red paper attached to gifts as tokens of friendship), *jubako* (tiered boxes with often exquisite decoration and lacquer coating used to store food prepared in advance for special occasions), *pochi-bukuro* (small gift envelopes exhibiting gorgeous patterns such as flowers or the animals from the Chinese zodiac) and, of course, the proverbially iconic *hashi* (chopsticks) and *hashi-oki* (chopstick rests).

The gestural vocabularies entailed by all of the aforementioned crafts and related products places considerable value on the creator's physical actions not merely as a means to an end — i.e., as a vehicle for the creation of an object — but also as artistic enunciations in their own right. This proclivity reaches its culmination in the tea ceremony, where ritual gestures carry pivotal importance as both expressive tools and symbols of autonomous worth. The actions performed in the context of the *chanoyu* are not only instrumental in the communication of emblematic messages: they also stand out as independent symbols themselves. This proposition is eloquently substantiated by Kakuzou Okakura's seminal text *The Book of Tea*, a beautiful record of the tea ceremony's concurrently performative and philosophical significance. The body, and hence the material dimension of creativity, are enthroned as the fundamental underpinnings of creation: as producers of meaning whose impact is capable of surpassing that of all immaterial sign systems and attendant concepts. At the same time, in making the creative gesture an artwork unto itself, the Japanese approach to creation declares its freedom from the notions of causality and teleology which have shackled much mainstream Western art for centuries. As seen earlier in relation to Zen thinking, Japanese aesthetics is not, as a rule, haunted by an obsessive focus on either outcomes or goals.

Highly laborious and diversified, all of the items and arts referred to in the foregoing paragraphs partake of a cultural heritage committed to the steady cultivation of first-class workmanship and, beyond this, to the promulgation of a profound sense of respect for the natural world as the cradle of ubiquitous spiritual forces. It is in keeping with this ethos that Japanese architecture has been environmentally sensitive for centuries, utilizing and recycling natural materials long before words like "green" and "eco-friendly" penetrated everyday Western discourse. A veritable paean to the indigenous tendency to live in harmony with the natural environment is the *machiya*, the nineteenth-century townhouse of the kind one sees in Kyoto, for example, where the use of bamboo shades and paper screens ensures that natural sunlight filters gracefully into the home, thus evoking the impression of outdoor living in the urban interior. Japanese art's regard for nature in all its manifestations finds philosophical expression in the theory of the Five Elements (*godai*), Japan's counterpart to the aforementioned Chinese *Wu Xing*. The philosophy of the Five Elements posits earth (*chi* or *tsuchi*), fire (*ka* or *hi*), air (*fuu* or *kaze*), water (*sui* or *mizu*) and the void (*kuu* or *sora*) as the essential powers shaping the universe, regarding both their intrinsic individual properties and their ongoing interplay as the generators of the life energy on which all species depend. The Five Elements are reflected in the traditional construction of numerous pagodas (*buttou*) and of the sorts of stone lanterns (*ishidourou*) one sees in gardens and temples, which consist of five tiers representing the gradual ascent of life energy from earth to the void.

This philosophy reverberates in novel guise in the works of contemporary artists such as Ando and Kengo Kuma, where the fluid interaction of stone, wood, water and air is innovatively encouraged. Ando himself has emphasized this concept as follows: "I do not believe architecture should speak too much. It should remain silent and let Nature in the guise of sunlight and wind speak" (cited in Lim, p. 19). Furthermore, Ando's conception of the natural world is clearly drawn to its most intangible expressions—those pervasive yet imperceptible fields wherein animistic forces continually renew themselves. "Such things as light and wind," the artist maintains, "only have meaning when they are introduced inside a house in a form cut off from the outside world. The isolated fragments of light and air suggest the entire natural world. The forms

I have created have altered and acquired meaning through elementary nature (light and air) that give indications of the passage of time and the changing of the season" (cited in Frampton). Ando's uniquely fluid designs and exquisite handling of the play of light and shadow, shrouded in tersely minimalistic silk-smooth concrete structures, consistently encourages the natural to seep into his works, therein to discover a congenial dwelling of its own.

Japan's sartorial fashion is likewise instilled with a deep sense of regard for materials and textures: a crucial aspect of native aesthetics resulting from a deeply ingrained commitment to the autonomous value of the creator's medium over and above its functional applications. Simultaneously, the ultimate roots of all art in the natural world are consistently emphasized. This ruse is abetted by the use of shades which are instantly reminiscent either of organic forms themselves (e.g., plants, animals, earth and water) or of their graphic and sculptural rendition in Japan's traditional arts. Most importantly, the tactile attributes of materials are everywhere foregrounded, though discreetly so. These stylistic preferences finds a direct correlative in the recent history of Japanese fashion and its international reception. When Japanese fashion designers first came into prominence on an international scale in the 1980s, it was primarily through their innovative approach to fabric that they made their impact on Western audiences.

As Frankel explains, these designers' creations typically exhibited "an extraordinary richness of texture, from unbleached, wrinkled felt to distressed or boiled textiles, dyeing in the style of *aizome* (a traditional indigo-dyed fabric) and subtle pattern woven in black on black." These imaginative fabrics owed much to highly inspired collaborative efforts engaging at once the couturiers themselves and indigenous "textile designers and technologists," their primary goal being the conception of silhouettes which seemed to flow "organically from the inherent characteristics of the fabrics used" (Frankel 2010b, p. 85). According to Fukai, Japanese fashion designers have also demonstrated a steady commitment to the establishment of "a new relationship between clothes and the body" which recognizes the importance of "the superfluous 'space' between the garment and the body." This interstitial site, traditionally "referred to as *ma*, is more than simply a void: it is a rich space that possesses incalculable energy" (Fukai 2010b, p. 16). By playing with *ma*, Japanese fashion departs significantly from Western perceptions of the correct relationship between the body and its clothes.

As Barbara Vinken emphasizes, Issey Miyake's designs are especially notable, in this regard, insofar as they offer a radical alternative to the Western notion of "dress as a 'second skin'" by assuming that "the space between dress and the body is where fashion takes place." Hence, "his trademark has become pleats ironed into the fabric." Enabling the materials to "project from the body," this device gives rise to garments that transcend "the normal dynamic of concealing and revealing to become a surprising and sophisticated, wholly abstract rhythmic sculpture" (Vinken, p. 33). In refusing to pander to the ethos of concealment and revelation, Japanese fashion simultaneously debunks conventional notions of erotic titillation based on "peekaboo voyeurism." Kawakubo cultivates this ethos by promoting "a symbiosis of clothes and body" which pursues "neither the sublimation nor the hiding away of the body but rather a new mode of embodiment." Kawakubo, in Vinken's view, protects the body's intimacy without trapping it: she "does not veil the body; she wraps it up; she packages it. By rewriting the Western history of classicism, she reveals the relationship between the nude, the naked and the dressed in a new light" (p. 35).

In exploring the fine collusion between the body's three-dimensionality and the fabric's two-dimensionality, Japanese fashion echoes one of the principal technical issues addressed by anime in recent decades: namely, the relationship between 3D and 2D graphics. On the whole, even though anime has incorporated a number of digital techniques conducive to the evocation of 3D effects, its dominant thrust remains oriented in the direction of 2D drawings (both manual and computer-generated). This bears witness, once again, to Japanese art's enduring preference for flat surfaces — a proclivity which, in the domain of fashion, is encapsulated by the flatness of an unworn kimono as the foundational point of reference. Western designers, by contrast, have traditionally sought to adapt clothes to the body by constructing them as 3D objects by recourse to devices such as pleats, tucks, darts and curvilinear cuts. No less importantly, the Western obsession with symmetry as an axial precept of classical aesthetics (and attendant conceptions of the perfect body) are exploded by Japanese fashion's cultivation of radically asymmetrical silhouettes. It is worth noting, on this point, that according to the philosopher, sociologist and literary critic Roger Caillois, asymmetry is actually the most distinctive aspect of Japanese aesthetics (Caillois).

As noted, the tendency to revamp local styles from the past constitutes a potent drive in the most disparate fields of Japan's motley culture. In the context of vestimentary fashion, this propensity sometimes manifests itself as a form of resistance to the authority of rationalism and scientificity conventionally associated with the notion of progress. According to Toby Slade, this is especially true of Japan's experience of modernity as a "cultural phenomenon" concurrent with "the period after the Meiji Restoration of 1868," and hence "the development of consumer culture" (Slade, p. 3). Indeed, while modernity is supposed to dispel the shadowy beliefs enforced by myth in the name of reason and clarity, it inevitably ends up erecting its own myths, often turning reason and clarity themselves not into instruments of truth but into mythical giants in their own right, and hence into ideologically oppressive agencies. Where fashion is specifically concerned, this equivocal situation finds expression in the paradox whereby "modernity everywhere repeatedly clothes itself in reconstructions of the past.... Even as tradition and superstition were consigned to the past, they were resurrected in the culture of modernity, in the sartorial uncanny, where the magical — romantic dress — and the irrationality of arbitrary ornamentation persist despite Enlightenment thought's insistence that they be abolished." Japanese culture entered modernity — and, with it, "this process of dialectical sartorial antithesis"— later than the majority of Western European cultures. Concomitantly, "most of its forms were borrowed" and yet, "they were equally irrational" (p. 5). Therefore, in the particular case of Japan, the revamping of traditional vogues and the absorption of foreign influences are virtually inseparable phenomena. In addition, Japan's inveterate delight in ornamentation, encapsulated by the aesthetics of *kazari*, would have easily encouraged the resurgence of this particular facet of fashion within the context of modernity itself.

It is also important to recognize, in this respect, that Japan's peculiar relationship to modernity is largely a corollary of the stringently isolationist policy maintained by the Tokugawa government in the Edo era. While securing a protracted period of peace and stability through the perpetuation of the ancient feudal system, this regime prohibited extensive transactions between Japan and the outside world, limiting the country's mercantile connections with the Chinese and the Dutch to the city of Nagasaki. As Masaru Katzumie observes, "the new government that overthrew the Tokugawa regime in 1868 (the year of the so-called Meiji Restoration) decided to reverse the existing policy of national isolation," and sought to "establish a modern state by introducing science and technology from advanced Western nations." Nevertheless, traditional lifestyles and mores which had flourished unchallenged for centuries could not be simply erased by the new dispensation in one fell swoop, and this inevitably led to "a kind of dichotomy" whereby Japan has since operated "in a state of perpetual oscillation between the opposed phenomena of tradition and progress" (Katzumie, pp. 7–8). Thus, the country has not moved gradually from feudalism to modernity through intermediate stages of economic and broadly cultural evolution but rather leapt somewhat mercurially from one condition to the other with scarce time for adjustment. The coexistence of the old and the new, the functional and the magical, the rational and the irrational in fashion typifies this dyadic state of affairs.

In the art of anime itself, we witness both the revamping of past styles in contemporary contexts, and the imaginative integration of local and imported elements. In this regard, anime functions as a commentary on Japanese culture in general, reminding us that its periodic reorientation toward the past has impacted on an ample repertoire of quotidian objects, including garments, household accessories, school equipment and toys. In addition, anime shows that the rekindling of the old has evolved in tandem with the reconfiguration of traditional native trends in light of novel cultural realities. To cite an illustrative instance from the vestimentary sphere, the revival of time-honored elements to satisfy the demands of a rapidly changing world is borne out by the popularity of the *yukata* as a fashion item of enduring appeal which women and young girls still don quite enthusiastically at traditional events such as festivals (*matsuri*) and attendant firework displays. Even more solemn situations, such as traditional weddings or coming-of-age ceremonies, still call for magnificent full-fledged kimonos and appropriate accessories, such as *geta* sandals, *tabi*, hair combs and purses. The *yukata* is also often favored as a casual evening garment to be worn at home after work by businessmen who are normally garbed in Western-style suits during the day.

In anime, traditional Japanese apparel makes regular appearances not only, as one might logically expect, in the context of costume drama but also in the presentation of ceremonial situations of the kind mentioned above. At the same time, local traits can be seen to influence daily apparel of basically Western orientation as this is more or less explicitly instilled with a sense of regard for materials and textures. Numerous outfits worn by female actors, in particular, show a dedication to the innate properties of disparate fabrics, leading to adventurous combinations of both practical and quirky details. Anime's take on uniforms, a common presence in the context of school-centered drama in particular, also evinces an integration of Western styles and native values, insofar as outlines of essentially European derivation merge with Japan's historical attitudes to the concept of the uniform as both a functional and an ideological entity. (This idea will be examined in some depth in the context of Chapter 3.)

The domestic interiors typically portrayed by anime set in contemporary or quasi-contemporary periods corroborate the overall impression of hybridity exuded by Japanese culture. They achieve this effect mainly by bringing together indigenous and Western elements of design, harmoniously juxtaposing Western-style furnishings such as sofas, tables and chairs with quintessentially Japanese materials: paper, straw, bamboo, clay, cypress and pine, among others. Kitchens, cooking appliances and accessories, aspects of the home which make frequent appearances in anime, supply a perfect example of cultural cross-pollination, insofar as they exhibit many salient features of their Western counterparts while retaining a sense of their origins in traditional native layouts (e.g., in the representation of alcoves and shelves for the storage of pots and pans, and of utensils hung from the walls).

Japan's customs are also reflected in the tendency to adapt the home's décor to the changing seasons, drastic climactic fluctuations being a major aspect of the indigenous environment and largely responsible for the culture's sensitivity to ideas of transitoriness and continual renewal. The synthesis of disparate elements and influences reflects the evolution of residential Japanese architecture over the past century. As Katzumie elucidates, "before the war, middle-class households preferred to live in one-family houses, which included, as a status symbol, at least one room in Western style complete with piano and sofa. Post-war apartment blocks are, generally speaking, in Western style, but the planners of such buildings have always to bear in mind the fondness of the people who will live in them for rooms floored in Japanese style with *tatami* straw matting" (Katzumie, pp. 8–9). The materials used in the modern anime home emit a feeling of tactile immediacy which serves to underscore the unabated influence of natural substances in the entire galaxy of Japan's artistic practices, while also conveying a deeply ingrained desire to enter into intimate communion with their sensory and sensuous qualities. A connected message is encapsulated by the ongoing popularity of traditional pieces of furniture such as the *chabudai*, a short-legged table devoted to a variety of activities from eating to study and needlework, the *zabuton*, a sitting cushion, and the aforecited *tatami*, adaptable flooring mats. All of these items convey the inclination to live in close proximity to the ground without the interference of artificial mediators and thus communicate directly with the dwelling's natural substratum.

The material dimension also proclaims itself in the frank admission of artificiality accompanying virtually any artifact. In this matter, Japanese art differs radically from canonical Western art, where classic realism has expected artists to efface or elide any obvious indicator of productivity from their final creations, taking care to eliminate all traces of the corrections and amendments to which the work has been subjected in the process of its execution. In fact, as Joan Stanley-Baker observes, "the human qualities of imperfection" are deeply "built into the artwork" (Stanley-Baker, p. 11), and even the raw signs of productive practice which many Western artists strive to hide in the service of perfection are candidly exposed. These often include graphic presences as elemental as "rough edges, fingerprints or chisel marks" (p. 13). The finished objet d'art is not Japanese art's ultimate objective. By implication, the work's presumed impregnability and immutability are not absolute priorities for the Japanese artist, designer or craftsman. Anime itself promulgates this world view by recourse to the self-reflexive strategies which, as noted in the opening segment of this discussion, have increasingly stood out as one of the art form's principal features. These tactics repeatedly draw attention to the process of production itself, alerting the viewer to the animation's constructed, and hence deconstructable, status.

Virtually all areas of artistic production, moreover, appear to be informed by a specific approach to work, which Lonsdale sums up as follows: "historically, craftsmen, each a specialist in their own field, have worked together. For example, a lacquer bowl requires a woodworker to craft the bowl, then someone else to apply the lacquer. This ethos is seen in the world of industrial design where in-house design teams at large corporations such as Sony and Canon work closely with the technical side and the marketing division to produce innovative and style driven products representative of the company as a whole as opposed to any individual designer or developer" (Lonsdale, p. 147). These comments offer an appropriate note on which to close this segment of the discussion insofar as they capture the intensely collaborative spirit which distinguishes the production of anime itself as an integral aspect of the art and is still honored even by the wealthiest and most acclaimed of studios.

Chapter 2

THE SEARCH FOR A LANGUAGE

> *Nowadays, the word "style" is frequently misinterpreted, since it is used to highlight the formal, even decorative aspects of various phenomena of mass culture. This confusion has reached the point where the unfortunate term "stylist" has been coined to refer to a person who could never exist: someone who creates style. In fact, style is the result of a complex process of personal and social transformation (and as such not attributable to a single person), one that gives rise to images capable of representing values that are profound and enduring, not ephemeral like fashion which, by definition, must constantly be changing.* — Gian Carlo Calza

Japanese culture's elevation to artistic status of activities not commonly considered art in the West is largely a corollary of its focus on the activity itself as an ongoing search for a language. Engaging potentially any individual who seeks to give form to a talent or vision, and not solely the so-called genius, this quest entails both the acquisition of an existing repertoire of tools, techniques and precepts, and the striving for novel methods and expressive molds. At both levels, what distinguishes the Japanese take on art inherited by contemporary anime is a deep appreciation of the value of an activity regardless of its goals. What seems to challenge most severely the West's mental constructs is the application of this attitude to activities which actually appear to be wholly geared toward — and dependent upon — tangible outcomes. The arts of gastronomy and horticulture are clear cases in point. The anime examined in this chapter show that the search for a language is inseparable from the ability to honor the practice per se: its enactment, its juggling of tested and groundbreaking possibilities, and its painstaking attention to the tiniest detail. Ideally, the greater the exertion fueled into this task, the more natural and effortless its products will seem. This facet of Japanese aesthetics echoes the principle of *sprezzatura* promoted by Western aesthetics in the Renaissance. This refers to the adoption of a casually relaxed attitude to one's accomplishments intended to dissimulate any vestige of toil beneath an appearance of spontaneity. At the same time, in treating even the most prosaic quotidian activities as actual or potential art forms, Japanese culture dismantles the barrier between performer and spectator. In so doing, it also explodes the idea that creators carry out their tasks so that others will admire the products of their efforts in an essentially passive mode. In fact, creators are also spectators, and therefore implied evaluators, of their own performance.

While different activities entail different approaches and routes through which their specific languages might be explored, they all share one vital factor. This consists of their emphasis on creative endeavor as inextricable from an honest acknowledgment of ephemerality — and hence as a potent reminder of the mutability and transience of all things, both embodied and conceptual. The frank recognition of evanescence is crucial to each and every art's distinctive search for a language. Moreover, it bolsters the Japanese aversion to valorize the attainment of timeless masterpieces — the goal conventionally pursued by Western art since Greco-Roman antiquity — as the ultimate end of creativeness. The indigenous attitude to the natural world evinces an analogous disposition, as exemplified by the culturally embedded preference for flowers which drop their petals one by one rather than in a single clump. Thus, even as evergreens such as the pine, the cypress and the cedar are deeply revered as emblems of eternal life and continuity, the feeling of transience associated with the cherry tree plays a major metaphorical role both at home and abroad in capturing Japan's special sensibility. The search for a language is rendered especially tantalizing by the penchant for vagueness and adumbration typically fostered by native aesthetics. Indeed, this preference prioritizes hints to direct statements, and discreet clues to precise meanings, all the while drawing attention to the philosophical value of emptiness as a source of infinite potentiality.

Emptiness, far from being perceived as a bleak state of negativity, presents itself as a uniquely valuable means of intimating a whole galaxy of possible worlds which viewers might ideate for themselves in accordance with their own disposition and sensibility. By bringing into play the imaginative potentialities of disparate individuals, emptiness becomes a space wherein opportunities for personal creativity, and hence both inner and outer growth, may be discovered and pursued. In order to stimulate the beholder's imagination, artifacts frequently rely on strategies intended to generate a sense of intermission or partial occlusion — such as the interposition of clouds, screens or foliage between distinct compositional planes — which cause the eye to pause and thus encourage speculation about what might lie beyond the immediately discernible. What might initially come across as an amorphous mass gradually evolves into a novel reality. Japanese art's seemingly spontaneous attraction to allusiveness over explicit description is consistently matched by its preference for penumbra over full light, for imperfection and incompleteness over plenitude and resolution, for subdued chromatic gradations over loud effects, for dynamic and asymmetrical composition over rigidly codified perspectivalism, for a fluid combination of naturalistic and geometrical forms (as well as flesh and metal) over strict iconographic distinctions.

The fascination with the image of a world suffused with mist and haze, with transient sparks and refractions, emanates directly from an aversion to mutually exclusive absolutes in favor of a capacious approach to the real which does not merely tolerate but actually honors the coexistence and collusion of apparent opposites in a never-ending dance of possibilities. This is a vision wherein "light and darkness," as Souseki Natsume maintains in *Kusamakura* (*The Grass Pillow*), "are but opposite sides of the same thing, so wherever the sunlight falls it must of necessity cast a shadow.... Try to tear joy and sorrow apart, and you have lost your hold on life. Try to cast them to one side, and the world crumbles" (Natsume, pp. 13–14). Moreover, blurring and veiling effects enable the creation of areas that are invisible not in the sense that they are altogether absent from an image but rather in the sense that they can exist within its imaginative map as sites of imponderability and wonder. In this context, the aesthetics of emptiness deploys interposition to problematize the conventional opposition between presence and absence by emplacing a presence made of absence as vital to the artifact's identity. Emptiness serves to enhance the scope of a picture, to invest it with folds of meaning wherein visibility and invisibility, being and non-being, ironically interact. The aesthetics of emptiness finds an important expression in one particular facet of the multiaccentual concept of *iki*, examined in Chapter 1, which Shuzou Kuki describes as "renunciation": namely, "a conscious distancing of the self from attachment" (cited in Calza, p. 51). The kind of renunciation entailed by *iki* with its endeavor to communicate a sense of effortless elegance through understatement and modesty is by no means synonymous with deprivation. In fact, it proceeds from an individual's ability to embody tastefulness unostentatiously and with no concern for public acclaim and for confirmation of his or her self-importance.

In this respect, the ethos of renunciation located at the heart of *iki* could be said to encapsulate Zen's positive perception of emptiness. This, as Shigenori Nagatomo explains, results from a dispassionate acknowledgment of the self as "a groundless ground that is nothing." It is its inherent nothingness that renders the self capable of experiencing freedom (*jiyuu*) as "the spontaneous creative act of living nature." Such a state is not, as is often proposed by Western perspectives on the subject, automatically equated to "a lack or absence of external constraint" meant to allow for the unrestrained expression of "ego-desire." The self's fundamental nothingness actually entails that *jiyuu* "arises out of the self on its own." Insofar as it emanates from nothing, Zen's "free action" is not restricted by "ego-desire." On the contrary, "it 'kicks through the bottom of the bucket,' that is, it purifies all the 'defilements' interlaced with the activity of the ego-consciousness, as well as the personal and collective unconscious. For this reason, there is no issue involved in the Zen person's action that addresses the will of ego-consciousness. For what motivates the Zen person to action is a *thrust* he or she feels, surging from the creative source in the bottomless ground" (Nagatomo). The West's inveterate susceptibility to *horror vacui* would be displaced, were Zen to give in to fear, to *horror plaeni*— or better still, to avoid any concessions to a sentiment alien to Zen, to *amor vacui*. In the anime here studied, the ethos of emptiness fluidly intermeshes with several of the aesthetic predilections fostered by Japanese culture for centuries. Their search for a language, accordingly, resonates with more or less sonorous echoes of that time-honored legacy, and acquires particular connotations and colorations depending on the specific art and expressive vehicles with each they engage.

Focusing on the art of music, *Piano: The Story of a Young Girl's Heart* examines the collusion of the search for a language with a process of psychological and emotional development akin to a bildungsroman. The anime's integration of a coming-of-age formula with the topos of creative expression is rendered most memorable by the fact that it does not derive its power from an especially innovative story line or from a passion for spectacle so much as from a disarming ability to communicate the intensity of the protagonist's search for a language in the most candid tone imaginable. Miu Nomura is portrayed from the start as a character whose commitment to music is so innately, even viscerally, deep as to have defined her identity since childhood. However, as the child's innocently unrestrained knack of self-expression has gradually given way to the self-critical and doubting tendencies of the introverted adolescent, Miu has been finding it increasingly difficult to play freely, and keenly share her gift with anyone willing to listen in the way she was wont to. Thus, the very music which would once provide Miu quite unproblematically with an uplifting sense of freedom has by and by grown into a burden, weighing on her soul as her innermost feelings simply refuse to flow unhindered. The girl's performance is severely impaired by this expressive impasse, and her failure to live up to the expectations of her temperamental tutor, Mr. Shirakawa, only adds to her mounting sense of frustration. In keeping with the classic bildungsroman of Romantic orientation, the protagonist's developmental curve is appropriately fraught by the incremental emergence of hitherto unknown emotions, with the experience of first love, of course, high on the agenda. At first, friendship itself is complicated by Miu's realization that while she is afflicted by the twin pressures of artistic unfulfillment and unrequited desire, her closest friend, Yuuki, may be too wrapped up in her own sentimental issues to have much time to spare comforting Miu.

However, it is precisely with the sustaining power of friendship, allied to an imaginative approach to familial solidarity and ties, that *Piano* ultimately locates the highest creative capacities. Miu and those around her manage to confront and, by and large, negotiate satisfactorily both the petty irritations of daily existence and some momentous life choices because they are able to instill their relationships with the energy of imagination and intuition at their most selflessly creative. In their handling of interpersonal responsibilities, the key characters are actually akin to artists ready to embrace their tasks for the sake of the creation itself and not as mere vehicles (or, worse still, weapons) for the self-centered assertion of personal values, ambitions and desires. Thus, even though music is the art to which the series devotes its attention on the thematic plane, it is with the crystal-faceted art of human interaction that its deeper ethical lessons reside. At one point, the two arts are actually posited as interdependent constituents of one composite creative endeavor as the drama discreetly hints at a parallel between its heroine's gradual discovery of a musical language able to convey her distinctive artistic vision and her somber piano instructor's search for a means of transcending his own affective inhibitions and thus releasing the submerged energy of his true feelings. The value placed by *Piano* on human interaction as an art sui generis could also be regarded as a metaphor for the interaction of visual artistry and music: a process of coalescence to which the anime owes its very identity as a creative construct of an essentially visual nature in which music is ascribed thematic dominance. The fluidity of the boundaries which supposedly separate the pictorial and the sonoric domains is thereby highlighted with admirable dramatic grace.

A potential solution to Miu's stultifying block emerges, in a quintessentially Romantic vein, with the suggestion that the protagonist's heart troubles could actually prove instrumental in freeing up her suppressed creativity by helping her release once again her soul's intrinsic melody and, most importantly, enabling her to discover a novel language through which she might satisfyingly articulate and share her vision. The most dramatic phase in Miu's bildungsroman coincides with the spring recital requiring the girl to create her own composition at Mr. Shirakawa's behest. While the stern teacher cannot overtly compel Miu to take part in the prestigious event, he sneakily pressurizes her by using every opportunity at his disposal to remind her that if she decides to withhold, none of his students will be participating. Thus, Mr. Shirakawa implicitly requires his pupil to reflect on the communal implications of her creative talent — on the duties and responsibilities she bears as an aspiring artist not merely toward her personal practice, let alone herself as an individual, but also toward the social ensemble to which she belongs. The crucial role played by group affiliation in Japanese society is here alluded to in the subtlest of ways.

Miu postpones the final decision for months while vacillating between the extremes of bravery and timidity — proclivities to which her personality seems innately inclined in equal measures — but suddenly resolves to confront the challenge when she realizes that in composing her own piece, she will enjoy a uniquely precious chance of playing with feeling for the sake of her sweetheart, Takahashi. This goal eventually rescues Miu from the deadlock of lack of inspiration which, compounded with concern about Takahashi's health, nearly prevents her project from coming to fruition. The philosophy of group loyalty comes prominently into play once more, underpinning Miu's eventual decision to stick with both the recital and piano playing in general. This indeed stems from the girl's epiphanic discovery of the capacity to visualize the people she plays for in spontaneous recognition of both her own and their feelings — and, by extension, the very reasons for which she plays *at all*. Throughout its unfolding, and increasingly in the last third of the series, *Piano* draws attention to the interrelation of its heroine's developmental journey with the emotional and psychological evolution undergone by other key personae, especially her teacher. Hence, while concentrating on Miu's search for a language, the anime is no less sensitive to the ethical perplexities besetting Mr. Shirakawa's task. Echoing a conundrum which many devoted teachers are likely to have at some point confronted, this aspect of the anime focuses on the tension between the piano instructor's dedication to Miu's artistic advancement, which prompts him to push her to extremes for her own ultimate good, and his implicit awareness that in so doing, he might end up alienating the girl altogether from the joys of music.

Like *Piano*, *NANA* frames the search for expressive tools capable of voicing its characters' creative drives within the generic parameters of a coming-of-age drama. Persistently subordinating the requirements of neat narrative ordering to the pursuit of psychological acuity and emotional range, *NANA* asserts most memorably its bildungsroman leanings by refusing to contain its characters' experiences into tight plotting devices. Relatedly, the anime does not seek to chronicle events by submitting its story to the rhythms of a neatly cresting drama but rather aims to supply a dispassionate anatomy of the vicissitudes attendant upon the transition to adulthood, and of the role played therein by artistic endeavor. The unusual relationship around which the anime winds its tortuous tale of cosmopolitan life, astir with the chords of thriving and aspiring bands, is pivotal to its creative project. Nana Komatsu and Nana Osaki are so profoundly different in background and outlook as to initially appear fundamentally mismatched. Nevertheless, they forge a uniquely close relationship of a kind infrequently witnessed in anime or indeed cinema at large.

The tie uniting the two young women virtually from the moment they meet on a snowbound train to Tokyo is a hybrid creature of a rare breed. So uncommon as to occasionally verge on the bizarre, yet tender and stirringly real, the relationship which the two Nanas gradually establish is neither a conventional friendship nor a romantic liaison. In fact, it approximates the exceptional status of an attachment which magically manages to partake of the distilled qualities of both types of relationship at their most refined. As the bond between Nana Osaki, the disaffected and brooding punk rock musician, and Nana Komatsu, a naive and childish girl with an unfortunate proclivity for poor romantic choices, progressively unfolds, artistic and emotional aspirations progressively blend in mutual suffusion. While they chase their respective dreams of music, love and self-discovery, the two Nanas come to resemble the long-lost of twins of Shakespearean drama: one feels that prior to their accidental encounter and discovery of unforeseeable affinities, each was akin to a drop of water, to paraphrase an especially beautiful line from *The Comedy of Errors*, seeking another drop in the vastness of the ocean.

The coming-of-age topoi dramatized in *Piano: The Story of a Young Girl's Heart* and in *NANA* find notable equivalents in a range of musical ideas, images and motifs which have been recurrently captured by the visual arts over the centuries in their interdisciplinary dialogue with music. In the history of Western painting, specifically, visual themes such as musical instruments have been often utilized in order to represent the ages of man (or the dance of life) in an allegorically capsulated fashion, each symbolically significant image serving to convey the supposedly characteristic mood of each phase of human existence. Musical motifs, moreover, have underpinned many pictorial allegories aiming to express the balancing power of music as a means of promoting an amorous ideal based on the principle of sublimation, on the salubrious harmonization of discordant emotions, and hence on the suppression of love's carnal dimension — the *voluptas* demonized by the chivalric tradition as inimical to spiritual growth and self-ennoblement. Music, in this particular context, has been elevated to the status of a mirror of virtue (*speculum virtutis*) whose delicate resonances — especially the ones generated by string instruments — are meant to emblematize harmonious interaction, mutuality, emotive refinement and, ultimately, marital concord. Ironically, when associated with unruly legendary figures such as Dionysus, Pan or the Sirens music serves the very opposite purpose, operating as a supreme symbol of lust, excess and dissolute behavior.

Music-oriented anime will be returned to later in this analysis. It is first worth noting, however, that the bildungsroman element also plays a conspicuous role in the creative quests dramatized by anime devoted to arts other than music, as attested to by the series *Skip Beat!* Combining a generous dose of enthusiasm with a hearty appetite for humor and no less liberal a helping of iconoclasm, the series articulates a twofold search for a language. On the one hand, it dramatizes the passionate quest for avenues of innovative self-expression in the devious realm of show business embraced by its heroine, Kyoko. The girl embarks upon her mission when she fortuitously discovers that the man to whom she has wholeheartedly devoted herself, Shou, is merely exploiting her in the solipsistic pursuit of his own artistic ambition, that of becoming an idol. On the other hand, the anime articulates a formal and generic search for a language centered on its own determination to subvert the conventions of *shoujo* anime — and, most crucially, their emplacement of kindliness, meekness, sweetness and cheerfulness (traits cumulatively conveyed by the word *yasashii*) as a young woman's ideal qualities. In fact, Kyoko reacts to her shocking discovery by giving vent to a raging storm of emotions abetted by a fair amount of food-throwing — a number which appropriately culminates with her fiery resolve to get her revenge at any price. This requires, in the first place, a creative act of self-reinvention resulting in the visible construction of an alternate — and much more glamorous — persona which abides in memory as one of the anime's most inspired artistic gestures. The protagonist's and the anime's respective quests for alternate expressive molds thus mesh into a deftly balanced dramatic whole.

Like *NANA* and *Skip Beat!*, the anime *Tsuyokiss — Cool x Sweet*, *Kaleido Star*, *Whisper of the Heart* and *Only Yesterday* knit the search for a creative language with an arduous process of personal maturation. In all four, it is intimated that when people are given the space and freedom to pursue their artistic ambitions, they are likely to develop a sense of confidence and purpose which is instrumental in their psychological evolution and assumption of mature responsibilities. Conversely, if those goals are frustrated, their overall chances of development are likely to be stunted and warped. In *Tsuyokiss — Cool x Sweet*, Sunao's determination to found a drama club as the basis of her devotion to the acting profession eventually wins the day despite the impervious obstacles thrown in her path by spiteful antagonists. This victory, in turn, helps her acquire the ability not only to secure her own artistic fulfillment but also to assist other people's creative development in distinct areas of self-expression. *Kaleido Star*, likewise, focuses on the challenges which its heroine, Sora, faces and eventually overcomes in the pursuit of a circensian career wherein her unique acrobatic talent may be maximized. Similarly, Shizuku, the heroine of *Whisper of the Heart*, is able to understand what kind of person she really is, and hence to refine her goals, thanks to her parents' recognition that the girl's dedication to the art of writing far exceeds in importance, on her journey to adulthood, her academic performance. *Only Yesterday* dramatizes the opposite scenario, intimating that the suppression of Taeko's desire to embrace a thespian career when this is brutally nipped in the bud by her father's prejudices, marks the inception of a lukewarm existence of frustration and unfulfillment which may only be redressed if the protagonist is willing to confront her frozen dreams and failure to pursue her true objectives.

Both *NANA* and *Skip Beat!* interweave the search for a language with projects of self-development grounded in the solid worlds of the music and show biz industries and of contemporary fashion. *Shinkyoku Soukai Polyphonica* and its subsequently released prequel, *Shinkyoku Soukai Polyphonica Crimson S*, develop the pursuit for artistic vocabularies and voices in an alternate direction, taking it straight into the spiritual realm and choreographing a quest whose ultimate goal is the sustenance of otherworldly entities. It is indeed the chief peculiarity of the continent of Polyphonica to accommodate spirits who survive wholly on the music played by human beings, thereby coexisting in harmony with their providers and even materializing, on occasion, in human or animal form. The beauty of the anime's artistic vision is not confined to its soul-enhancing deployment of music, however. In fact, it could be argued that it reveals its full colors in the incremental, yet discreet, celebration of the key relationship around which its diegesis is constellated: the cooperative bond between Phoron, a "Dantist" (i.e., a player of divine music known as "Commandia") and the "Crimson Spirit" Corticarte, one of the most ancient spirits in the entire universe. Moreover, their interactions with a diversified gallery of friends and colleagues consistently enriches that focal connection. Therefore, it could be argued that in this yarn, the ethos of collaboration pivotal to Japan's artistic practices for time immemorial finds unique and poignant articulation.

The mystical dimension of a search for a language centered on music is likewise axial to *The Melody of Oblivion*. The anime's pseudohistorical premise is that in the twentieth century (i.e., one hundred years prior to its unfolding), humanity was caught in an epic struggle against preternatural beings dubbed simply "Monsters," which ended with its complete domination by that race. Even though the Monsters are supposed to rule the Earth unchecked, they remain hidden from the public, capitalizing on a sophisticated virtual apparatus redolent of the scenario portrayed in the *Matrix* movies, which effectively occludes their very existence. The sole human beings who are still cognizant of the rulers' presence and strive to vanquish them so as to restore the human race to its original freedom are the "Warriors of Melos." These heroic champions of a beleaguered breed rely not only on their unique ability to sense and oppose the evasive oppressors but also on a creative gift based on the capacity to perceive a ghostly girl who goes by the evocative name of the "Melody of Oblivion" ("*Boukyaku no Senritsu*"). The spiritual energy released by this creature is held capable of emancipating humanity from its current state of subjugation once and for all. Bocca, the male lead, is an ostensibly ordinary adolescent who suddenly discovers his potential as a Warrior when he hears the otherworldly melody in the course of a confrontation between a Warrior of Melos and a Monster. Hence, Bocca determines to seek out and liberate the *Boukyaku no Senritsu* at any price, which hauls him into a dizzying spiral of adventures and trials revolving around countless demons, alongside new friends and allies. Even this rapid survey of the series' trajectory ought to leave no doubt as to its emplacement of the art of music as a force of cosmic proportions.

As several of the titles discussed in the preceding paragraphs indicate, the coming-of-age parables traced by anime in its anatomy of disparate quests for creative expression are often fraught with psychological conflicts and emotionally tortuous relationships. The dark side of the topos examined in this chapter is even more prominent in anime which focus explicitly on the artistic pursuits embraced by characters afflicted by traumatic and disabling legacies. In such instances, the search for a language is cast as a struggle for self-redefinition through creative endeavor necessitated by especially harrowing experiences. *Ef—A Tale of Memories* provides a classic illustration of this trend. Chihiro, one of the anime's principal personae, is the victim of a peculiar form of amnesia which reduces her memory span to no more than thirteen hours at a stretch. The girl has unremittingly fantasized about writing a novel but has been hindered from accomplishing her goal by her strange predicament. Taking it upon himself to grapple with the ephemeral specters haunting Chihiro's mind, her boyfriend Renji embarks on a singular mission: enabling the girl to realize her creative aspirations at all costs. This entails some stoic perseverance on the youth's part, since Chihiro's initial reaction to the suggestion that they collaborate on her project is self-protectively cynical. Even when the girl yields to Renji's proposition and agrees to lend him the notebook hosting her ideas in an embryonic guise, her aide's objective is thwarted by Chihiro's ineluctable proclivity to forget who he is from one day to the next. The only counteracting strategy at her disposal, in the circumstances, is to write about Renji and their meetings every day in the diary she treasures in a brave effort to retain some tenuous connection with the passage of time.

When Chihiro's project is eventually embraced, the anime delivers a stunning interpretation both of the creative process per se and of the materials and tools deployed in its pursuit, unleashing a multimedia carousel in which the intersection of graphics, colors and sounds — deftly punctuated by tasteful allusions to a wide range of stylistic influences of both Eastern and Western provenance — succeeds in evoking powerful synesthetic impressions. Most notable, in this respect, are the sequences devoted to shots which are intended to provide direct insight into the world of Chihiro's novel. At times, these are placed within arty borders reminiscent of picture frames, which figuratively replicates the depiction of Chihiro's protagonist as a painter. At the same time, it also mirrors the anime's self-referential leanings and unabated fascination with a metaworld of screens within the screen: traits of its cumulative makeup which find expression in myriad forms of visual play and technical experimentation. This is paradigmatically borne out by the frequent interspersal of regular footage with hand-drawn sketches, monochrome frames, character silhouettes in which parts of the actors' environment appear to flow, stylized depictions of climatic elements such as snowflakes or raindrops, stylishly manipulated photographs and recurrent shots of a sky in nearly continual motion enhanced by subtly diversified textures.

The self-reflexive tendencies consistently exhibited by *Ef—A Tale of Memories* throughout its dramatic unfolding are sustained by the animation's assiduous emphasis on textuality—an effect it achieves by foregrounding in uncompromising terms the underlying materiality of language. This phenomenon is powerfully highlighted in a sequence devoted to Chihiro's voicing of her creative anxieties: "the obstacle," the girl frankly admits, "is that I can't finish writing in one day ... I forget memories and details. The story, setting, and even my impression of the characters change." The climax of Chihiro's revelation is visually matched by shots in which the background is flooded by whirling fragments of sentences and even single typographical marks in disparate fonts which are superimposed, assembled and disassembled by turns across the screen. Writing is also deployed in the scenes meant to dramatize various aspects of Chihiro's story, with its protagonist, setting and props, where ample chunks of text scroll over the background, traverse the visuals or flicker intermittently through the frames. In this respect, the anime could be said to pay enthusiastic homage to one of the most vital characteristics of the form it adapts, the visual novel, as a digital creation whose graphic, narrative and pictorial identity is vitally intertwined with textuality.

Traumatic experiences are also pivotal to the dramatic premises of the search for a language elaborated by *Clannad* in both its movie version and as a two-season TV series. The crux of *Clannad*'s engagement with the topos of the creative quest resides with the thespian ambitions nourished by its heroine, Nagisa. Though generally hesitant and insecure, largely due to her protracted absence from her lessons as a result of ill health and resulting lack of friends, the girl is determined to revive her school's disbanded drama club and to perform a play of her own conception, which she has been tirelessly rehearsing in private. Nagisa's search for a language is instilled with a humorous note by the revelation that despite her passionate attraction to theater, she has never actually seen an onstage performance in her whole life. The jocular element does not, however, detract from the swelling sense of pathos pervading the girl's quest: a vital aspect of the anime's mood which gains momentum as we learn that Nagisa'a artistic dream is inextricably intertwined with painful childhood experiences and a latent urge to exorcize their legacy. Central to her ordeal is a haunting feeling of inadequacy ensuing from her parents' self-sacrificial choices, and particularly their resolve to put an end to their own successful dramatic careers for her sake. At the same time, the play ideated by Nagisa comments metaphorically on her current situation by focusing on a girl stranded in a spectral realm — "a world that has ended" — who fills time by indefatigably crafting a doll out of "pieces of junk" in an effort to alleviate her own dreadful isolation.

In *True Tears*, traumatic experiences are artistically processed by recourse to an especially imaginative form of allegorical distillation. The picture book revolving around the chickens Raigomaru and Jibeta, created in the course of the story by the protagonist, Shinichirou, works as a fable of Aesopian caliber in reflecting allegorically both on the youth's innermost feelings and on his relationships with the two girls vying for his romantic attention, Hiromi and Noe. Pervaded by a potently oneiric and almost magical atmosphere, this story-within-the-story incrementally acquires independent artistic force: so much so that at times, the techniques deployed in Shinichirou's watercolor paintings spill over into the main body of the anime, and numerous shots invested with special dramatic resonance are presented in an analogous style. With *Full Moon O Sagashite*, we witness quite a different variation on the thematic interplay of creative ambition and emotional trauma, as this moves resolutely into the realm of the supernatural. The diagnosis of a malignant throat tumor annihilates in one fell swoop twelve-year-old Kouyama Mitsuki's aspiration to become a singer — a goal she has promised to achieve to the boy she loves, Eichi. When the *shinigami* (angels of death) Takuto and Meroko materialize in order to inform Mitsuki that she has no more than one year left to live, the girl resolves to take her destiny in her hands and do her best to fulfill her dream before time runs out — a quest she embraces with a good deal of otherworldly support.

Another sensitive exploration of the potential for emotional healing held by a quest for creative self-expression is offered by *Myself; Yourself*. Nanaka, the anime's female lead, is portrayed as a deeply tormented adolescent, blessed by remarkable talent as a violin player in childhood but now unable to even touch such an instrument due to traumatic experiences leading to her family's disintegration. The causes of Nanaka's current predicament are not fully revealed until an advanced stage in the series, insofar as her amnesia and concomitant disruption of her essential personality inevitably hinder their emergence. Nevertheless, the trauma-related motif implicitly operates as both an effective storytelling catalyst and a connective thread right from the start. Indeed, it is hinted at as early as the opening installment, insofar as Nanaka's farewell present to Sana, the male lead, prior to his departure from their hometown in childhood is presented as an unfinished composition which she vows to complete and play for him upon their reunion. It is only in the anime's finale, by which time Nanaka has managed to regain both her submerged memories and the core of her original personality, that we see her playing the violin again and performing in public the old composition. Complete at last, the piece has been assigned "Myself; Yourself" as the title most apposite to the description of the journeys of self-discovery which both she and, by implication, Sana, have had to endure.

The search for a language may even manifest itself in the guise of an imaginative redefinition — or reinvention — of an existing language steeped in ritual lore. The classic anime movie *Swan Lake* dazzlingly exemplifies this trend in taking the figure of the swan maiden and the repertoire of dramatic and iconographic motifs embedded in its worldwide diffusion as the starting point for the elaboration of a distinctive animational language of its own. Advancing an adventurous, yet lyrically disarming, take on the time-honored legend, the film paradigmatically illustrates the extent to which the creative interpretation of an established language, far from constituting a simple act of literal adaptation, may in fact prove conducive to an inspiringly novel language. Nowadays, the *Swan Lake* legend is commonly associated with the Tchaikovsky ballet premiered in 1877. However, it actually originates in an ancient mythos shared by countless cultures which well predates the Russian composer's particular interpretation of the story. It is to that venerable substratum of images and affects, and especially to its graver undertones, that the anime version of *Swan Lake* harks back at the levels of both its mood and its thematics in the articulation of a distinctive search for a language. Unlike the animated feature directed by former Disney artist Richard Rich, *The Swan Princess* (1994), the anime indeed comes across as a somber interpretation of the classic tale courtesy not solely of its visual style but also, to a significant extent, of scriptwriter Hirokazo Fuse's infusion of his adaptation with some unpredictable twists and turns. This tonal shift holds in spite of the movie's decision to chronicle the drama from the perspective of a pair of comic squirrels, the timid Hans and the arrogant Matilda. *Swan Lake*'s employment throughout of Tchaikovsky's music as the animation's very soul magisterially reinforces the film's wistfully dark atmosphere. The mood evoked by the original composition matches Fuse's rendition of the story much more fittingly than it ever could in the case of the Rich production. The legendary roots of the *Swan Lake* anime will be returned to later in this discussion. Some of its most salient narrative and formal elements first deserve some attention.

2—The Search for a Language

The drama finds inception with a chance encounter of visionary poignancy as prince Siegfried, out with his friends on one of his hunting trips, sees a bevy of swans drifting peacefully on a lake. A crowned white swan captures the young man's attention by intently looking at him in such a way that he feels he is being gazed at by a gorgeous lady. Mesmerized by its otherworldly charm, Siegfried follows the creature to a ruinous castle, where it abruptly morphs into precisely such a person. It soon transpires that the beautiful woman is the ill-fated Odette, a princess who has been laboring for three long years under a curse placed on her by the wizard Rothbart, who demands her hand in marriage. The wizard's mighty spell has transformed Odette into a swan and condemned her to be able to regain her true form only at night, when the moon shines upon the lake. The sole antidote to this cruel sortilege is supposed to be a man's unconditional love — a gift which Siegfried would be only too happy to provide if Odette were to attend his birthday ball at the castle and agree to be his bride.

Since Rothbart has no intention of losing his beloved, he conveys his daughter Odile to the castle in Odette's guise. An inexperienced youth, the prince proves fully vulnerable to the crafty Odile's seductive advances and, bewitched by her dancing, soon ends up pledging his love to her and announcing her as his future wife. Odette, who has meanwhile managed to flee Rothbart's prison with Hans and Matilda's help, reaches Siegfried's castle and, witnessing the prince's unwitting betrayal, loses her senses in the wizard's rapacious arms. The action reaches a memorable climax, which even some seasoned viewers find spine-tingling to this day, as Siegfried realizes that he has been duped, and engages Rothbart in a duel meant to prove beyond doubt his love for Odette and thus put an end to the iniquitous enchantment. As even a rapid assessment of the film's basic storyline suggests, the anime evinces remarkable formal balance, largely as a result of its intelligent division into three main segments corresponding to the lovers' initial meeting, the orchestration of Rothbart and Odile's deceitful plan, and the ball-related incidents. The anime's form concomitantly gains, in its achievement of a cumulatively harmonious impression, from a well-balanced distribution of action and reflection, dynamic and dialogical sequences, interpersonal exchanges and solitary meditations.

An especially interesting moment consists of the scene in which Rothbart's fiendish daughter, attired in the costume of the black swan, introduces herself to the prince as Odile. When the latter expresses his surprise, having believed that his beloved's name was actually Odette, Odile tersely declares that Siegfried must simply have misheard her the previous night and should now drop the issue. The prince is so delighted at the sight of the girl that he does precisely that, simplistically concluding that names are not that important. Siegfrid is painfully wrong, of course, and his superficiality with regard to the naming issue is a concise measure of his naivety. Keen on pursuing the object of desire without pausing to ponder his circumstances with the maturity of the king he is just about to become, the youth appears to be totally blind to the mystical significance of names and naming. In fact, as Kristen Hanley Cardozo maintains, "the power of a name is as ancient as naming. All throughout mythology, examples can be found of secret names, names that had the power to destroy, and names that had the power to bring great rewards" (Cardozo). In some cultures, moreover, names still carry magical connotations due to their latent connection with ancient spells. In others, names are associated with the soul, supporting the belief that no person could exist without a proper name.

While Hans and Matilda bicker relentlessly about the courtship, though they seem resolved to bring the lovers together at any price in keeping with their restorative comedic role, the drama itself oozes with conflict and malice. The complexity of the dark forces confronting the protagonists from beginning to end is most effectively conveyed through the juxtaposition of diverse versions of evil. On the one hand, we witness the overt, at times deliberately formulaic, evil embodied by the wizard Rothbart and his sensational spells. While portraying Rothbart as unquestionably formidable (and potentially murderous) in the expression of his sorcerous skills, the anime concurrently alludes in an almost affectionate vein to his relative immaturity and naivety as a man in love. The character's overall standing as an incarnation of preternatural wickedness is, accordingly, mellowed down or even underplayed. On the other hand, we are faced with the covert, cleverly disguised nefariousness of the cunning Odile, the archetypal femme fatale. It is Odile, after all, who comes up with the plan intended to dupe Siegfrid and stunt his romantic pursuit of the innocent Odette. The black swan, therefore, ultimately comes across as a far more scheming, sinister and unpredictably astute screen presence than her father.

In order to grasp the genuine import of *Swan Lake*'s artistic vision, and most pointedly of its search for a novel creative language, it is helpful to inspect some of the story's narrative precedents. It is in relation to this rich background, as anticipated earlier, that the anime's efforts to develop an identifiable register can be best appreciated. As Midori Snyder points out, "it is hard to imagine a more visually beautiful image in folk tales than the one presented by the figures of the swan maiden and her sisters. With a flurry of wings, they swoop down from the sky to glide elegantly across a clear pond." The anime fully corroborates this contention, positing the early image of the swans resting serenely on the lake as more vividly illustrative of its unmistakable timbre than either the youthful energy of Prince Siegfrid and his friends or the hauntingly beautiful setting in which they ride. That image indeed offers a memorable distillation of the sense of the numinous which seldom leaves the anime as the action unfolds, emanating at all times an aura of mystery tinged with sensual exoticism and delightful innocence in equal proportions.

Swan Lake might appear to dispel the shadows which haunt the main body of the action with its supposedly happy ending. Yet, the film's resolution can only be called "happy" in potential terms. It does not truly provide a categorically reparative or consolatory rounding-off of the dramatic experience — and hence does not qualify for definition as unequivocally joyous — mainly due to its intentional precipitousness. The incidents by means of which the villains are defeated and the lovers united are presented at such breakneck speed, and therefore with so little chance of reflection or comment on their actual import, as to hint at a slew of utterly unexamined developments and complications which could feasibly befall Siegfrid and Odette once the final frame has faded from the screen. The audience is invited to train its attention exclusively on the protagonists' mutual infatuation as an instinctive and immediate force without having to ponder the longer-term implications of their hybrid liaison.

According to Snyder, the swan maiden legend harbors sinister ethical implications which find expression in a series of unsavory occurrences. These typically become evident in the aftermath of the preternatural creature's union with her human suitor. The critic trenchantly describes these recurring narrative motifs as "crimes" perpetrated by the legend's male hero (normally a young prince or a hunter) "against the very object of his desire for the sole purpose of keeping such a magical creature within his grasp." These misdeeds typically "culminate in marriage and the attempted domestication of the wild, fantastical swan maiden, turned into a wife and mother," which renders the classic swan maiden narrative "less a tale about love than one about marital coercion and confusion." Even though the anime does not explicitly dramatize the legend's more baleful components, it does not rule them out either. In fact, *Swan Lake*'s finale hints at the ominous situation described by Snyder in a tangential fashion, in much the same way as many of the closing scenes of Shakespeare's love comedies intimate a hypothetical sixth act following the happily-ever-after moment. Thus, they induce us to wonder what real life might actually yield for their protagonists once the lovers have been preposteroulsy and arbitrarily brought together by chance and contingency. It may well be the case that Siegfrid will not, ultimately, prove as different from Rothbart in his handling of marital affairs as one might wish or believe, and will turn out to be just an alternative incarnation of the predatory male stereotype — just a more liberal one, if we focus on appearances, or a more legitimate one, if we look at the situation in terms of power and hierarchy. A young prince is bound to come across as more generous and lenient than an evil wizard but these positive attributes may only be formal and circumstantial offshoots of his privileged social standing.

At the same time, however, *Swan Lake* does not quite fit the mold presented by many popular variations of the tale in which attention is drawn, with variable degrees of emphasis, to the idea that "the husband has done nothing to earn such a powerful wife, and the swan maiden has no opportunity to choose her own fate." In those versions, the central relationship lacks both harmony and balance, and discord is sooner or later destined to tear apart the flimsy walls of the shell wherein it has been precariously and forcefully housed. "No matter how compliant a swan maiden may appear as a wife," Snyder comments, "there remains an unspoken anxiety and tension beneath the surface of her marriage.... Conflict is never far beneath the veneer of the swan maiden's compliance" (Snyder). Moreover, several versions of the legend actually refrain from divulging any information regarding the swan maiden's existence as a human wife and mother to concentrate entirely on her burning desire to revert to her original life and status.

On the whole, *Swan Lake* is keen to foreground the more positive aspects of the mythos on which it draws. Siegfrid does, after all, engage in mortal combat with the fearsome Rothbart, while Odette appears drawn to the prince not simply as a means of escaping the magician's cage but also, and more importantly, out of genuine affection. The crucial difference between the swan maiden portrayed in the anime (on the basis of Tchaikovsky's model) and the traditional swan maidens discussed by Snyder is that unlike those creatures, she is originally human, and her longing to resume her natural form is therefore bound to consist of a return to humanity, not otherworldliness. Furthermore, the anime consolidates its positive message by yielding an ardent celebration of the powerful bond connecting the human and the supernatural realms. In this regard, the movie could be said to communicate a critical philosophical message by reminding us of the omnipresence of mysticism and magic as realities always lurking just beneath the surface of our familiar world. Their hold endures in spite of our tenacious efforts to dodge or disavow their ascendancy through the glorification of rationality and logic—an ideology which, upon inspection, turns out to be simply a smarter name for fear. All in all, the anime version of the swan maiden story declares the originality of its creative language by hinting at bleak potentialities which haunt the action from the wings in the guise of virtual actors as yet unlisted in the cast. Relatedly, it allows us to imagine promising alternatives to the darker variations on the classic tale without, however, ramming them down our throats and hence implicitly curtailing our interpretative freedom.

In the search for a language capable of capturing the spirit of an age-old legend in anime format, and hence making it relevant to contemporary sensibilities without sacrificing its timeless appeal, *Swan Lake* studiously relies on stylized visuals and tersely refined dynamic rhythms. In this regard, the film finds an apt correlative, in the history of classic Western animation, in the fairy tale movies of the pioneering German artist Lotte Reiniger, which span the early 1920s to the mid–1950s. This animator is justly renowned for her knack of visualizing the eternal essence of fairy tale by recourse to an unprecedented form of stylization stemming from the invention, and indefatigable perfection over the years, of silhouette animation. With this technique, Reiniger has created many memorable worlds, endowed with aesthetic sophistication and distinctive screen presence. In the process, she has also brought to life a kaleidoscopic gallery of characters, intimating that all of her figures are engaged, in different fashions, in the search for an expressive language: a code able to help them negotiate an unsettling reality and to face all manner of trials and challenges. The compilation *Lotte Reiniger—Fairy Tales* (2008) provides exhaustive evidence for the uniqueness of Reiniger's vision. The fabulous personae it presents can realistically be regarded as avatars of the animator herself in her progressive elaboration of a novel animational language. Comparably, the magical reinventions of reality effected by *Swan Lake*'s main characters could be seen as metaphorical equivalents of director Koro Kabuki's sparkling artistic vision.

With *Tenpou Ibun Ayashi Ayakashi* (a.k.a. *Ghost Slayers Ayashi*), the search for a language unfolds over a decidedly self-referential terrain since the activity elected as instrumental to the quest is the art of language itself. In this respect, the anime can be regarded as an original interpretation of an archaic belief surrounding the spiritual vigor of the graphic sign promoted by Chinese Taoism. This credence, as Mitsukuni Yoshida explains, held that "words (characters) written on paper" harbored "divine power." In China, specifically, the written sign was often held to "possess the power of the word whose meaning was expressed therein" (Yoshida 1985, p. 27). Set in 1843, the fourteenth year of the *Tenpou* era in Edo Japan, the anime chronicles the war waged by the "Ayashi," members of an organization publicly known as the *Bansha Aratamesho*, against a race of preternatural monsters, the *Youi*. The Ayashi's special gifts derive from the power of "Ayagami": namely, the ability to draw out the power of words, and hence to discover a creature's true name and to turn it into a lethal weapon. The protagonist is Ryuudou Yukiatsu, the son of a powerful samurai whose life has been warped by a vision of the "Other World" whence the power of Ayagami ensues. This experience, which Ryuudou is held to be the only person to have survived, has totally deprived him of the capacity to find any satisfaction, let alone joy, in the normal human world and turned him into an eternal fugitive.

The anime's supernatural dimension gains credibility from its cogent situation in a historically accurate context, which records a moment of political insecurity marred by political sleaze, corruption and intrigue, on the one hand, and extreme poverty, on the other. While destitute nomads, branded as "floaters," are routinely captured, tattooed and relegated to derelict ghettos, facing decapitation if they escape, the authorities pursue blindly their inane power games and dubious pleasures. A further touch of historical realism capable of infusing the supernatural yarn with an atmosphere of historical concreteness lies with the name of the organization responsible for fighting the *Youi*. Officially presented as a scholarly body, the *Bansha Aratamesho* is indeed related to the *Bansha no goku*: the suppression of Western studies and scholars launched in 1839 in response to criticisms of the Japanese government's isolationist policies.

The art of language is also accorded a special part in *Mushi-Shi* with a focus on the practice of calligraphy. This is especially true of the episode, which stands out as one of the entire anime's most remarkable adventures, where the pictographs diligently traced by a boy's brush on paper progressively detach themselves from the page, morph into living creatures and fill the space around them with a swirling profusion of forms. The idea that calligraphic characters are innately endowed with vitality operates as a compelling trope for the spirit of the art of animation itself as an activity able to imbue inert matter with dynamism and sentience. The creatures brought beautifully, albeit inadvertently, into existence by the boy's brush call attention with lyrical conciseness to the most salient attributes of the entire imaginary biology coursing the anime's universe, and providing the narrative premise for its adventures. Epitomizing the notion of life at its purest, the multifarious entities known as *Mushi* give the impression of being amorphous and polymorphic at once. When they come to be embodied in graphic marks, their ambivalent status implicitly replicates the divided status of the art of language itself—a corollary of its signs' unsettling tendency to mean something other than what they say and, at the same time, say something other than what they mean. In addition, the physical depiction of the flowing and undefinable beings peopling the drama's interstices calls attention in a metaphorical vein to the concreteness, evanescence and intrinsic aliveness of the art of language itself: a system made up of tiny shapes which can be thought of both as inchoate and as latently capable of gaining a dizzying variety of shapes.

Calligraphy is likewise prominent in *The Tale of Genji*, which is entirely consonant with the Heian valorization of this practice as a pictorial art of autonomous aesthetic caliber. The anime underscores this proposition by emphasizing the intrinsic nature of Japanese writing itself as a composite ensemble of signs of pictographic provenance. It thus throws into relief the materiality underpinning the art of language even when this seems to refer to exclusively abstract ideas, drawing attention to the corporeal origins of storytelling, theater and indeed all arts dependent on language in the broad sense of the term. In this matter, *The Tale of Genji* bears witness to a distinctive semiotic sensibility keen to underline the kinetic power of textuality by allowing writing to function as a dynamic agent unfettered by the limitations of the static physical page. The shots deployed by the series as a means of foregrounding the calligraphic skills of diverse personae are particularly worthy of notice: as the *kanji* take shape on the screen stroke by stroke, without the visible involvement of anybody's writing hand, they appear to be endowed not only with solidity but also with independent energy.

In this context, the written word is overtly promoted to the status of an art form in its own right. Concurrently, we are unobtrusively reminded of its intimate connection with the traditional Eastern art of "wash painting" known in Japanese as *sumi-e*. In Heian scrolls, as Joan Stanley-Baker explains, every "painting has its own tempo, fast or slow, which engages our viewing to the extent of conditioning the speed at which we unroll the scroll. In the *Genji* scrolls, for instance, the pictorial sections are different paintings interleaved with a continuous calligraphic narrative" (Stanley-Baker, p. 97). Calligraphy itself, as Yukio Lippit points out, provides a kind of visual "meter" by means of which artists could "choreograph the tempo and columnar flow of the writing" (Lippit, p. 59). An illusion of acceleration can be communicated, for instance, by fluidly compressing a large number of characters in the shape of a vertical cascade: a technique overtly employed by the anime in the scene where the protagonist is portrayed in the act of writing his farewell missives prior to his forced departure from the capital so as to convey economically the urgency of his situation.

Anime's treatment of this chapter's designated topos reaches an apotheosis with *Honey and Clover* and its sequel, where the search for a language is investigated with both affection and clinical precision through a panoramic journey across a broad range of arts — including painting, drawing, photography, architecture, carpentry, pottery, fashion design and cuisine. Given its sheer thematic scope, which is unremittingly abetted by both remarkable production values and imaginative flair, the anime deserves election as a major case study. *Honey and Clover*'s premises are neither groundbreaking nor inherently exciting, since the series merely aims to chronicle the everyday experiences of three art students who share a decrepit apartment block and attend the same college — second-year Yuuta Takemoto, seventh-year veteran Shinobu Morita and graduand Takumi Mayama. The drama focuses on these characters' emotional attachments and especially on the romantic triangle involving Yuuta, Shinobu and the first-year student and artistic prodigy Hagumi Hanamoto.

For both youths, the experience is a clear case of love at first sight of the most epiphanic, life-transforming and disconcerting kind conceivable by either classic or modern romance.

At first, Shinobu seems mainly disposed to frighten Hagumi with his excessively overt demonstrations of affection, compounded by an addictive yearning to photograph her or otherwise employ her cute appearance as an ostensibly inexhaustible source of creative inspiration: e.g., by preserving an impression of her exquisite footprint in clay. (Shinobu's obsession with Hagumi as his ideal subject matter will shortly be returned to). Yuuta, conversely, maintains a reserved stance and endeavors to befriend the girl by engaging with her in activities which one would tend to associate with young children more than with college students. This character contrast is further sustained by persistent indications that Shinobu is so unprincipled and unscrupulous, though endearingly so, as to transcend morality altogether, whereas Yuuta is affable and thoughtful to a fault, and inclined to place the well-being of others, Shinobu included, well ahead of his own. The pathologically unsocialized Hagumi does not initially relate to either of these potential suitors. She feels simply uncomfortable in the company of boys — at least not until she discovers in Yuuta an unthreatening playmate — and would rather spend the time she does not devote to her art to consolidating her friendship with the popular pottery master Ayumi Yamada. Ayumi herself is a fatality of unrequited love, her longstanding affection toward Takumi remaining unreciprocated as the latter pines in vain over Rika Harada, the designer and owner of the innovative architecture studio in which the student finds temporary employment as he is about to graduate.

Given these unassuming premises, it may come as a surprise to those who are as yet unacquainted with *Honey and Clover* to hear that it ranks among the most cherished series of its generation. The anime was initially targeted at older female audiences with the intention of encouraging young women who did not habitually watch anime to conceive a budding interest in this art form. However, it proved instantly popular not only among its intended viewers but also among audiences well beyond the target demographic. What fascinated these unexpected admirers was not the anime's choice of thematic or generic formulae but rather its outstanding take on characterization, insightful narrative style and judiciously experimental visuals: qualities which unobtrusively demonstrated its ability to feel more amusing than many mainstream comedies and more moving than many dramas in other the animated or live-action formats. One would have to be emotionally defunct — or, at any rate, severely allergic to romance — not to feel touched by a scene like the one in which Takumi, looking at Yuuta's expression as he gazes at Hagumi, suddenly realizes that this is the first time he has witnessed the precise moment at which a person falls in love.

It does not take inordinate effort, therefore, to appreciate that *Honey and Clover*'s strength does not lie with its dramatic premises — in fact, it does not claim these as assets either at the start of the series or in its unfurling — but rather with its perceptive interpretation of the timeless coming-of-age curve and, most critically, of the paramount role played therein by the quest for artistic expression. Indeed, the trials of self-development and the anxious search for a creative language are posited as twin components of one and the same ethical, aesthetic, and finally existential mission. What allows this task to affirm its prominence unhindered is, above all else, a refreshing avoidance of grander or more theatrical ploys of the kind one often encounters among *Honey and Clover*'s contemporaries — such as the unraveling of some byzantine conspiracy, the completion of an epic save-the-world task or the attainment of the supreme prize in a preposterously challenging tournament. The affective predicaments outlined earlier could easily appear banal and stereotypical were it not for *Honey and Clover*'s unflinching dedication to the achievement of psychological realism and attendant capacity to formulate a wholly original poetry of feeling in the anime realm. At the same time, the story's touches of authenticity would come across as tokenistic concessions to mimetic verisimilitude if they were not sustained by an intelligent search for a distinct stylistic register and vocabulary: namely, a discourse able to let both its own and its personae's creativity shine forth even in the most unassuming of scenes. This is a language which does not abide by mimesis but, in fact, by its very opposite: that is to say, a deliberate cultivation of dreamlike and surreal effects, distinguished by mellow palettes and softly drawn silhouettes, which exude the kind of ethereal grace of which watercolor painting alone is capable. These stylistic traits pervade the representation of the characters' physiognomies and myriad facets of nature and architecture alike.

On the dramatic plane, one of *Honey and Clover*'s principal strengths lies with its power to interweave situations and personalities of a convincing stamp with totally imaginary circumstances in a seamless tapestry. As a result, the fantastic dimension does not come across as an escape from reality but rather as a well judged metaphor for the complexities of real life, and is therefore in a position to operate as no less credible a commentary on the actual than its down-to-earth counterpart. We are able to recognize the figurative significance of the fantasy as a convincing scenario in spite of its apparent distance from reality because it is portrayed in such a manner that it feels entirely logical within the parameters of the medium and genre in which it is couched.

Honey and Clover unambiguously revels in the expression of an artist's total dedication to the artistic practice per se over and above its tangible outcomes or its intended goals. The anime elaborates this theme to great dramatic effect throughout its diegesis, and particularly through the character of

Hagumi. The young artist's typical attitude to creation is indeed characterized by unparalleled levels of absorption indicative of a total synthesis of creator and performance. W. B. Yeats' lines "O body swayed to music, O brightening glance, How can we know the dancer from the dance?" ("Among School Children," 1926) spring to mind as one observes Hagumi in the act of creating — regardless of whether the project in hand is a cyclopean stone sculpture, a dainty decoration, a sublime chromatic experiment or a balloon installation (Yeats, p. 217). The sheer intensity of Hagumi's absorption in her work offers some precious moments of solemn spectacle: for example, in the scene where she gazes intently at a giraffe in a melancholy wintertime zoo and appears to be painting the view in her own mind in its entirety even before touching a single brush.

Even more memorable is the scene in which Yuuta and Takumi hear from Shuuji Hanamoto, Hagumi's uncle and current guardian, that the girl is engrossed in her artwork and instantly fantasize about her likely output in the guise of pastelly and cute images. When they actually peer into the studio where Hagumi is working, they find that she is busy molding a colossal male nude of grim demeanor redolent of both Michelangelo and Rodin. It is at this early point in the series that we are also informed that Hagumi's talent has already been recognized by the upper echelons of the art world, that she is therefore already prestigiously employed despite her status as a first-year student, and that this particular piece has been commissioned for the lobby of a new art museum about to open in Yokohama. Shuuji describes Hagumi's art as follows: "the birds, flowers, people and everything else that she makes look as though they may start moving at any time. The owner of the gallery and I often talk about how we want to see the world through her eyes. To make people feel like that, that's what talent is." The veracity of Shuuji's comments regarding Hagumi's abilities is compellingly borne out by the palpability of the tensile energy rippling through the statue's titanic musculature.

What is especially remarkable about Hagumi's attitude is that however enraptured in her task she might become, she never seems to be selfishly pursuing a personal goal. In fact, one senses an innocent, totally unprejudiced commitment to the elaboration of expressive vocabularies and registers which may reach disparate audiences and thus enlist the creative capacities of viewers of all ages and backgrounds. The only other character in the series whose stance to artistic production evinces a degree of engrossment so marked as to verge on obsession is Shinobu. His and Hagumi's characteristic attitudes to creation are indeed explicitly compared in the series. Yet, the elemental values underpinning the two characters' visions are actually quite different. With Hagumi, one gets a strong feeling of collaboration between the creator and the materials at her disposal, which suggests that the two parties are perceived as equal in their significance and rights. With Shinobu, conversely, the performance betrays a solipsistic drive tinged with megalomaniac ambitiousness, which at times mars the beauty of his visions despite their unquestionable genius and vigor. Thus, though the youth's art honors the materials' unique force, it occasionally appears to relegate them to ancillary status.

At the same time, Shinobu's artistic output is consistently distinguished by the unorthodox deployment of seemingly inexhaustible multimedia versatility. Channeling his talent into pieces which generally have nothing to do with school projects, the youth devotes his genius to the creation of myriad works based on Hagumi, including photographs, sculptures and conceptual artifacts, and finds a brilliant way of turning them into a lucrative venture. Placing several Hagumi-related images on the internet, Shinobu rapidly gains an ample fan base, and makes a handsome profit whenever a visitor to his website, eager to access more and more pictures of what he sees as an enticing bimbo, clicks on an advertisement banner. Interestingly, the very first photograph of Hagumi taken by Shinobu, which he then uses as the site's home page to captivate potential acolytes, features the girl in the guise of *Korobokkuru* (a semilegendary race of diminutive creatures in Ainu folklore) with the caption "Finally Discovered." This preference for unconventional artifacts, allied to a pathological inability to get to school in time, unsurprisingly results in Shinobu's legendary failure to graduate.

The young artist's creative makeup harbors a basic conflict insofar as his selfish tendency to overindulge personal desires stands in stark contrast with the intuitive generosity intrinsic in his astounding eclecticism and expansive understanding of creativity. Not only does Shinobu's mentality enthusiastically uphold the commodious conception of art promoted by indigenous aesthetics: it also translates it into action as the drama progressively reveals the sheer scope of the youth's gifts. Alongside sculpture, photography, painting and drawing, Shinobu also practices — and excels at — the art of music, as evinced by his ability to play beautiful melodies on a Mongolian *morin khuur* brought back by Shuuji from his travels. He is likewise proficient at the art of costume design: a skill often fueled into the execution of wacky outfits for fictional characters which he wishes Hagumi to impersonate, such as "Mouse Number One," as well as for his own spurious roles as a rock musician and popular entertainer. Last but not least, Shinobu is veritable CGI wizard: his talent in the field, refined with the instruction of esteemed Hollywood director "Peter Lucas," culminates in the youth's achievement of an Academy Award for the movie "*Space Titanic*" (the spoofing is so clear as not to necessitate elucidation). Liberality of spirit is undoubtedly the principal quality able to counterbalance Shinobu's self-centeredness. His mentality is further enriched by the redeeming virtue of humility, as attested to by his decision to return to college after his belated graduation to enroll in the Japanese painting department as a third-year student: a move predicated on Shinobu's humble recognition of his failure to receive orthodox academic training as long as he was pursuing his private projects and missing lectures for weeks on end.

Hagumi's personality, largely defined by her creative flair, is rendered additionally intriguing by the ironical tension between the maturity of her commitment and the childish cuteness of her physique — graced by honey-gold tresses and azure irises — which could indeed be regarded as the very distillation of *kawaii* at its most fetching. Takumi affectionately describes the girl as a "tiny person" upon her first appearance at the art college, thus hinting at her doll-like or even fairy-like air. Gentle hues and graceful forms which mirror her personal appearance undoubtedly feature within Hagumi's varied repertoire. Yet, as noted earlier vis-à-vis the statue of the male nude, figures of forbidding bulk and grave mien are among the subjects capable of enlisting most powerfully her exceptional abilities. As the series develops, we discover that Hagumi's physical infantilism is in fact psychosomatically related to an excessively sheltered upbringing which has severely impaired the girl's sociability and interactive skills. It is also worth noting, in this matter, that Hagumi's character is allowed to evolve gradually — and by no means uniformly — from childishness to maturity as her initial blindness to her feelings, and particularly to the experience of being in love, gives way to a considerate appreciation of other people's desires. The girl's selflessness is poignantly demonstrated by the episode in which she asserts Shinobu's right to pursue his objectives unfettered, even though she is well aware that this entails a painful period of separation from her beloved.

The conflict between Hagumi's artistic wisdom and adorably petite body does not only provide the basis of an entertaining dramatic irony. In fact, it bolsters in vital ways the anime's overarching aesthetic priorities, and specifically its tendency to engage with the darker facets of the human psyche, and with the more tormented moments of the bildungsroman revolving around its characters' search for a language. *Honey and Clover*'s pervasive — if often submerged — somberness emanates primarily from the tortuous affects incessantly generated by its interactive alchemy: a brew of lacerating timidity, lack of confidence, diffidence, irrational apprehension, churning desire, dread of rejection and abandonment and, most poignantly, dusky loneliness. So pervasive are these emotions that even when flickering rays of ostensibly unpolluted hope and delight puncture the shadows, a ubiquitous atmosphere of melancholy and insatiable longing dominates the drama, impeccably matching its deliberate lyrical rhythm. The potent, albeit nameless, pull of the unknown is communicated right from the start by the first installment's pre-credit sequence — a moment revisited at several junctures later in the series through the emblematic metonym of a bicycle wheel. The sequence alludes at once to a positive effort to open up to the indefinite and the unpredictable, and to a bewildering sense of uncertainty. In this sequence, Yuuta revisits his childhood in a dreamlike flashback, recalling his habit of riding his bicycle far and wide, always wondering for how long he might be able to move on without looking back and never being able to ascertain where this urge originated.

In painting a comprehensive picture of the art world, *Honey and Clover* does not forget to deliver a jocular stab at the pompous shallowness of the academic enclave and its pretensions at superior aesthetic sensitivity. Upon first beholding the preposterously tall, rickety, bizarre — and yet mysteriously elegant — tower created by Yuuta for the art festival, the two critics responsible for its evaluation are at a total loss. However, the moment Shuuji affixes an extempore title onto the piece and proclaims its excellence, the two characters instantly proceed to express their appreciation of its greatness in the most inflated, absurd and incongruous of terms — ultimately commenting neither on the work's quality nor on its creator's genius but on their own pathetic self-importance. The same clownish professionals enjoy further opportunity to wax lyrical about the youth's presumed talent — and thereby alert us to their own inanity — when they witness the outcome of his drastic demolition of the tower in a fit of chagrin triggered by the sudden realization that he lacks a clear goal in life. On this occasion, it is the budding artist's "destructive urge" which appears to send them into a paroxysm of bliss. At a later stage, when Yuuta eventually resolves to focus on the execution of a more orthodox, albeit far less enticing, project and constructs a tower which according to Shuuji simply shows how "obvious" the boy can be, the critics tearfully bemoan the likelihood of his having matured too quickly — a development which they seem to resent not so much because it is inimical to the boy's own artistic growth but because it deprives them with pretexts for stereotypically rapturous evaluations.

Swift transitions between light and darkness, and between hilarious comedy and heartbreaking introspection, are one of *Honey and Clover*'s most salient attributes. It would indeed be hard to think of an anime which captures this tonal oscillation more loyally and dispassionately. Each episode offers vivid examples of the show's propensity to shifts of gears with the mercurial rapidity of a twinkling star, displacing a mood of intense pathos through eruptions of clownishness one moment, and an atmosphere of joviality and warmth with presages of loss and sorrow the next. As the drama is intent on following Yuuta's ruminations about evanescence, for instance, quiet contemplation may be suddenly disrupted by a farcical flurry with the quirky Shinobu at its center. Alternately, the action may be recording a boisterous party involving all of the key personae and abruptly transition to an atmosphere of nostalgic reverie focused on the perceptions of singular characters, and keen to intimate that the appearance of gregariousness is powerless to dispel conclusively those individuals' ultimate isolation — in others' company and in their innermost being alike.

The atmospheric fluctuations which distinguish *Honey and Clover* at the tonal level find an apt parallel in the series' eschewal of stark characterization in favor of portrayals which accommodate contrasting personality traits and affective propensities. For example, while Yuuta is depicted as almost undilutedly amiable and selfless, there are suggestions that his qualities are partly the result of psychological repression: a defense mechanism developed in response to painful childhood experiences revolving around his father's untimely demise and his mother's remarriage. Thus, we are implicitly invited to evaluate even the most positive of character traits against a background of thwarting, if not downright negative, affects. Shinobu is an even more blatant bundle of disparities. Despite his pervasively playful and nonchalant attitude to both his mates and his academic commitments, the youth is actually very caring, able to provide counsel and comfort when these are most needed, to rescue others from thorny situations and, most refreshingly, to voice some unpalatable truths when nobody else seems prepared to either articulate or hear them. In addition, he helps his brother Kaoru obtain revenge on the company responsible for ruining their father out of generosity more than of a desire for personal gain. Shuuji likewise evinces a composite personality. Risibly juvenile in the face of Hagumi's *kawaii* appearance, as shown by his tendency to dissolve into pathetic jelly whenever he is exposed to its most enticing manifestations, he is nonetheless very conscientious in his assessment of the rights, responsibilities and duties entailed by guardianship. Moreover, he displays a deeply meditative streak in the sequences devoted to his reminiscences, punctuated by poignant flashbacks, where we catch glimpses of his past life and especially of his intimate connection with Rika and her husband prior to the latter's tragic death. Shuuji's image emits a bittersweet aura whenever he reflects on his lack of any notable artistic gifts, and decision to opt for a teaching career instead of pursuing a fruitless dream of creative fulfillment simply because he happens to be clever at handling conceptual issues in areas like anatomy and art history.

While the characters themselves can be seen to harbor conflicting dispositions, their personal histories and related influences often lend themselves to discordant interpretations. Hagumi's background is a clear case in point. There can be little doubt that the girl's inordinately protected upbringing in her irascible grandmother's shadowy home has yielded detrimental effects in impairing her interactive skills. Yet, it is in the context of that very home that Hagumi has developed her creative skills by painting again and again the same scene — the only view to which she has had access from the remote dwelling — and thus given birth to embryonic masterworks without for a moment realizing it by recording the impact of the passing seasons on the world's colors and light. It is at this early stage in her artistic evolution that Hagumi begins to foster, with no ulterior motives in mind, the immense gifts soon to be recognized by all who witness her art, including several professionals eager to have her submit her work for public exhibition. Moreover, Hagumi seems to sense at a primarily instinctual level her ancestral connection to the world in which her art found inception. This is suggested by her intention, after graduation, to return to the countryside, tend the chickens and devote herself to her art wholeheartedly in such a secluded setting: a plan to which her chief teacher sternly objects, claiming that it would be selfish of such a uniquely talented artist to shut herself off from the artistic community and thus deprive the world of her gift.

The anime's attentive representation of psychological ambiguity, evident in its treatment of both the characters and their contexts, could be regarded as a correlative for its take on art. *Honey and Clover*'s methods of characterization indeed replicate its highly diversified and nuanced attitude to creative expression. These two aspects of the anime's special makeup flawlessly support and enhance each other as the drama progresses. Few symbiotic integrations of theme and technique work as beautifully in either anime or the entertainment universe of storytelling at large. Claiming that *Honey and Clover*'s aesthetic partakes of the genius of the sublime may sound like a presumptuous exaggeration of the kind one could expect to issue from an undiscriminating fan. Nonetheless, there are moments when the anime invokes precisely that vision, conveying the pathos of the indefinite at its most wrenching and yet most unnamable. A case in point is the episode where all of the key personae coincidentally gather in a field to look for a four-leaf clover which Hagumi hopes to give Shuuji as a good luck charm prior to his departure for a one-year research trip. As the characters pursue their hunt throughout the afternoon seemingly oblivious to any other worries or duties, canopied by a blue sky and caressed by a suave breeze, the scene captures the force which incrementally binds their lives and destinies together with a poignancy rendered especially memorable by its wordlessness. Despite its mundane parameters, the sequence has the power to evoke a cumulative sense of the numinous.

Another affecting instance of the same stylistic tendency is the scene in which all of the main characters wander around the aforementioned zoo and suddenly realize that they are the only visitors, at which point Takumi wonders about the fate of the lonesome giraffe, born and trapped in a land far away from its natural habitat, and destined to die without ever having met a free member of its species and plausibly as an outcome of malnutrition — a hypothesis based on the scarcity of visitors and hence of revenue to be spent on food for the alienated captives. As Takumi dispassionately outlines his somber reflections, the other characters start shivering visibly as strongly drawn shadows cloud their faces in the clutches of a rigor which cannot be attributed solely to the inclement season, as though seized by undescribable anguish — by "thoughts," to adapt a line from Wordsworth's "Immortality Ode," "that do often lie too deep for tears" (Wordsworth, p. 704).

The aesthetic preference for adumbration and subtle clues to the underlying meanings of a situation, relationship or state of mind, pervasive in Japanese art since ancient times, finds a parallel in the anime's melancholy mood. This disposition is in fact ideal to the evocation of a drama of continual and anxious search for voices and forms in preference to black-and-white statements or flashy sensationalism — for twilight hesitation to stark tenebrosity, for gradations, delicate nuances and modulations to definitively polarized feelings. While celebrating the aesthetic principles of absorption and allusiveness, *Honey and Clover* concurrently upholds the primacy of matter in various ways. Yuuta, for instance, decides to become an architect because he is good with his hands, and has demonstrated since an early age a proclivity to deal spontaneously and affectionately with practically any materials and objects his environment has had to offer. Hence, he is not governed by the urge to master matter at any stage in his development. The art of pottery provides another glorious example of the ascendancy of the material dimension in the anime's aesthetic sensibility, being hailed by the pottery master Professor Shouda as "the art of using dirt"— namely, the earth from which, according to countless belief systems the world over, we are all supposed to come and to which we are all bound to return. No substance, we are thereby reminded, is ever too lowly or undeserving for the truly devoted practitioner. At no point, relatedly, is the concept of human mastery over the natural domain upheld as an artistic objective. Professor Shouda emphasizes that pottery is essentially an art whose performance requires the artist's engagement in an honest dialogue with the clay in his or her hands, and a humble preparedness to let the energy intrinsic in the substance penetrate the human body's very core. "You have to listen to its voice," the elderly master advises, "by allowing your soul to become an empty vessel. Only the ones that can do that and see eye to eye with the dirt can hear its voice."

A veritable gem of both anime per se and the celebration of matter as the protagonist of artistic endeavor is the scene in which Hagumi, having accidentally destroyed one of Ayumi's recent and as yet unset creations, instinctively proceeds to remold the fresh clay into a stunning little artwork in its own right. The enthusiastic response to the object displayed by Professor Shouda indicates that the creation can be regarded as a genuine impromptu masterpiece in the field — not least since the old man's keenness is accompanied by a bout of nose-leaking, which could be seen as a gracious variation on the nose bleed trope normally used by anime as shorthand for ecstatic and orgasmic states. The work brings to mind, in mood even more than in shape, the prehistoric figurines traditionally located in the vicinity of the tombs of Japanese rulers and members of their family, the *haniwa*. Geometrically stylized, these artifacts nonetheless succeed in evoking a potent sense of vitality, and thus symbolize a pleasant and jovial courtly atmosphere of the kind the departed would have been likely to enjoy while alive. Yet, despite their vibrant energy, the *haniwa* figurines are distinguished by facial features which deliberately allude to lifelessness, thus providing emblematic reflections on the reality of death with which they are ceremoniously associated. As Gian Carlo Calza observes, this idea is clearly illustrated by the celebrated artifact portraying a couple of singers, where the characters' posture immediately conveys an impression of aliveness which is subtly contradicted by their visages. "The arms of each figure are raised in a dramatic gesture," which is quite consonant with their emblematic role. Yet, the ultimate pathos is conveyed not so much by this manifestation of dynamic gaiety as by each figure's "expressionless face," which alludes to the experience of an entire "culture waiting for a miracle that will make it rise again. The lack of expression comes from the sense of emptiness, emphasized by holes representing the eye sockets and the mouth that open on the flat surface of the face with a dark void behind them" (Calza, pp. 139–140).

Hagumi's creation is a paean to the aliveness of seemingly inert matter, yet is careful to convey an analogous sense of emptiness which can be interpreted as a symbolic reference to life's ephemerality: a fundamental trait, as argued throughout this study, of Japanese aesthetics and culture at large. The mood thus captured by Hagumi's unpremeditated work of genius hints at the fleeting substance of youth and pleasure which, like cherry blossom and autumn leaves, only enjoy the briefest of glory, swiftly to disperse across the firmament of time. The inevitably transitory beauty choreographed by Hagumi's art in all its forms is comparable to the charm radiated by a face drowned in inscrutable darkness as the light of a lantern briefly punctures the gloom only to fade again into its engulfing embrace. While the connection between Hagumi's extemporaneous piece and indigenous tradition cannot be overestimated, it is also important, however, to acknowledge its simultaneous ties with disparate Western periods, styles and influence, including Cycladic pottery, Etruscan funerary sculpture, Picasso and Matisse. This wide-ranging network of cross-cultural connections economically serves to remind us of the eminently syncretic proclivities of Japanese culture and arts over the centuries.

In the realm of painting, Hagumi's works reveal an urge to experiment unremittingly with the interplay of linear concepts and chromatic blends to express their unique perceptions of nature, space and time. In so doing, they encapsulate some of the most salient features of traditional Japanese painting traceable back to the fourteenth and fifteenth centuries. This even applies to creations which patently integrate autochthonous influences with diverse Western sources characterized primarily by avant-garde leanings. Most notable among those time-honored traits are the tendency to handle the relationship between vacant and occupied spaces in terms not of conflict but of fluid and continually evolving interaction. Even when the Japanese passion for flatness is allowed to rule the overall composition, Hagumi's visuals come across as highly dynamic: neither the turbulent nor the tranquil areas are ever static or stagnant. The sense of movement is so potent and pervasive as to generate the impression that the picture extends beyond its frame, and that the visuals contained within its boundaries are merely passing through it, briefly dwelling therein before flowing on along the river of life itself. At the same time, the paintings exhibit a flair for combining sparse and even minimalistic abstract designs with vividly convincing depictions of the natural world and its multifarious inhabitants which derive tangible credibility from their punctilious attention to detail and chroma.

In addition, Hagumi seems instinctively drawn to the art of fashion design, even though basic ineptness in the handling of tools incapacitates her from pursuing this calling to any notable effect. This thwarted vocation still manages to find expression in the execution of imaginative, albeit haphazardly constructed, doll outfits — her one concession to *kawaii* in art. Yuuta is utterly intrigued by these creations, and even though he is surprised to find himself playing with a cute girl and her dolls as an adult, he is aware that Hagumi's magic is in itself powerful enough to retain his interest. In fact, the youth even gets inveigled, though inadvertently, into demonstrating his own talent as an architecture student by designing and constructing a closet in which Hagumi may house her atelier. Unfortunately, the girl's tastes demand a closet in Rococo style, which poses a considerable challenge for the as yet inexperienced second-year student.

In its finespun exploration of the mysteries and promises of creativity, *Honey and Clover* emphasizes that people must learn to emancipate themselves from the past and its legacies if they are to develop emotionally, intellectually and, of course, artistically. This gesture should never amount, however, to an arrogant elision of past experiences and of the lessons they entail, since honoring their enduring influence is also pivotal to the individual's maturation and to the discovery of rewarding creative languages. According the past a metaphorical interment is necessary but remembering the location of the burial ground is no less important.

In the specific fields of painting and drawing, *Honey and Clover* finds a sympathetic relation in *GA: Geijutsuka Art Design Class*: a series likewise eager to underscore its protagonists' commitment not merely to the cultivation of existing skills but also to the incessant exploration and perfection of new modes of expression, new forms and new compositional methods. The anime centers its dramatization of the search for a creative language on a class that specializes in the arts at Ayanoi High School, and specifically on the daily adventures of a group of five friends with divergent personalities brought together by their artistic passion: Kisaragi, Nodamiki, Kyoju, Tomokane and Namiko. *GA*'s structural organization echoes its pivotal preoccupation by devoting virtually all of its installments to the exploration of a distinctive facet of the prismatic cosmos of the visual arts. These include both specific techniques and media, such as pencil drawing, still life, costume design and photography, and stylistic modalities associated with particular movements, schools or aesthetic ideologies, such as conceptualism, surrealism and trompe-l'oeil. The high level of intimacy characterizing the relationship between the artist and the artistic activity is repeatedly communicated, often with the addition of humorous touches, as borne out by the episode in which Kisaragi's sleep is invaded by surrealist dreams. Color plays a crucial role in the anime in both literal and metaphorical terms, as various palettes are deftly matched and contrasted with the chromatic rhythms of the protagonists' creative adventures.

What is most remarkable about the search for a language undertaken by the anime explored in this context, and is indeed most pointedly instrumental in the communication of the maturity of their efforts, is their awareness of the status of the arts they embrace as texts — i.e., discourses, or signifying practices, embedded in a large tapestry of intersecting traditions, voices and intertextual echoes. Hence, they do not claim to assert their autonomous standing, to pretend that they came into being in a free-floating neutral point in time and space. Rather, they seek to pay homage, both explicitly and tangentially, to the cultural configurations wherein their languages emerge and gradually accrue meaning in the manner of a fractal formation and with the modest perseverance of a coral reef. In articulating their creative voyages through music, drama, dance, painting and sculpture (among other arts), the anime alert us to the cultural construction of the characters and settings they depict, emphasizing that the search for a language is not an enterprise on which human beings embark from the external and privileged standpoint of transcendental artificers insofar as human beings themselves are inexorably constructed within and by language. The search for a language is therefore a mission whereby the anime's protagonists strive to fashion not only particular artworks and contexts for the display of their creations but also — and no less critically — their own contingent identities. Any language ensuing from the artistic (and varyingly experimental) gestures ostensibly associated with specific individuals and specific groups must be approached as a culturally positioned palimpsest of multisubjective creative moments inscribed by vectors of desire, aesthetic taste, ethical judgment, learning and entertainment.

The anime's intersection with the broader fabric of culturally defined meaning-making practices is paradigmatically exemplified by their approach to color. Japanese art's striking use of color is an essential component of its unique cultural beauty. Since ancient times, its practitioners have relied on adventurous combinations of contrasting hues (such as scarlet and black, gold and green, green and red, dark blue and brilliant white) in the conception of artifacts as diverse as armor and screen paintings, furnishings and pottery. Colors are deployed both to honor their intrinsic aesthetic charm and as a means of conveying feelings and beliefs in material form. The titles under scrutiny posit color as an element shared by all of the arts with which they engage either visibly or affectively. Such ubiquity tersely demonstrates the centrality of the chromatic dimension to Japanese culture, intimating that color should not be dismissed as a purely cosmetic supplement since it emanates directly from nature — namely, Japanese art's supreme guide and primary source of inspiration.

The predominant hues adopted by countless artists over the centuries are themselves drawn from Japan's landscape, pride of place being traditionally accorded to indigo (*ai*), green (*midori*), scarlet (*beni*) and purple (*murasaki*) — with black (*sumi*) as a key player in the rendition of silhouettes and calligraphic elements which, in the capacious logic entertained by Japanese culture, are considered no less worthwhile, as artistic designs, than floral, animal or aquatic motifs. The names allocated to the vast majority of colors originate from the designations initially used for the plants, the animals and the aspects of both terrestrial and marine environments which they echo. Relatedly, particular colors have been inspired by seasonal variations and studiously matched to the requirements of different times of the year and attendant climactic circumstances. This trend is exemplified by the custom of employing cool shades in the manufacture of summer clothes and accessories to counteract the more unpleasant effects of heat and humidity. As Tohru Haga observes, "when wearing a *yukata* on a hot summer evening, one could not be without an *uchiwa*, or round fan, both to stir the breezes and banish the persistent mosquitoes. These bamboo frame fans covered with paper were usually printed with designs using *ai* blue as the main color in order to accentuate the image of coolness." The use of *ai* in the production of "mosquito nests," likewise, "was an attempt to create at least the illusion of coolness" (Haga).

The unparalleled care placed by traditional Japanese culture in the conception, orchestration and display of particular color combinations in accordance with nature's cycles is proverbially epitomized by the layering of colors in full-fledged kimonos, where both the patterns and the hues themselves vary with the season or even the month. The essay "Japanese Traditional and Ceremonial Colors" elucidates this proposition by listing the main hues at play in the intricate and sophisticated game of layering:

- **January** *Pine:* sprout green and deep purple
- **February** *Redblossom plum:* crimson and purple
- **March** *Peach:* peach and khaki
- **April** *Cherry:* white and burgundy
- **May** *Orange Flower:* deadleaf yellow and purple
- **June** *Artemesia*: sprout green and yellow
- **July** *Lily:* red and deadleaf yellow
- **August** *Cicada wing*: cedar bark and sky blue
- **September** *Aster:* lavender and burgundy
- **October** *Bush Clover*: rose and slate blue
- **November** *Maple*: vermilion and grey-green
- **December** *Chrysanthemum:* lavender and deep blue ["Japanese Traditional and Ceremonial Colors"].

Indigenous palettes have been traditionally informed by a distinctive and multi-layered chromatic symbolism. The combination of red and white (*kouhaku*) has been consistently elected as an auspicious symbol, as borne out by its prodigious prominence in a wide range of traditional Japanese artifacts of both ceremonial and daily usage. Furthermore, vermilion red is the color of the *torii*, the traditional Shinto gateway leading to a shrine, and is hence central to the indigenous religion and stance to the spiritual. White also carries mystical meaning as an emblem of supreme purity: to communicate with the *kami*, Japanese people have traditionally resorted to "delicate white symbols made of the bleached fiber of the bark of the paper mulberry or other trees. Such symbols, called *yushide*, were affixed to the ever-greens or other trees that were considered to possess the spirit of the divine" (Yoshida 1985, p. 26). Furthermore, birds "with pure white wings, like the crane (*tsuru*) and the snowy heron (*sagi*) seemed half-mystical ... the white wings suggested something under the power of the *kami*. The rooster that crows at dawn, for example, was thought to drive away the evil deities of darkness, and herald the return of the deities of light and goodness" (p. 74). Alongside *kouhaku*, the colors favored by Japanese culture on the basis of their emblematic powers are green, a symbol of eternal life and of the animating sap coursing through all forms; blue, the living expression of water as the epitome of life-giving energy; black, the emblem of the mysterious depths which daylight existence must respect if it is to achieve harmony within its own rhythms and tasks (it is worn, incidentally, for both traditional funerals and weddings); gold, the color of heavenly glory and prosperous harvests; and the multicolored (*tasai*) as an expression of vitality, enthusiasm and good fortune: for instance, the traditional *temari* balls presented as toys and intended to wish their recipients happy and fulfilling lives, while also promising friendship and loyalty, consist of multicolored pieces of fabric cut out of old kimonos adorned with intricate embroidery.

It is crucial to note, when considering the symbolism of *tasai*, that Japanese culture has rarely relied on undiluted and primary colors on their own. As Haga emphasizes, "intermediate" hues and the countless "variations" to which these lend themselves have been characteristically favored, giving rise to "neutral tints" combining various colors. Some of the available blends are so subtle as to seem impenetrably infinitesimal to many Western viewers—a case in point is "the color *moegi*, a neutral tint corresponding to the green tinged with yellow color of onion tops as they sprout, and slightly darkened by the addition of gray so that it is more like strong green tea." At the same time, one and the same basic hue can be associated with a wide spectrum of poetic associations depending on the local variations it displays. A perfect example is supplied by the color terms used in different seasons or times of the day to describe the morning glory (*asagao*), typically elected by artists and poets as the supreme symbol of uncomplicated beauty. "When the indigo blue or deep blue of the morning glory is somewhat paler," Haga explains, "it is known as *ao* (blue) or *mizuiro* (sky blue). It is the color of an early summer or early autumn sky or of shallow lakes or rivers that mirror such skies. When blue is dark, it is known as *kon* (dark or navy blue). In some case, when all strong light is eliminated and a shade of purple added, it is *shikon* or purplish blue. The range of indigo hues is wide, from a bright blue, clear midsummer sky dotted with puffy white clouds and the billowing ocean that reflects it to the towering gray-blue silhouette of Mt. Fuji viewed from the adjacent seacoast, to the purplish blue of the delicate *nasu*, the small Japanese eggplant. All these hues may be found in the morning glory as well" (Haga).

In the anime under investigation, the cultural ascendancy of color expresses itself at three interrelated levels—i.e., through the color schemes adopted by the arts they dramatize, through their own distinctive palettes, and through their emphasis on the metaphorical value of color both within those areas and, by extension, within the culture whence they emanate as an art form sui generis. *Piano: The Story of a Young Girl's Heart* is especially notable, on the chromatic plane, due to its inspired interpretation for the contemporary screen of Japanese art's long-standing preference for neutral shades resulting from the combination of numerous colors into minutely differentiated and genially refined mixes. No less importantly, the series provides a sensitive dramatization of the interplay of color and sound: a major component, as argued in detail in the preceding chapter, of the evolution of sonoric-visual relations since classical antiquity. Thus, *Piano* diligently explores diverse ways of translating the chromatic values of music into appropriate visual correlatives, often relying on backgrounds which bear witness to the rolling seasons by recourse to color variations, and on different types of clothing likewise connected with the seasonal cycle or else with specific personalities. *Piano*'s take on fashion is made especially effective by its ability to come across as pervasively elegant without in the least pandering to the pressures of trendiness for its own sake. The adoption of subtle palettes and blends is largely responsible for the achievement of this cumulative effect and, in refusing to make any cheap concessions to faddishness, serves to instill the anime with a timeless feel. Most notable, in this regard, is the use of muted, mellow and gracefully harmonized hues with a preference for plum, lavender, magenta and indigo palettes, all of which are ingrained in the indigenous sensibility. *Piano*'s chromatic genius ultimately lies with its ability to deploy consistently a relatively limited range of colors, yet impart this scheme with myriad prismatic variations by tirelessly experimenting with the interrelated properties of hue (a color's distinctive characteristic), value (its brightness), and intensity or saturation (its chromatic purity—a.k.a. chroma). Few words could describe the anime's atmosphere more fittingly than Ralph Waldo Emerson's metaphorical interpretation of life at large in eminently chromatic terms: "life is a train of moods like a string of beads; and as we pass through them they prove to be many colored lenses, which paint the world their own hue, and each shows us only what lies in its own focus" (Emerson).

Swan Lake is another cogent example of the enduring legacy of tradition in anime's treatment of color. The film indeed yields a veritable paean to the centrality of blue in all its variants, renewing an aesthetic preference evinced by Japanese culture at large, and paradigmatically exemplified by the wide range of lyrical associations utilizing the morning glory as their focal point. This is especially evident in the rendition of the movie's setting, where blue and blue-related tints and shades predominate in the portrayal of both peaceful and forbidding scenarios. At one point, the concurrently environmental and symbolic significance of blue is thrown into relief by its subtle infusion with elements of red (particularly in the regions of garnet and carmine) in order to impart the locale with intense feeling of vitality and urgency. This effect accompanies the key sequence in which Prince Siegfrid, unable to take the image of the crowned swan out of his head and troubled by the imminent prospect of having to choose a bride out of beauty rather than love, resolves to seek out the noble creature. Throughout the sequence, the majestic afternoon sunlight is shown gradually to give way to the reddish palettes of dusk, inserting novel symbolic connotations into the scenery.

Swan Lake's sensational metamorphoses provide some of the most remarkable chromatic effects, especially in the scenes dramatizing Rothbart and Odile's prodigious transitions between their human and owlish physiques, and those charting the drastic changes undergone by the habitat as the wizard's nefarious spells are dissipated and the world's pristine beauty is attendantly restored. Most notable, in this regard, is the film's handling of its palettes (and related lighting effects) in conjunction with the setting's elemental shapes. In the climax, color and light magically collude as the wizard's tenebrous castle is stripped of its disquietingly bizarre appendages and finally returns to its original form, that of a massive solemn rock. This is a spiritually poignant moment when one reflects on the paramount importance attached to rocks (and mountains) in the Shinto belief system. The world's regeneration is simultaneously conveyed by the metamorphosis undergone by the vegetation, as bare brambles and contorted roots suddenly appear bedecked with blossom and tender leaves.

Swan Lake also relies on the extreme polarity of white and black in a fairly conventional fashion, placing the former on the side of purity, innocence kindness, spirituality and hope, and the latter on that of corruption, cruelty, spite, greed and vengefulness. At the same time, however, it captures a less obvious set of symbolic associations by equating white to submissiveness and sterility, and black to power and energy. Therefore, while the white swan Odette is portrayed as virginally pure, chaste and peaceful but effectively unproductive due not only to the curse but also, one feels, to her innate passivity, the black swan Odile comes across as colorfully spirited even though corrupt, pernicious and mean. Strictly speaking, the impostor is presented as a far more creative presence than the praiseworthy heroine. It is also worth recalling, on this point, that certain conventional beliefs and assumptions regarding black are suspended, or even discredited altogether, by the preference for dark and shadow-laden locales evinced by traditional Japanese culture. In this context, the Western valorization of niveous luminosity as synonymous with goodness holds no authority. For beauty to resplend, in fact, a modicum of gloom constitutes a major prerequisite. Given the global and seemingly timeless prominence of the swan maiden mythos, moreover, it should be noted that there are other cultures, alongside Japan, in which black does not carry incontrovertibly negative connotations, just as there are also cultures in which white is not always coterminous with either virtue or beauty.

Darkness — and, by extension, black — have been traditionally associated in numerous societies with the baser drives, primeval chaos, horror, grief and the absurd: the condition which most befits humankind and its pathetic weakness in the face of an incomprehensible cosmos. Christianity has implicitly damned the color black by depicting the Devil, the Prince of Darkness, as the ultimate threat to the triumph of God's Logos. In Hindu mythology, darkness symbolizes Time the Destroyer; in Iranian mythology, it is a power associated with Ahriman, Lord of Lies; in Islam, it connotes recklessness. Yet, light is not unanimously regarded as synonymous with either probity or integrity. In fact, countless ghosts populating the most disparate traditions are rendered terrifying by their very paleness, transparence or even pearly-white radiance. The "jack-o'-lantern" (a.k.a. "will-o'-the-wisp," "fairy light," "demon fire," or "fox fire") is a potentially charming light but is also commonly paired with baleful presences, such as witches, vengeful spirits and ill omens. In addition, light is often posited as the hallmark of dangerously enthralling delusions such as the ones beckoned by the mermaid-like Breton "Morganes" and the Italian "Fate Morgana," all descendants of the ill-fated visions summoned by the Arthurian figure of Morgan le Fay. Worldwide folklore also suggests that the most daunting of all conceivable chromatic effects is, as Marina Warner maintains, the "absence of colour: the whiteness of negation, found in night-flyers such as barn owls and certain moths.... The owl that hunts and screeches, gleaming ghostly in the shadows ... has a paralyzing effect on its prey" (Warner, pp. 180–181).

Furthermore, the association of blackness and darkness with the amorphous does not necessarily make them dangerous, since the state of apparently shapeless undifferentiation often provides the natural substratum of the light and forms which may grow out of it. Germination, for instance, occurs in the darkness of the soil, while embryos develop in the darkness of the womb. Finally, it should also be remembered that darkness and blackness have frequently been associated with rites of passage and concepts of spiritual initiation analogous to the coming-of-age stories central to the plots of many of the anime examined in this study. This proposition is corroborated by the trope of the "Dark Night of the Soul" famously promulgated by St. John of the Cross. Derogatory assessments of darkness have conventionally accompanied the propensity to perceive that dimension as incontrovertibly black in keeping with colonial and patriarchal prejudices eager to demonize blackness itself as the realm of feral, destructive and inscrutably alien instincts. Like all myths, those defamatory attitudes are contingent constructs, not natural givens, and are therefore bound to dismantle themselves the moment their constructedness is recognized, their spuriousness is detected and their contextually limited currency is thereby exposed. A simple example indicating the cultural instability of the symbolic connotations of blackness can be found in its variable relationship with the concept of goodness. Whereas in the West it has been common, as Warner observes, to "scare the young into obedience" by invoking people such as "Gypsies, Jews, Turks, blacks" (p. 161) — as attested to by the Italian designation of the bogeyman as "l'Omo nero" (literally, "the black man") — a "lullaby from the plantations of Gran Canaria" describes the monster keen on devouring children as "the white devil" (pp. 162–163). It is therefore beneficial to bear in mind that images of whiteness and figures of light are not, in themselves, absolutely and unproblematically auspicious.

In deploying particular color schemes within a well-defined natural and social environment, virtually all of the anime addressed in this chapter alert us to the cultural codification of color, whereby hues come to constitute a crucial means of organizing, identifying and maintaining a whole world picture. In this context, certain learned cultural associations contribute vitally to the definition of diverse ways in which people perceive and respond to the colors around them at both the conscious and unconscious levels. As Frank Vodvarka observes, in this matter, "*symbolism* is, in some sense, an outgrowth of association and custom; colors forever associated with a particular phenomenon, and sanctified by time and usage. They are the colors of our uniforms, social and religious icons, and institutions" (Vodvarka, pp. 9–10). This realization does not, however, automatically render the theoretical investigation of colors and color-related symbolic associations a straightforward enterprise — let alone an activity likely to yield universally applicable results — due to the intrinsically context-bound character of those associations. The conflicting interpretations of black and white outlined above attest to this contention. "The factors that make up a study, and application, of color are many," argues Vodvarka, and are rendered especially "complex by the difficulty in knowing color's role in particular situations" (p. 10). The conscious connection of a color to a distinct symbolic meaning or set of meanings can be regarded as an intellectual exercise. Albeit important, this activity is never totally divorced from purely sensory and emotional reactions of an intensely corporeal, even visceral, nature — as resplendently borne out by color's penchant for inducing specific moods and, at times, also manifest patterns of behavior. As psychologist Ulrich Beer maintains in *What Color Tells Us* (1922), "seldom, surely, is the psychological part of an appearance in nature so great as it is in the case of color. No one can encounter it and stay neutral. We are immediately, instinctively, and emotionally moved. We have sympathy and apathy, pleasure or disapproval within us as soon as we perceive color" (cited in Mahnke, p. 6).

Swan Lake offers an apposite instance of this phenomenon in the scene where Prince Siegfrid is shown to react with alarm to the sight of Rothbart's castle. At this point, the character is not simply responding to the edifice's grotesquely distorted and asymmetrical forms but also, at a deeper level, to the blue-black color scheme in which those macabre shapes appear to be not simply painted but actually immersed — as though color held a material existence of its own independently of the objects it touches. In so doing, the youth is bringing a cluster of culturally sanctioned associations to bear on the object of his perception. However, insofar as the sight instantly affects his mood, causing his erstwhile adventurous and plucky attitude to degenerate into apprehension and doubt, those colors are seen to host great affective significance, and hence to have the power to impact on the character's conduct in ways which bypass and, to a certain extent, altogether defy, intellectual rationalization.

In *Swan Lake*, the emotive import of color is reinforced by its studious integration with the film's musical score, light effects and the dance of radiance and shadow abetting the coalescence of the two dimensions to great dramatic effect. With its magisterial synthesis of sonoric and visual effects, the movie implicitly echoes Charles Baudelaire's interpretation of musicality as described in the foregoing chapter. Handling its lines and hues on the basis of the overarching principles of tone and rhythm, *Swan Lake* posits harmony as the foundation of its musical-visual experiments, striving to evoke a unifying melody which is able to embrace all local and contingent variations and to abide in memory well after its images have departed the screen. At the same time, without diminishing in the slightest the affective substance of its elegantly stylized character portraits, the film invites us to appreciate the rhythmic and tonal qualities of its colors and lines independently of the actual forms these are supposed to define and delimit. Our attention is thus steered away from the level of representational verisimilitude and encouraged to venture into the enchanted realm of as yet undefined possibilities — a world in which amorphousness is not a flaw but the precondition of creativity: the cauldron accommodating the virtually infinite range of potential realities which may generated in the mind through subjective sensation and memory, and not through unquestioning obedience to the authority of mimesis.

The codification of the relationship between sound and chromatic effects endorsed by the early twentieth-century composer Alexander Scriabin provides a precedent of considerable aesthetic relevance to the present context. Seeking to bring out the chromatic value of harmonies and musical structures as the simultaneous projection of colors and lights, Scriabin associated particular musical keys with particular colors in a fundamentally intuitive fashion, arranging the keys in a circle of fifths (the shape showing the relationships among the twelve tones of the chromatic scale). The code of seasonally determined color symbolism outlined earlier vis-à-vis Japan's vestimentary tradition, with its matching months, hues and natural forms, finds an intriguing musical-visual correlative in Scriabin's template of correspondences:

C = Red
G = Orange
D = Yellow
A = Green
E = Pale Blue
B = Very pale blue

F# = Bright blue
D♭ = Violet
A♭ = Purple
E♭ = Metallic gray/blue
B♭ = Blue-gray
F = Dark red [cited in Peacock].

Swan Lake's symbolic use of landscape also recalls the tradition of the poetic landscape, a form of painting in which geography and architecture are depicted from a markedly subjective perspective in order to maximize their emotional import, while mythological, fantastic and elegiac motifs are also brought consistently into play. In its purest form, the poetic landscape exhibits a wholly imaginary setting. Unshackled by the dictates of mimetic verisimilitude and empirical experience governing the topographical tradition, artists devoted to the evocation of imaginary places are free to fathom the world of emotions and distill the poetry of color and light into their paintings. It is precisely from this highly refined interpretation of the poetic landscape that *Swan Lake*'s most memorable locations derive their force. Several of its recurring visual elements echo quite overtly the principal motifs found in that pictorial tradition: for example, the nostalgic golden light of early morning and twilight, the gloomy shadows dancing on gnarled trees and craggy rocks, gently expanding vistas and rolling hills imbued with pastoral serenity, and horizons fading into radiant mist. At the same time, the film's handling of color strives to match the distinctive emotional palettes of Tchaikovsky's music, which it logically adopts as its score (as indeed does *Princess Tutu*, here examined in Chapter 4). So intimate is the sonoric-visual bond that the anime's visual drift and rhythm often appear to be determined by the score itself. In the process, *Swan Lake* encapsulates the affective potency of the Russian composer's art as portrayed by Rich Di Silvio: "Tchaikovsky's music was marked by a sensuously rhythmic pulse and an innate melodic flow that enabled him to create some of the world's greatest ballet music; music that shows a mixture of playful classicism and romantic verve. His deep-sensitivity saturated his music producing lush melodies that have enamored listeners for over a century" (Di Silvio).

In offering the most comprehensive of the quests at stake in the selected titles, *Honey and Clover* concurrently delivers a richly nuanced interpretation of the culturally axial part played by color in the creative heritage to which the art of anime is heir. The series proclaims the affective import of color so enthusiastically — more often, it must be emphasized, by tasteful allusion than by spectacular display — as to bring to mind the Expressionist painter Emil Nolde's reflections on the subject: "colors, the materials of the painter; colors in their own lives, weeping and laughing, dream and bliss, hot and sacred, like love songs and the erotic, like songs and glorious chorals! Colors in vibration, pealing like silver bells and clanging like bronze bells, proclaiming happiness, passion and love, soul, blood, and death" (cited in Vodvarka, p. 1). Foregrounding color's power to affect qualitatively all aspects of a composition (its forms, play of light and shadow, dynamic rhythms and overarching structure), *Honey and Clover* posits it as a force capable of imbuing both the immediately visible aspects of surface and mass and the imperceptible interstices of space, connecting and differentiating by turns the natural and human-made components thereof. In a sense, the energy of colors is so pervasive as to acquire an independent existence and to exude a simultaneously sensual and mystical aura. Therefore, the anime's multifaceted exploration of the languages of painting and sculpture, fashion and interior design, architecture and photography enthrones the chromatic dimension as a uniquely effective means of kindling and appealing to the emotions. At the same time, it is profoundly sensitive to other aspects of color which are no less instrumental, if often less obvious, in enabling particular artistic registers to emerge. These encompass psychological and physiological phenomena alongside the array of figurative associations on the basis of which, as shown, a culture comes to forge the aesthetic principles and perspectives which guide the ongoing flow of its creative productivity.

A comical perversion of the Japanese commitment to the ideation of subtle chromatic blends and nuances is supplied by Hagumi and Ayumi's bizarre gastronomic exploits. These flaunt dishes such as chocolate-chip mint ice cream in a nest of warm pumpkin, and a curry concoction containing whole apples laced with an unspecified syrupy substance served on a bed of rice garnished with grapefruit. Though abysmal to the palate, these admittedly innovative recipes look weirdly charming on the chromatic plane. Culinary genius finds more orthodox expression, on both the gustatory and the chromatic fronts, near the end of the first season when Yuuta, in the course of a soul-searching journey round Japan on his bicycle, is temporarily employed by a troupe of itinerant workers who specialize in yet another noble art, that of temple and shrine repair. Having quickly realized that none of the things he has learned as an architecture student are of any practical use when it comes to real manual labor, the youth adopts the role of a surrogate housewife and focuses, specifically, on the thorough preparation of nutritious indigenous dishes, receiving unanimous praise from the famished men. While the basic task of delivering tasty meals constitutes the core of Yuuta's job, he does not fail to revere the local devotion to the aesthetic value of cuisine and food display by presenting the dishes as not only corporeally satisfying but also visually attractive and stylishly colored artifacts.

The fascination with color-centered play is also married to culinary artistry in the anime's first opening animation, which feature a wide variety of vibrantly colored spinning plates containing a selection of both indigenous and international dishes endowed with bizarre morphing tendencies and somewhat disturbing motility. The piece echoes the style of Czech surrealist artist, filmmaker and stop-motion animator Jan Svankmajer, and especially his fascination with grotesque and disturbing imagery. As a self-consciously arty gesture, this opening animation offers the first taste of a tendency, exhibited by the anime's producers throughout its progression, to accord creativity pride of place, and thus mirror in emblematic form the mentality of its cast of art students.

A downright farcical interpretation of the aesthetic preference for deftly modulated colors comes with the sequence dramatizing a game of Twister. On this occasion, the players' task is rendered absurdly difficult by Shinobu's impromptu creation of color circles painted in highly refined chromatic gradations which would be perfectly at home in Japanese traditional costume but are quite incongruous with a festive pursuit. Dissatisfied with the customary range of red, blue, yellow and green utilized in orthodox versions of the traditional party game, Shinobu proceeds to incorporate not only colors which could be deemed just about acceptable (such as purple, orange, pink, brown and beige) but also obscure tints and shades bearing culturally resonant names — e.g., moss green, mineral violet, carmine-red and, most importantly, passion blue: a hue invested with climactic prominence in accordance with the anime's primary thematics as well as in implicit recognition of its privileged position in Japan's chromatic pantheon.

In adopting an eclectic approach to the role played by color in art, *Honey and Clover* could not fail to engage with fashion design. As noted, Hagumi embraces this art with remarkable enthusiasm in spite of an inherent lack of any genuine vocation in the field. However, it is in its presentation of the characters' clothes that the anime asserts most vividly its distinctive vestimentary sensibility. In the execution of day-to-day apparel, the visuals assiduously refrain from the use of either bright palettes or adventurous silhouettes, opting instead for sedate hues which by and large harmonize with the natural colors of their wearer's hair, eyes and complexion. This stylistic choice is consonant with the series' overall preference for mellow tones and watercolor softness. At the same time, it is an economical means of foregrounding the actors' personalities at the expense of superficial decoration, insofar as it allows their special qualities and foibles to manifest themselves unfettered by frills or fripperies. Even Hagumi's costumes, despite their occasional allusions do Victorian children's fashion in their cuts and tasteful use of lace trimmings, are rendered in muted, even nondescript, shades to ensure that her complex personality is allowed ample room for self-expression.

Alongside everyday outfits, *Honey and Clover*'s sartorial range accommodates carefully chosen instances of traditional attire and related color schemes. Samurai and ninja costumes are hinted at in comical vignettes intended to translate a character's aggressiveness or anger into condensed dramatic moments — such as the one capturing Shuuji's inner turmoil as he storms into Hagumi's bedroom late at night suspecting that Yuuta and his charge might be up to no good. Traditional costume finds more extensive portrayal in the depiction of a traditional summer festival — replete with stunning fireworks as is customarily the case in Japanese *matsuri* held in the warm season — and especially in the main female characters' preparations for the event. The shapely Ayumi rapidly finds in the available domestic collection a *yukata* adorned in a classic floral style which fits her perfectly. Hagumi's childlike physique, by contrast, makes all of the full-size *yukata* available totally unsuitable to the purpose. With each successive attempt to adapt such a garment to her form, she simply ends up looking more and more ridiculous — until, with a genuine flash of genius, one of Ayumi's elders comes up with a child's costume adorned with a correspondingly infantile marine motif which not only fits Hagumi but actually does her special beauty the justice it deserves. Traditional Japanese costume also comes briefly into play in the sequence devoted to a traditional wedding, where the bride wears the traditional robe known simply as *shiromuku* ("pure white"), and coily wonders about the garment's symbolic appropriateness given that she has been married before — at which point, Ayumi's unflinchingly optimistic aunt reassures her that such details do not truly matter because there is no limit to happiness.

In its interstitial engagement with fashion, *Honey and Clover* confirms the passion for colors already manifest in its opening treatment of cuisine. The *yukata*, in particular, paradigmatically exemplify this tendency, according greater dramatic value to the chromatic blends evinced by the fabrics than to the silhouettes themselves, gracefully alluding to the symbolic connotations carried by their emphatic use of a variety of traditional colors — and especially by the culturally pivotal *ai* with its spellbinding blend of mysticism and poetry. Traditional costume makes an additional cameo appearance with the Mongolian *dels* (knee-length tunics with sash) brought back by Shuuji from his field trip as presents for Hagumi and Ayumi alongside a vast assortment of exquisitely crafted bracelets and hair ornaments. (The male characters, incidentally, are regaled with comparatively stingy souvenirs in the forms of a stamp, a postcard and a stone.)

Honey and Clover's fascination with the colluding languages of color and fabric is meticulously documented by the companion volume *Honey and Clover Illustrations*, an artbook showcasing the works of Chika Umino, the creator of the manga on which the anime itself is based. The volume as a whole can be viewed as a vibrant testament to Wassily Kandinsky's theorization of the interrelation of color and line, and specifically to the artist's reflections on the capacity held by particular organizations of lines to convey vibrant dynamic oppositions as a quality they share with specific colors. For example, the power to communicate "tensions of advancing and retreating" characteristic of "acentric free straight lines" is posited by Kandinsky as a property which also distinguishes "the 'colourful' colours," and most notably "yellow and blue" (Kandinsky 1979, p. 62). Important correspondences are also seen to obtain between "angular lines" and particular colors. Thus, the right angle is associated with "red, which represents a midway point between yellow and blue and carries within it cold-warm characteristics" (p. 72), while the "acute angle" is linked up with "warmth" and the "obtuse angle" with "coldness" (p. 73). Kandinsky's theories suggest that colors inhabit all shapes, however implicitly or latently, insofar as the states of motion or rest expressed by different lines and planes are themselves endowed with color. In this perspective, "only the point, so long as it remains isolated, offers complete 'rest'" while individual "horizontal or vertical" lines, though seemingly quiescent, possess "a coloured rest, as warmth and coldness" which are intrinsic in their dynamic potentialities. Relatedly, "of all the forms of the plane, the circle tends most toward colorless rest as it is the result of two forces which always act uniformly and because it lacks the violence of the angle," which, by implication, can be regarded as the most vividly colored of shapes (p. 124).

Although Kandinsky's theories are supposed to apply to eminently non-objective painting, the propositions outlined above find some intriguing parallels in Umino's experimental fusion of chromatic and linear elements as a means of producing a variety of dynamic effects. Stark lines organized independently of any unifying or guiding centers, for instance, tend to come into play whenever the artist's main goal is the expression of a marked state of tension, and this geometrical strategy concurrently relies on the power of warm hues (especially yellow) to convey the sense of advancement and the inverse capacity held by cool hues (most notably, blue) to communicate the sensation of retreat. Angular and quasi-angular forms are employed as economical indicators of various degrees of either kinesis or stasis. These, too, correspond to specific hues, the warm end of the spectrum coinciding with dynamic energy, and the cool end with stillness. Circular shapes, in turn, are repeatedly utilized to evoke a restful atmosphere or an emotive striving toward peace.

One of the most salient traits of Umino's art, in this regard, is its synthetic orchestration of geometry and chromatism (in both the pictorial and the musical conceptions of this term). Umino's drawings offer an intriguing variation on Kandinsky's compositional and coloristic grammar insofar as they do not conform with the Russian artist's proverbial prioritization of primary hues.

In fact, they characteristically capitalize on the distinctive properties of watercolor to create a wide range of mellowed out palettes replete with the subtlest gradations and modulations. In so doing, they endeavor to hint at the dormant presence of coolness in warm shades, and of warmth in cool ones, by placing side by side contrasting hues in a fashion which leads them to interplay rather than clash. For example, pale blues and blue-grays are often twinned with pastelly reds and yellows so elegantly as to induce the eye to sense in each end of the spectrum the emotive potentialities of the opposite end. This is paradigmatically exemplified by the illustrations — of which there are several in the companion volume — portraying pairs, triads or larger ensembles of characters. In many of these drawings, one observes a preponderance of curvilinear rhythms in the depiction of both individual personae and the interactions between them, which serves to evoke an overall impression of harmony and peace. The curves and arcs defined by the characters' bodies and body language (as well as by the verbal communication one can imagine to be taking place between them) are juxtaposed with the lines which define the patterns on their clothes. These typically consist of assemblages of more or less sharply contrasting circular and straight lines whose cumulative effect is the evocation of vitality and energy. The geometric contrast, moreover, is sustained by the simultaneous juxtaposition of cool and warm hues in the coloring of individual elements of both those patterns and the sartorial accessories associated with each garment. At the same time, Umino's vestimentary sensibility evinces a fascination with color duets which is deeply embedded in Japanese fashion, stretching back to Heian times and still governing present-day assemblages of kimono and obi. This is based on the cultivation of delicate contrasts between a warm major tone and a cool minor tone, or vice versa, which are capable of achieving highly dramatic effects in the most economical of styles.

The examples delineated above indicate that the linear vigor of Umino's visuals is inextricable from their chromatic properties insofar as colors, instead of merely adding a pleasing ornamental effect to the drawings' geometrical properties, actually play a critical role in bringing out their inherent aliveness or even imparting their forms with animating afflatus. Thus, it could be argued that an aesthetic vision analogous to Kandinsky's own does come to fruition in Umino's manga art as the interdependence of color and line is enthroned as the central marker of *Honey and Clover*'s distinctive language. The overall effect is that of a gracefully smooth visual and performative flow — a compositional current which transcends the staccato rhythms inevitably attendant on the frame-by-frame constitution of animation as an art form to evoke the feeling of a fluid chain of impressions. This places the book on virtually the same dynamic level as the anime itself, rendering it a joy to behold even for people who do not customarily favor visual guides, companions and the like insofar as they view their content as a poor substitute for the moving image itself. At the same time, the volume's presentation style echoes the ancient pictorial tradition of the narrative tableau — a typology often favored by Japanese artists — as a work in which logically sequential and discrete elements coexist and finally coalesce in mutual suffusion.

Few works in the realm of anime, and indeed animation at large, approximate as closely as *Honey and Clover* does the philosophical ideal of the *Gesamtkunstwerk*. Conceived by Richard Wagner to designate the synthetic fusion of all the separate arts, this process of amalgamation is intended to occur under the aegis of music. The historical roots of the *Gesamtkunstwerk* in the art of painting are of even greater relevance to *Honey and Clover* in consideration of the anime's eminently pictorial leanings. The concept can indeed be traced to Romantic landscape painting, and most pointedly to the allegorical works of Caspar David Friedrich. This artists played a crucial part in emancipating landscape from its Cinderella status as a mere backdrop to the unfolding of human dramas into an autonomous emotive subject. Friedrich's goal was to reach all of the viewer's senses with the synaesthetic experience of art as an intrepidly hybrid integration of multiple forms. Thus, the spirit of music is always latent in Friedrich's images as a phantasmatic presence even when they do not allude in an obviously recognizable fashion to an actual melody or instrument. Likewise pivotal to the promotion of artistic integration in the service of both synaesthesia and interdisciplinarity was the painter Otto Philip Runge, Friedrich's contemporary. To this end, Runge planned a series of symbolic paintings entitled *The Times of the Day*, meant to be viewed within a purposely designed architectural structure to the accompaniment of poetry and, most intriguingly, ad hoc music.

The description of *Honey and Clover* as a *Gesamtkunstwerk* of sorts may sound bizarre in consideration of the substantial gap separating Wagner from contemporary anime in both historical and generic terms. It is worth bearing in mind, however, that this is by no means the first time Wagner's notion of the total work of art is used figuratively to designate a creative gesture beyond the scope of the German composer's own purview. Indeed, as Peter Vergo points out, Wagner's "notion of an integration or synthesis of all the arts, which he had envisaged taking place on the operatic stage, was soon applied to other, quite unrelated areas of artistic endeavour in ways that he would probably never have sanctioned and might scarcely have been understood. By the early 1900s, the term *Gesamtkunstwerk* had already been associated with a wide range of activities that included book illustration, interior design and decoration, even architecture and urban planning" (Vergo, p. 109). What matters here is the relevance to *Honey and Clover* of the concept of the total artwork as a form able to encompass disparate artistic and artisanal practices in an ongoing dialectical exchange.

Although *Honey and Clover* may seem to accord uncontrasted priority to the visual arts, this is hardly the case. For one thing, as shown vis-à-vis Shinobu's Hollywood exploits, it accommodates the performance arts to great dramatic effect. More importantly, in its eclectic purview of art, *Honey and Clover* does not neglect to integrate the art of music into its fabric. This is not, by and large, thematically foregrounded — except in the aforementioned scene in which the supremely multiskilled Shinobu plays the *morin khuur* with astonishing competence. Nevertheless, the art of music does assert its power throughout the series by means of a beautiful soundtrack. A vital component of the anime's cumulative aesthetic identity, this proves capable of operating as a cohesive force on both the thematic and the structural planes. Carlo Santos' analysis of the series propounds this idea so precisely that it deserves full citation in the present context: "if music is the language of emotion, then few shows speak it as eloquently as this one. With just a few studio instruments, the soundtrack is able to express the gamut of emotions that each character runs through. The energetic opening theme by YUKI converts into a gentle piano solo, and even Morita's bouts of insanity are accented by charming comedic themes. The most effective emotional tools, however, are the insert songs by singer-songwriter Suga Shikao and rock group SPITZ" (Santos).

Director Kenichi Kasai's commitment to the exploration of graphic creativity, so pivotal to *Honey and Clover*'s entire diegesis, reproposes itself with *Bakuman*: a sensitive anatomy of the universe of manga production. While focusing on the creative act itself, the anime simultaneously adopts a quasi-documentary approach to the art at issue, offering an intriguing insider's look at the manga industry at practically all levels of the design, serialization, distribution and consumption processes. It thus supplies us with fascinating insights into the creative, ideological and commercial trials surrounding the emergence of a specific market or fanbase in accordance to which the artist's genius may or may not grow beyond the sphere of a purely personal — indeed solitary — vision. In this respect, *Bakuman*'s approach to the topos of artistic self-realization presents the search for a language not solely as a personal quest but also as a widespread social phenomenon which defies age, status and gender boundaries.

Most importantly, the style in which the anime delivers its behind the scenes information about the manga industry is never so detached or formal as to resemble a TV documentary, which would deprive the story of its dramatic vigor and feasibly discourage the audience from empathizing with the protagonists' creative quest. In fact, *Bakuman*'s insider knowledge bears witness to its creators' genuine devotion to both manga and anime, and to a desire to reach viewers who harbor germane feelings toward those arts. In other words, it is a work conceived by manga and anime lovers for manga and anime lovers. It even finds an ingenious way of appealing specifically to practitioners of drawing (both within and outside the boundaries of the manga universe) by intermittently reflecting on details such as the thickness and suppleness of lines drawn with different types of pen (e.g., the "G pen," the "*kabura* pen" and the "*maru* pen"), as well as dynamic, shading and background effects. On these occasions, the anime takes care to intimate that such considerations are critical to a *mangaka*'s success not so much because of their technical significance as by virtue of their ability to determine the visuals' emotional impact, and hence affect significantly their reception by readers. While excessive emphasis on the technical dimension could easily have alienated the less arty (or more action-oriented) members of the audience, *Bakuman*'s exploration of the affective implications of drawing has the potential to appeal to virtually anybody.

At the same time, Kasai's keenness on delving into the interaction of different art forms seen in *Honey and Clover*— and also demonstrated, as argued in Chapter 4, by *Nodame Cantabile* and *Kimikiss Pure Rouge*— is eloquently confirmed by *Bakuman*. The male protagonists, Moritaka Mashiro and Akito Takagi, pursue their dream of becoming *mangaka* and being serialized in *Shounen Jack* (a publication evidently modeled on *Shounen Jump*, the prestigious magazine in which the manga version of *Bakuman* is published). Simultaneously, Moritaka's girlfriend, Miho Azuki, strives to become a *seyuu* (voice actor) in the anime sector. Moritaka and Miho's aspirations intersect as he vows to marry her once they have realized their respective ambitions, and jointly brought them to fruition with her performance in an anime based on the youth's own manga.

As noted earlier, *Skip Beat!* transgresses the conventions of *shoujo* anime (as does *Princess Tutu*, a series explored in Chapter 4). *Bakuman* cultivates a parallel vision by superficially embracing the classic format of the *shounen* anime only to reinvent it with unparalleled gusto. Thus, while typical *shounen* characters fantasize about becoming superheroes endowed with preternatural powers, and are routinely involved in high-octane battles, tournaments and chases featuring countless prodigies and monsters, *Bakuman*'s protagonists pursue a relatively realistic goal in comparably realistic settings and among credible human beings. This is not to say that Moritaka and his associates have it easy. Early in the series, in fact, Moritaka dishes out a detailed set of figures documenting the obstacles and risks besetting any aspiring *mangaka* in strictly arithmetical terms — and highlighting the incidence of failure attendant upon their dreams with chilling dispassionateness. It is not until their work has proved durably and dependably successful that would-be artists come to deserve the designation of *mangaka*: until then, they are mere "gamblers." Relatedly, *Bakuman* does not show lack suspense in comparison with more conventional *shounen* series. On the contrary, it repeatedly proves able to generate a gripping atmosphere through the feelings of trepidation and anxiety preceding any crucial decisions concerning the future of Moritaka and Akito's creations — rather than by recourse to martial or athletic exploits in the way a typical *shounen* title would do.

The anime's title is in itself worthy of notice. A blatant demonstration of the Japanese passion for portmanteau terms combining the first syllables of two separate words into a new whole, the word *bakuman* lends itself to different readings depending on the meanings one chooses to attribute to each of its components. The *man* segment is almost certainly an abbreviated form of the word "manga," though it could also be taken to signify "ten thousand." The *baku* segment is more multilayered since it could equally well derive from the word for "explosion," *bakuhatsu*, which could be interpreted as a reference to the potentially explosive impact of Moritaka and Akito's creative gesture, from the word for "gambling," *bakuchi*, which would allude to the dicey nature of the enterprise, or from the word *baku*, the chimeric nightmare devourer of Eastern lore, and hence a possible symbol of manga's power to usher the reader into ideal alternate worlds. There is no way of knowing for sure which of these meanings is correct as long as the word *bakuman* is written entirely in *katakana*, as it commonly is, rather than with the employment of *kanji* highlighting its likely root.

As the protagonists' understanding of their art deepens, they increasingly realize that the successful interplay of words and visuals on which manga production pivots requires a sensitive grasp of the fundamental strategies capable of triggering the most visceral, and yet most baffling, of human experiences: enjoyment. Pleasure in art, Moritaka and Akito come to appreciate, springs to a significant extent from an instinctive desire for exploration and understanding: a drive which finds maximum satisfaction in artifacts which know how to fulfill and frustrate by turns their recipient's curiosity, expectations and fantasies. In order to guarantee the integrated progression of the text's visual and verbal strands — ideally over several months of steady serialization — involves the development of ruses through which particular narrative patterns may be regularly deployed for the sake of continuity without these degenerating into bland repetitiveness. Such models include templates which can steer the action from conflict to resolution, from menace to solace, from obscurity to clarity. At the same time, *Bakuman*'s up-and-coming artists are well aware that in their world, the quest for novelty should never be posited as so overwhelming a priority as to obscure the value of reiteration as an essential component of the enduring popularity of manga over time. They have, in fact, learned from their personal experience as keen manga readers that the most enjoyable aspects of their art revolve to a significant extent on the appeal of the familiar — that certain character types, plot complications, verbal expressions and, ultimately, entire world views simply *work* by virtue of their recurrence in different contexts. The knack of handling well-known topoi imaginatively and with seeming spontaneity is a sine qua non of the *mangaka*'s chances of achieving a lasting reputation. Equally vital is the ability to contextualize the ideas at the core of a "name" or "sketch" in relation not only to specific genres but also to overarching transgeneric categories and their defining attributes, with special care always to acknowledge the distinction between "mainstream" and "cult."

This facet of *Bakuman*'s philosophy deserves special attention insofar as it taps directly into a major vein of Japanese aesthetics which finds expression in many of the culture's most distinctive art forms — e.g., Noh and Kabuki. This consists of a systematic cultivation of repetition, centered on the use of recurrent ritualized gestures, postures and other kinetic elements. In Japan's theatrical tradition, performers do not customarily court originality, the frisson of improvisation or the communication of contingent messages. Rather, they endeavor to depict, by recourse to fundamentally unchanging and highly conventional movements, a stylized portrait of recurrent states and emotions. The objective, in observing this aesthetic value, is to preempt the dangers of equivocation and misconstruction. It is crucial to acknowledge, however, that the elimination of these elements of potential semiotic instability is not intended to inculcate dogmatic teachings into a passive audience. In fact, it aims to show that the yearning for continual surprises is a form of escapism, and that it is only from repetition that we may access deeper and more rewarding perceptions of the world. Relatedly, the consistent resurgence of archaic techniques and vocabularies is a way of intimating that the desire for new-fangled tricks crudely disregards the existential substratum of performance — and indeed of the drive to perform — by rejecting the old as stolid and obsolete. In fact, those techniques and vocabularies carry a metaphysical weight which far exceeds their contingent embodiments (as stage plays, puppet shows, festivals or parades, for instance). *Bakuman* supports the contention that the return to the ancestral cannot be automatically dismissed as stubborn traditionalism but is actually a means of expressing lasting human concerns in changing cultural contexts. At the level of plot, the anime honors the principle of reiteration through the suggestion that the current state of affairs involving an aspiring *mangaka* and a girl in his class whom he loves replicates, at least partially, an analogous situation revolving around Moritaka's late uncle and Miho's time-defyingly cute mom.

As it takes us through the workings of manga creation, alternating between pragmatic assessments of the tasks and challenges confronted by budding authors and moments of quasi-visionary inspiration, the anime remains alert to the needs of its protagonists' prospective readership. It thus reminds us that the boys' success finally depends on the extent to which they are able to comprehend and challenge a whole series of desires and responses. David Bordwell's description of these affective processes in the comparably ritualized art form of Hollywood cinema is also relevant to *Bakuman*'s context: "when we bet on a hypothesis, especially under the pressure of time, confirmation can carry an emotional kick; the organism enjoys creating unity. When the narrative delays satisfying an expectation, the withholding of knowledge can arouse interest. When a hypothesis is disconfirmed, the setback can spur the viewer to new bursts of activity. The mixture of anticipation, fulfilment and blocked or retarded or twisted consequences can exercise great emotional power" (Bordwell, pp. 39–40). Simultaneously, the series echoes Christopher Butler's related evaluation of "pleasure in art" as a process entailing "a complicated dynamic interplay, between our *anticipation* of the experience (for example our sense of what makes a good colour harmony, our generic expectations about musical climax, or the function of our desires within narrative…), our *recognition* of what is currently going on in it, and our *retrospection* concerning the interaction between the two" (Butler, C., p. 133). By the end of the series, Moritaka and Akito seem not only to have fully assimilated these ideas but also, and more critically, to have turned them into a durable lesson.

Chapter 3

MYTHOPOEIA

When it is said that sumiye [ink and wash painting] *depicts the spirit of an object, or that it gives form to what has no form, this means that there must be a spirit of creativity moving over the picture. The painter's business thus is not just to copy or imitate nature, but to give to the object something living in its own right.* — Daisetz Teitarou Suzuki

The stance to mythology evinced most characteristically by the various anime here examined is indubitably sustained by Japan's distinctive interpretation of the relationship between human beings and their surroundings: an aspect of Japanese culture which can be realistically described as a lynchpin of its entire development and as the foundation of a striking variety of original styles and art forms. In mainstream Western thought, matter has been traditionally marginalized as an inert presence devoid of any spiritual substance, which has automatically posited its transcendence in the service of mind and soul as man's ultimate goal. Aiming to shape the natural environment in accordance with the requirements of its human inhabitants, and attributing humanity's supposedly inalienable right to mastery to its possession of the faculty of reason, Western thought has repeatedly promulgated the superiority of the Logos as the sphere of well-defined categories and forms over the realm of the fluid and the inchoate. The individual part, concomitantly, has been routinely accorded precedence over the whole, and the singular self over the communal ensemble. In other words, this tradition has typically endeavored to sever fantasy and magic from the rhythms of human existence in the name of a world view which celebrates the uncontrasted supremacy of the mental over the material.

By contrast, Shinto sees the cultivation of harmony between human beings and their environment as the prerequisite of the healthy functioning of both individuals and society. The individual, concomitantly, is seen as inextricably intertwined with a wide network of other beings and of both realized and potential interrelations. Spiritual energies course the whole universe and every minute facet of the land should therefore be regarded as a site of the encounter between the material and the numinous, the perishable and the eternal. For those who have eyes to see and use them — and any person is deemed capable of this skill, not only holy monks or hermits — all forms potentially host special spiritual energies. A rock or tree openly exhibiting the injuries of time on its scarred surfaces, for example, might deserve to be encircled with a *kumihimo*, or sacred rope, as a means of embracing the numinous force it has accumulated through its vicissitudes and its resilience. The lowliest of stones and the flimsiest of ripples on the surface of a pond is pregnant with implicit meanings, insofar as they harbor — less grandiosely but no less tenaciously than majestic mountains, sublime forests and tumbling waterfalls — the spiritual essence which human beings themselves share with nature's forms and host in their bodies no less than in their minds. The material dimension of all experience — which, as shown, plays a key role in Japanese art and aesthetics at large — asserts itself as an all-pervasive metaphysical principle able to blend seamlessly the corporal and the spiritual. Furthermore, the intrinsic aliveness of all natural forms is borne out by their material constitution as a record of their interaction with an incessantly mobile environment. An ancient pine tree, for example, bears its history as a textual mesh written by the onslaughts of wind, rain and snow upon its twisted branches, tenaciously clinging roots and textual mesh of intersecting marks deeply engraved into its venerable bark.

The animistic ethos outlined above strikes its roots in Japanese mythology, where the universe at large is ideated as a tripartite structure comprising the lofty celestial regions of Tamakanohara, where the supreme deities (*kunitsukami*) dwell; the human realm of Nakatsukuni, where the myriad divine forces engendered by two of those deities (one male and one female) find expression in all manner of natural phenomena; and the land of Yomi, the domain of darkness beneath the earth. The word Nakatsukuni translates literally as "middle world" to indicate precisely the liminal situation of the human zone as the threshold where the radiance of Tamakanohara and the gloom of Yomi intersect and blend. Although the three areas are, strictly speaking, separate, this does not render the Japanese cosmos hierarchical in the Western sense of the term. Thus, while it is commonly accepted that human beings cannot aspire to godly standing, the realm of the gods is not posited as an ideal location in the way Christianity tends to conceive of heaven. Most crucially, the world's three regions are ultimately seen to share one and the same spiritual essence. As Mitsukuni Yoshida explains, "every thing and creature that exists in the earthly realm, just like all the deities of the earth that rule them ... are related by birth, so to speak. And like the *kami* that created them, all things and creatures possess a dimension of the divine.... This makes supernature a part of everyday life" (Yoshida 1985, p. 9). This conception of the natural world encompasses inert entities alongside living species, following the conviction that "if trees or stones possess their own anima, manmade objects made out of such materials must, too, possess that anima. Thus anima exist in all the articles and utensils of daily use. And it was these anima that in fact allowed man to live in harmony with his tools" (p. 23). Furthermore, insofar as they operate as "companions of man in life and work," such objects "are often given names" and felt to act as "extensions of their human users" (p. 90). Far from being perceived as obsolete, this cultural attitude still resonates in people's treatment of articles of everyday usage as well as in the context of contemporary manufacture. "In Japan," Yoshida maintains, "an operator of a modern industrial robot thinks of it in much the same way as a traditional carpenter thought of his tools — as his alter ego or extension of himself" (pp. 90–91).

The universe of popular entertainment has time and again articulated the animistic outlook described by Yoshida by striving to intimate the sentient nature of seemingly inanimate humanoid creatures. (The term "humanoid," in this context, is employed to designate any being whose body structure resembles that of a human.) Within the history of Western animation, this endeavor finds superb expression in the works of the Czech puppet master Jiří Trnka, an artist justly acclaimed for elevating puppets executed with loyal dedication to the traditional methods of indigenous puppetry and puppet theater to the unprecedented status of film stars. An interesting selection of Trnka's films, spanning the late 1940s to the mid–1960s, is offered by *Puppet Films of Jiří Trnka* (2000). In a field of Japanese animation other than anime, the yearning to infuse seemingly lifeless effigies with an aura of animateness reaches its apotheosis with the puppet animation of Kihachirou Kawamoto, one of Trnka's most eminent disciples. Kawamoto is especially renowned for his studious manual execution of stunningly animate puppets down to the minutest detail, and for the design of their gorgeous costumes. The result is a gallery of thoroughly individualized performers whose vigilant gaze appears to be continually monitoring the spectator's responses no less than the events unfolding around them. In addition, the uncanny fusion of artificiality and aliveness evinced by Kawamoto's puppets is compounded by their recurrent characterization as angelically graceful harbingers of portentous visions. The anthology *Exquisite Short Films of Kihachiro Kawamoto*, a compilation of works produced in the 1960s and 1970s, beautifully exemplifies the artist's vision.

The animistic world view is founded on a pervasive sense of humility (*kenkyo*) in the face of the innumerable and fathomless forces that shape the natural dimension and, in so doing, directly or indirectly guide our lives. Japanese art's proclivity to honor the beauty of its materials and acknowledge the power exerted by the corporeal substance of both the work itself and the instruments employed in its execution over the creator's hand could ultimately be seen as a logical corollary of that humble disposition. The value of humility is supported by an ethos of "integration" which the architect and woodworker George Nakashima posits as "one of the most important aspects of design" insofar as it plays a key role in harmonizing design not solely "to the process of manufacture, but to life itself and the creation of an environment" (Nakashima, p. 119).

The indigenous stance on the relationship between humanity and nature impacts vitally on Japan's reverential acknowledgment of the life coursing through all substances and objects — through human-made artifacts rooted in nature's bounties no less than in the environment's elemental gifts themselves — and is therefore central to its conception of art. Most importantly, it results in the assiduous encouragement of the artist's absorption in his or her task, whereby the creating agent does not seek to dominate either the media and instruments entailed by the activity or the rhythms of the performance but allows them instead to speak to, and act upon, him or her via the productive vehicles: i.e., via the spirit of nature which such tools are seen to host as an inscrutable force akin to a sort of mana. The experience of absorption constitutes a vital component of the creative act which tirelessly sustains and revitalizes the notion of art as a means of fostering a productive dialogue between the realm of matter and the numinous. The existence of such an information flow between artists and their arts by means of particular materials enthrones the lessons of Shinto as a philosophy which surpasses by far, in both its intensity and its enchantment, mere pantheism. Noh theater provides a paradigmatic example of total immersion in artistic practice insofar as its actors are not merely expected to be able to master a complex repertoire of symbolic acts and to assume a wide range of parts: they must also be able to become fully engrossed in their art.

The perception of the relationship between humanity and nature underpinning Japanese thought is borne out by a significant departure of indigenous art from its aesthetic models, especially those of Chinese provenance. As Yoshida points out, "all of the Chinese arts are based on the teachings of either Confucianism or Taoism. The goal of art was, above all else, to portray the spirit of nature in terms of the fundamental triad: heaven, earth and man." In the Japanese context, however, Chinese ideas were subject to a radical (albeit gradual) metamorphosis, since art was regarded chiefly as "a mystical medium that linked man and the supernatural" (Yoshida 1984, p. 11). This notably results in a distinctive approach to the depiction of nature, in particular, which does not posit the assertion of hierarchical tenets as its fundamental goal. This shift is evident in Japan's appropriation and transformation of Chinese monochromatic painting executed in ink (*sumi*): whereas the Chinese originals tend to emphasize humanity's insignificance in the face of an overwhelmingly vast universe, their Nipponic relations portray human beings and the natural surroundings as partners in a fundamentally harmonious relationship. In the sphere of religious doctrine, likewise, the teachings of Buddhism have been adapted by Japanese society so as to render than more compatible with people's mundane existence and day-to-day tasks.

The most rigorous forms of Buddhism hold that in order to break the endless revolution of the cycle of karma, it is vital to cut oneself off from desire, the root of all human misery and strife, through stern discipline and, by welcoming the belief that the self is non-existent, finally enter the enlightened state of nirvana beyond the rhythms of Eternal Recurrence. Strictly speaking, all human beings may aim to the achievement of this superior state. Yet, classic Buddhism makes it patent that only few special beings are equipped with the intellectual assets and moral firmness demanded by that task. Japanese culture, conversely, has promulgated a form of Buddhism known as Mahayana which, as Richard Bowring observes, adopts a "more compassionate" outlook insofar as it is "based on a shift from enlightenment for the few to salvation for all; a shift from meditation to devotion" (Bowring, p. 9). In this generous interpretation of Buddhism, the karmic wheel is not regarded as uninterruptible by common people, and salvation is hence attainable even by those who have not subjected themselves to strict disciplinary measures meant to pave the way to illumination. The character of Amida is the most prominent of the numerous figures inhabiting Buddhist mythology believed to have achieved nirvana but to have deliberately abided among ordinary humans to abet their quest for redemption. According to Bowring, Amida was held to have "promised eventual salvation to all who simply trusted him and had faith. His paradise (known as the Pure Land) was not nirvana itself but ... was certainly outside the karmic wheel and once gained there was no backsliding. This quickly became the paradise to which all aspired" (p. 10). It should also be noted, in this context, that contemporary Japanese society does not appear to sense any real tension between Buddhism and Shinto. In fact, the two religions are observed in tandem as alternate and mutually sustaining expressions of divinity, never losing sight of Japan's viscerally animistic tendencies.

The lessons of animism are of pivotal significance to both the existing mythologies borrowed and reconfigured by anime for variable dramatic purposes and the alternate mythologies fashioned by specific shows and directors over time. In this respect, the use of the term "anime" to describe animated images of specifically Japanese origin in preference to "animation" is itself worthy of consideration. The *Oxford Dictionary* defines "animation" as "the state of being full of life or vigor; liveliness" (with "the state of being alive" as a "*chiefly archaic*" companion definition), and as "the technique of photographing successive drawings or positions of puppets or models to create an illusion of movement when the film is shown as a sequence." The word "animation," therefore, lays emphasis either on the generalized state of being animate or on the productive act, implying a human agency behind it.

One possible etymological interpretation of the word "anime" (アニメ) is that it is an abbreviation of the Japanese word *animēshon* (アニメーション), which is based on the English "animation." However, it is also often maintained that the term actually derives from the French phrase for "cartoon," *dessin animé* (literally, "animated drawing") — an interpretation corroborated by the widespread pronunciation of the term "anime" itself. In the light of the latter interpretation, "anime" could be said to constitute not merely an indigenous adaptation of an imported lexical item but also the marker of a distinctive philosophical attitude whose aim is to foreground the entity endowed with animation. This implies a shift of focus both from the possession of liveliness as an abstract concept and from the human ability to generate the illusion of movement to the thing which is animated. This reorientation suggests a sense of respect for the artifact as such, a recognition of its autonomous standing which is entirely consonant with the animistic world picture.

The animated image metaphorically replicates nature's lessons. Like the plant progressively fashioned by nature as an ever-evolving text, the animated image displays the markers of its development as a living entity upon its very texture. Thus, it never invites us to forget its madeness. In fact, it persistently draws attention to the process of its coming into being through physical (as well as conceptual) labor. It is at this level that *animation*, *anime* and *animism* tantalizingly coalesce in a concurrently philosophical and experiential partnership of unique appeal. The anime discussed in this chapter communicate this message with variable degrees of emphasis. In so doing, they foreground the significance of an artistic practice (or of a cluster of practices) as a means of constructing alternate mythologies on the basis of both existing belief systems rooted in indigenous lore and novel visions. The latter, in turn, are inspired both by an anime's specific world picture and by actual cultural circumstances of local and/or global scope. All of these mythologies are variously underpinned by animistic concepts and values.

In *Yakitate!! Japan*, the focus is on the creation of a distinctively Japanese mythology, itself inspired by precedents supplied by other cultural mythologies, around a galaxy of gastronomic artifacts. These entities, in turn, are conceived of as pregnant with traces of a pointedly animistic world picture insofar as their identity as objets d'art sui generis is inseparable from the anima of the natural ingredients — and hence the vital energies — fueled into their making. The series focuses on Kazuma Azuma, a boy who has been striving since early childhood to create "*Ja-pan*"— namely, a bread recipe capable of capturing the hearts and palates of his people and thus come to represent a national symbol of global significance, able to epitomize Japan itself in much the same way as the baguette stands for France or the ciabatta for Italy. Endowed with a mysterious power of veritably mythical standing, *solar hands*, Azuma is in a position to fuel his creative talent with unique physical resources, imbuing the dough with special warmth and thus impacting on the fermentation process. Yet, the boy's artistic flair and ambitions are incessantly given precedence, on the thematic and narrative planes alike, to any preternatural capacities he may possess, thus distinguishing the anime from many formulaic renditions of a magical kid's exploits. The sweat and toil inherent in artistic production, accordingly, are never quite elided from the series' ethical priorities.

Azuma initially makes his way to Tokyo to work for Pantasia, Japan's most prestigious bakery chain, and thus refine his skills while also broadening his artistic horizons. The bulk of the anime consists of a sequence of tournaments, organized within a multi-arc format, which involve the protagonist alongside his Pantasia coworkers and members of the rival company St. Pierre. In this respect, *Yakitate!! Japan* can be regarded as a parody of the conventional *shounen* genre, where action and fighting are typically prioritized. This proclivity is reinforced by the employment of various *shounen* character archetypes and stereotypes, rendered ridiculous by their situation in utterly prosaic contexts where displays of heroism and vim appear utterly — and deliciously — irrelevant. Where the classic *shounen* plot would normally make its contests instrumental in the realization of splendid goals and rewards, *Yakitate!! Japan* unremittingly reminds us that this is a story *about bread* and has no intention whatsoever of hiding its humble premises. In fact, it is precisely through a frank admission of the disparity between its mundane subject matter and the quasi-epic fervor which it places in its articulation that the series asserts its identity — glorying in the inane no less than in the reasonable. One of the anime's most endearing qualities is its consistent reluctance to shy away from the absurd, and thus ultimately enthrone the genius of the ludicrous itself as the prime ingredient in its Rabelaisian 69-episode banquet.

The anime's title capitalizes on wordplay: a rhetorical preference evinced by the series throughout its unfolding. The word *yakitate* translates literally as "freshly baked," whereas *Ja-pan* carries a double meaning. While the term in its entirety can be taken to denote the country of Japan, the *pan* constituent represents the Japanese word for "bread." Stemming from the Portuguese *pão*, this word is one of several lexical items imported from the Portuguese language in the sixteenth century as Portugal's expansionist drives were taking its adventurers and explorers to corners of the globe hitherto regarded as *terra incognita*. Other common terms which are still part of the contemporary Japanese vocabulary alongside *pan*, incidentally, include *karuta* ("playing cards") from the Portuguese *carta*; *tempura* (a dish consisting of battered and deep fried seafood or vegetables) from *tempora* (the Portuguese word for "Friday," when the consumption of meat is proscribed and the preparation of such meals is therefore commended); *rasha* ("woollen cloth") from *raxa* ("felt" in old Portuguese); and *biroudo* ("velvet") from *veludo*. (The "b" and "v" sounds are virtually interchangeable in Japanese, as are the "r" and "l" sounds — hence, *biroudo* may easily be pronounced "*viloudo*")

For the sake of historical accuracy, it is worth noting that Spanish, Dutch and English navigators and traders also penetrated Japan in various waves, mainly from the late sixteenth century to 1638, when the Tokugawa regime resolved to cut Japan off from the outside world. When Japan eventually reopened its doors in the late 1850s through commercial treaties signed with Holland, France, England, Russia and the U.S., its culture was not just ready but actually craving for change and experiment and hence eager to absorb a remarkable range of imported ideas and objects with unprecedented gusto. These successive infiltrations of Japanese culture by foreign influences led to some of the most inspiring transgeographical dialogues ever witnessed in human history. Over the centuries, Japan responded both enthusiastically and inquisitively to a plethora of Western artifacts — firearms, clocks, leather products and wool garments, as well as plants (e.g., the passionflower or clockface flower, now a popular motif in Japanese design) and animals (e.g., horses, camels, elephants and parakeets), artistic techniques such as perspective, scientific (especially medical) texts, and the methodologies underpinning empirical observation and analysis.

As Yoshida maintains, "the Japanese taste for foreign things helped broaden their limited horizons with tangible proof that other cultures besides their own existed. It also nurtured an openness and flexibility toward the artifacts of other cultures completely independent of the people or the historical backgrounds of the places from which they came" (Yoshida 1984, p. 40). This tendency is largely responsible, it seems safe to assume, for the seeming effortlessness and creativity with which Japan has been able to reconceptualize its findings without having to worry excessively about their roots. The imported material is handled more in the spirit of a Surrealist *objet trouvé* than as a dauntingly immutable monument. Moreover, it would be fallacious to assume that the trends established four centuries ago have died out and been relegated to the pages of musty archives. In fact, "the uninhibited adoption of other cultures ... is still going on today. The Japanese cultural system, in other words, is characterized by its openness to other, different systems." What is most crucial to bear in mind, as an underlying philosophical message of which contemporary anime vibrantly partakes, is the intuitively discerning attitude with which the Japanese have time and again been able to abstract the structural essence of the imported material to ensure its suitability to their culture's specific needs. Thus, "just as when Chinese civilization was introduced centuries before," Japan has dealt with Western sources "as a matter of *forms*, not as something so fundamental that it posed a threat to human existence or identity" (p. 111).

Thus, while it may seem ironical that the anime's protagonist should aspire to create a quintessentially indigenous culinary artifact on the basis of a foreign import, this is perfectly consonant with Japan's character as an intrinsically hybrid culture — a network of interlocking, overlapping and multibranching flows and loops. Some of the most distinctively Nipponic styles, items and customs have indeed derived precisely from the imaginative adaptation and reconfiguration of foreign influences in the light of autochthonous sensibilities and in the service of concomitantly environmental and societal circumstances. Thus, while the anime's titular bread harks back semantically to an imported entity, it is nonetheless said to derive its unmistakeable identity from the dexterous manipulation of indigenous ingredients. The kind of bread introduced at the very start of the series, for example, is called *an-pan* after the word *anko* (a.k.a. *azuki*), i.e., sweet bean paste. The spiritual connotations carried by natural products, yielded by the land itself and shaped over time by the country's distinctive climate, are worthy of consideration, in this regard. As Yoshida explains, "it is believed that rice, millet, wheat, red *adzuki* [a.k.a. *azuki*] beans, soyabeans, and silkworms, the origins of agriculture, were created from the body of a female deity slain in an incident in Takamanohara. The grains, as well as the silkworm, represent life that dies and is regenerated. The grains created through the death of the goddess ... were gathered by the *kami* who presided over regeneration, and the practices of farming begun in Takamanohara were later transmitted to the earthly world of Nakatsumikuni by the deities who descended to govern the world" (Yoshida 1985, p. 11).

Azuma is tremendously eclectic in his adaptation of countless ingredients of diverse geographic and cultural provenance to the realization of his overarching creative project. Nevertheless, several of the dozens of bread types he creates in the course of the series derive their distinctive identities from the imaginative appropriation of fundamentally local components. These include not only the aforementioned *an-pan* but also (among many others) *taiyaki* bread (the term *taiyaki* referring to a traditional bream-shaped cake), soaked millet Ja-pan, autodigested Japanese barnyard millet, Mt. Fuji curry Ja-pan, *kamaboko* (a type of cured *surimi*) Ja-pan, *wasabi* (horseradish) dinner bread

Ja-pan, eel, nori (seaweed), silk powder and black-soybeans sports bread, sushi-style *melon* (a popular type of sweet bun) Ja-pan, *okonomiyaki* (savory pancake) sandwich with *yakisoba* (fried noodles) filling, *kabuki-age* (rice cracker) Ja-pan.

The anime's settings are atmospheric and beautifully individualized, and its character designs appealing in their subtle integration of stylized and naturalistic elements. However, it is in the depiction of its bread-based artworks that *Yakitate!! Japan*'s pictorial excellence fully proclaims itself. These evince so tactile a presence as to kindle a somewhat primal, instinctive desire to caress their surfaces, pick at their crusty edges and, ultimately, partake of their treasures through unrestrained gustation. Insofar as the screen does not permit such a level of audience participation (as yet), we must make the most of the traditional Japanese lesson according to which food should be consumed with the eyes no less intensely than with the mouth. Repeatedly, yet subtly, *Yakitate!! Japan* is itself keen to foreground the importance of the sense of sight in the preparation, reception and consumption of victuals. In so doing, the anime captures realistically one of the most distinctive aspects of Japan's culinary sensibility: namely, its painstaking approach to the incremental refinement of various techniques of visual presentation. In the anime, the importance ascribed to the visual dimension by Japan's attitude to food is neatly encapsulated by the suggestion that in a tournament, presentation alone can influence vitally how the food will taste to its assessors and how it will be judged.

In unremittingly prioritizing the requirements of visual appeal, Japanese cuisine devotes considerable attention not only to the processing of food but also to the selection of appropriate vessels, and to the arrangement therein of small portions of food on the basis of the overall interaction of color, consistency and shape within a comprehensively conceived design. With the eye at the forefront of its aesthetic priorities, Japanese gastronomy is able to summon to the table an extraordinary diversity of aromas, flavors and textures by deftly combining raw ingredients with simmered or deep fried items. Food, its manipulation and its consumption become interrelated players in the enactment of ritual events which time and again seek both to consolidate and to convey humanity's physical communion with nature. The traditional cutting of vegetables so as to make them resemble flowers tersely exemplifies this ethos by reinforcing our sense of the ingredients' material roots in nature and, at the same time, enhancing their spiritual reality. What we encounter, in the process, is a synesthetic feast wherein the eyes are no less viscerally involved than the other senses in the overall enchantment. *Yakitate!! Japan* pays homage to this indigenous skill with unmatched exuberance: even though its characters' responses to each new recipe are often ludicrous, they never fail to communicate the cultural significance not only of particular ingredients but also of the processes through which they are choreographed into a satisfying ensemble.

Yakitate!! Japan in its entirety bears witness to a characteristically Japanese attitude toward food. Thus, in offering a faithful reflection of Japan's distinctive approach to the art of cooking through its emphasis on the visual domain, it concurrently foregrounds a respectful recognition of the sensory and sensuous qualities of cooking materials — a tendency which, as noted, has resulted in the evolution of an extremely nuanced vocabulary of tastes denoting gustatory and visual sensations at once. Whereas Western gastronomy is generally characterized by a search for flavors based on principles of contrast and fusion, which tends to result in a more or less radical transformation of the basic ingredients' intrinsic properties, Japanese cuisine strives to maintain each element's innate traits. This applies not solely to the orchestration of tastes within a dish but also to the relational arrangement of their shapes and hues. Accordingly, the anime's chefs insistently endeavor to emphasize the natural flavors of the ingredients they employ to make the bread. Keeping disparate food items in their pristine state even as they struggle to ensure that the final artifact deserves to be called bread is a major priority for all the anime's key personae.

In Japanese food culture, the centrality of nature to all creative endeavor is underlined by the time-honored inclination to match particular dishes and both their chromatic and formal qualities to particular seasons. The subtlest gradations and modulations of flavor are thus released in accordance with the natural environment's inherent rhythms. *Yakitate!! Japan* highlights the concept of seasonality by repeatedly indicating that its characters, like any respectable Japanese cook, will spare no toil in guaranteeing the freshness, and the seasonal relevance, of the dishes they serve and consume. Furthermore, the anime draws attention to the value attributed by Japan's food culture to the use of local ingredients. This is clearly demonstrated by the suggestion that the contestants in a tournament are judged according to their ability to incorporate local specialties in their recipes with a flair for both diversity and subtle synthesis. In adopting those elements, the competitors are also shown to honor local traditions and mythologies by absorbing their heritage into new-fangled artifacts, and to express a grateful recognition of the efforts placed by local people into the raising and preservation of their distinctive produce.

Kanon, like *Yakitate!! Japan*, affords cuisine a vital role, portraying the preparation and sharing of meals as axial to both its diegesis and its sustaining imagery. Food, in this context, is comparable to a cementing agent capable of binding the anime's characters together and of gradually abetting their interactions. In addition, the particular food items cherished by each of the main female personae are accorded the privileged status of character markers.

These include indigenous recipes such as *taiyaki*, the traditional sweet bream-shaped filled pastry which the character of Ayu adores, *nikuman*, the meat buns avidly consumed by Makoto, and *gyudon*, beef bowl, the dish favored by Mai alongside other Japanese classics. These recipes feature alongside globally recognized favorites such as vanilla ice-cream (Shiori's most cherished food item) and home-made strawberry jam (Nayuki's treat). In each instance, the veneration for their favorite culinary items exhibited by the various heroines elevates those entities to the rank of objets d'art. Gastronomic mores are also axial, incidentally, to *Chocolate Underground*, an ONA (Original Net Animation) based on the children's novel *Bootleg* by British author Alex Shearer. Proceeding from the simple premise that chocolate has been rendered illegal by the electoral victory of the "Good for You Party" and its attendant establishment of the "Chocolate Prohibition" law, which proscribes all sweet things as detrimental to people's health, the anime posits the interconnected arts of chocolate manufacture, distribution and consumption as the nub of an intricate web of political and financial intrigue. Huntley and Smudger, the drama's young protagonists, pit themselves against the fascistic law and resolve to bootleg chocolate.

Yumeiro Pâtissière focuses even more emphatically on cuisine as the foundation of its particular mythology. No less importantly, it shares with *Yakitate!! Japan* a hearty appetite for crosscultural exploration insofar as it endeavors to synthesize local priorities with a foreign tradition through its desire to create a new mythology of cakes. The anime's protagonist is Ichigo Amano, an ordinary school girl who dreams of becoming a pâtissiere in the footsteps of her grandmother. Ichigo's aspiration finds a chance of fulfillment when she attends the Sweets Fiesta and is accidentally discovered by Henri Lucas, a genius pâtissier from France. Impressed by Ichigo's ability to identify each of the ingredients contained in his cake, Henri recommends the girl for enrollment in the Japanese branch of St. Marie Academy, an elite cake-making establishment where Ichigo's own grandmother received her training. Although Ichigo's skill is no doubt impressive, she lacks practically all of the typical talents expected of a top-notch pâtissier or pâtissière — a reality which quickly hits her as she enters the academy and proceeds to meet its immensely skilled pupils.

However, Ichigo discovers that alongside its regular human students, the esteemed establishment houses a team of Sweets Spirits hailing from the Sweet Kingdom: preternatural entities who are also held to be learning the art of cake-making, and team up with humans to help them give form to their most ambitious fantasies while pursuing their own education. Known simply by the names of the sweet substances with which they are elementally associated, such as Vanilla, Chocolate, Caramel and Café, the Sweets Spirits have the ability to enhance a recipe's overall charm by recourse to magic but are also unfortunate enough to be among the first to sample their partners' gastronomic fiascos — which leads to several moments of refreshing comic relief. Although *Yumeiro Pâtissière* is more closely related to *Yakitate!! Japan* than to any of the other anime discussed in this chapter, its treatment of the drama's magical dimension bears affinities with *La Corda d'Oro*, especially at the level of imagery. This is most evident in the representation of the Queen of the Sweet Spirits: the supernatural being employed as St. Marie Academy's mascot and accordingly revered by means of a statue located in the school's courtyard and of a portrait watching over the principal cooking room. *La Corda d'Oro*'s magical creature is accorded an analogous role and likewise enshrined in the traditional visual symbolism of the school to which he is bound.

If *Yumeiro Pâtissière* echoes *Yakitake! Japan* through its emphasis on the crosscultural dimension, *Moyashimon* shares its fascination with animism as manifested in the land's produce. Animistic thinking is amusingly reimagined in the light of the protagonist's idiosyncratic sensitivity to the spirit of the land as a dynamic web of flickering energies. With the series *Moyashimon*, Japan's commodious take on creativity — and, by extension, on the range of practices entitled to definition as art — reaches a veritable apotheosis as the supposedly prosaic discipline of agriculture rises to unprecedented artistic status. This imaginative gesture enables the anime to deliver a refreshingly imaginative interpretation of the meaning of animism in contemporary society. The series posits as its fundamental premise the unique gift harbored by the anime's protagonist, Tadayasu Sawaki. A first-year college student at an agricultural university, the youth is concurrently blessed and haunted by his power to perceive and interact with even the most elusive micro-organisms and bacteria. Moreover, the configuration exhibited by such entities to Tadayusu's eyes differs substantially from their ordinary appearance under a microscope. The anime's own artistic caliber gains immensely from its ongoing visual experiments with the depiction of uncannily large, multicolored and unremittingly bouncy creatures, thereby evoking the image of a consummately animated universe in quite exceptional ways. The land itself, in the process, is enthroned both as an ideal setting for the unfolding of an innovative animistic mythology and as the living text on whose pages such a mythology incessantly reinvents itself as the seasons roll by.

Quite a different vision emerges from the attitude to nature permeating *Speed Grapher*, an anime which subjects the principles of animism to a tantalizingly dystopian reconceptualization, consistently matching this gesture to the invention of an alternate mythology buttressed by the art of photography. In *Speed Grapher*, art's power to collude with the world's spiritual energies is invested on photography. The anime's male lead is Tatsumi Saiga, an ex-war photographer who has witnessed some of the most harrowing moments of human violence in history, including the Vietnam conflict, and been reduced to the status of a lowly tabloid freelancer by his confinement to a darkly dystopian Tokyo in the wake of the "Bubble War." In this unprincipled and anomic society, the rift between the wealthy and the destitute has widened to unprecedented extremes and corruption reigns supreme. In the course of one of his assignments, Saiga infiltrates a secret Roppongi club where a choice elite of politicians, celebrities, media moguls and industry CEOs revel in all manner of forbidden pleasures, including sadistic Satanist rituals performed in a setting that uncannily brings to mind the relevant sequences in Stanley Kubrick's *Eyes Wide Shut*. At this point, Saiga's chance encounter with a beautiful young woman named Kagura, an abused teenager elevated to the status of a goddess by the club's members to preside over their pursuit of the most perverse and fetish-laden primal fantasies, steers his whole existence in an utterly unpredictable direction.

Instructed to kill the intruder, Kaiga chooses to kiss him instead, thereby endowing Saiga with a most unusual gift which horrifies and captivates its recipient in equal proportions: the supernatural power to cause any entity he photographs to explode. Thus, Saiga's urge to give vent to his artistic passion, as deeply ingrained in the core of his being as the instinctual tendency to breathe, becomes inextricable for the unleashing of catastrophically destructive energies. Saiga's supernatural ability finds worthy companions in the powers enjoyed by several other members of *Speed Grapher*'s multifarious cast known as the "Euphorics"— people coursed by unique spiritual forces emanating directly from their most intimate desires. Combined with photography's knack of releasing an alternate mythical reality, the many sequences in which these baleful powers are deployed serve cumulatively to evoke a sinister distortion of animism which is perfectly suited to the anime's gritty vision and setting.

Sola echoes the artistic project pursued by *Speed Grapher*, capitalizing at once on a dramatic premise of an eminently mythological character and on the use of the art photography as an ideal instrument to recreate and enhance its pivotal mythology. The adventures embarked upon by Yorito, the male protagonist, in his effort to solve the mysteries surrounding Matsuri, a peculiar girl with magical connections, constitutes the core of a quasi-epic quest of a kind often seen in anime. However, the series announces its distinctiveness by interweaving its drama's action-oriented strand with an emotional component by focusing on the protagonist's mission as a brave attempt at artistic self-expression through the art of photography. This aspect of the series gradually asserts its ascendancy over the more formulaic elements of the story, so much so that the very relationship between Yorito and Matsuri is ultimately inconceivable independently of the art of photography. An especially endearing aspect of that bond, established right from the start and echoing throughout the show, resides with the tension between Matsuri's incompatibility with daylight (a trait inherent in her status as a *yaka*) and Yorito's almost compulsive attraction to the sky in all of its imaginable manifestations, which he satisfies by both gazing at it endlessly and taking pictures of it at any time of the day and the night. Fascinated with the concept of the daytime sky as a dimension which her nature forbids her to enjoy, Matsuri experiences that unknown reality vicariously via Yorito, his photographs, his passionate descriptions of all sorts of light conditions and cloud formations, and the photorealistic panorama of an azure sky speckled with wandering clouds which adorns his bedroom's whole ceiling.

One of the most potent anime demonstrations of the coalescence of creativity and animism in a mythology's evolution is offered by *Touka Gettan*. The series is especially relevant to the present discussion insofar as it conveys that philosophical proposition by interweaving a consummately animistic universe, pervaded by both time-honored and freshly envisioned legends, with a prismatically varied range of artistic pursuits. In so doing, the anime offers an artistically comprehensive dramatization of the principles of animism. The saga is set in the alternate world of Kamitsumihara, where powerful magic holds sway and humans coexist with *youkai*, demons which are capable of behaving both destructively and supportively, depending on the circumstances. However, while the *youkai* are not necessarily evil, their coexistence with humans often gives rise to unpleasant conflicts which can easily carry world-shattering repercussions in their wake. The liminality of the human realm of Nakatsukuni referred to earlier comes to the fore with the anime's emphasis on the status of its own fictional land as the site of intersection of discordant energies.

Central to the anime's animistic world view is the divine triad comprising the goddesses Sei, Fuu and Juna. Sei (a.k.a. Momoka when she features in the role of an ordinary teenager), acts as the chief representative of spiritual light and concord — qualities she pursues in tandem with the gentle and peace-loving Fuu, even though their preservation increasingly requires her to sacrifice personal fulfillment to the general good. Juna, by contrast, is a darkly vengeful creature seemingly governed by entirely disruptive urges though in her case, too, as in Sei's, the public and the private dimensions unfold in opposite directions. Thus, in the context of her personal liaison with the character of Kikyou, Juna surprisingly exhibits a tenderly affectionate disposition. In order to preserve Kamitsumihara's precarious equilibrium, the disparate energies released by the three deities must be harmonized and synthesized into a coherent whole. The dire alternative is the land's infiltration by larger and larger contingents of *shikigami* (i.e., undilutedly noxious *youkai*). The drama's pseudo-historical backdrop tersely intimates that for Kamitsumihara's spiritual balance to disintegrate into chaos and hatred, all that is needed is a single moment of unruly or irrational conduct. The state of affairs portrayed in the anime, specifically, is retrospectively shown to ensue from an ancient incident: a ritual in which Juna's brother loses his sanity and blasphemously interferes with the ceremonial sacrifice of his beloved Sei.

The art of writing plays a prominent part through the character of Yumiko as an author of romance novels with strict standards and expectations, and a tendency to be especially fastidious about the achievement of proper dramatic effects. At one point, for example, she is most upset by the realization that she has inadvertently indulged in the dubious pleasure of a happy ending. In consonance with the consummately animistic universe in which she operates, Yumiko does not write solely of her own volition. Much of the time, in fact, her creativity is shaped by the otherworldly force supposed to possess her: namely, the mighty Juna herself. The Platonist concept of Fine Frenzy springs to mind, in this context. The mischievous Butterfly Triplets — i.e., Hibari (butterfly), Tsubame (swallow) and Suzume (sparrow) — cultivate their own eccentric authorial ambitions by creating *doujinshi* and indulging in an area of the entertainment industry often associated with manga and anime, cosplay.

Music is also presented as a major player in *Touka Gettan*'s animistic realm. It indeed proves pivotal to the climactic restoration of Kamitsumihara's equilibrium with the episode devoted to the traditional "*Joumi* Concert" and to the attendant purifying rite involving the three goddesses' self-immolation through disappearance — and subsequent relinquishment of all human bonds and human passions. Sei, Fuu and Juna are here reunited alongside Touka, the character intended to operate as a catalyst in the harmonization of their discordant powers, and Makoto, a student endowed with a preternatural melodic sensibility enabling her to awaken the "Great Dragon" dormant within her and hence channel its unparalleled spiritual energy into the ceremony. The conception of music as a balancing force of cosmic proportions can be traced back to ancient Greek philosophy. Pythagoras, in particular, is renowned for his theorization of a system of harmonic correspondences whereby the celestial spheres are believed to generate sounds which express the numerical relations through which the harmony of the cosmos reveals itself. Plato's *Republic* developed this idea with its vision of the universe as a system held in motion by melodies conforming to the designs of *Ananke* (Necessity). Christian theology inherited these views, as famously attested to by the concept of *harmonia mundi* or *musica universalis* (the harmony or music of the spheres) elaborated by Boethius and St. Augustine in order to represent the relationship between God and the whole of Creation.

It was also in the Middle Ages that musical theory came into being as a discipline separate from musical performance per se, which took it upon itself to determine the numerical relations on which cosmic balance was supposed to depend. While music, thus regarded as a scientific, rather than mechanical or representational, art was accorded superior standing over practices such as architecture, sculpture and painting, painters themselves sought to capture in images the theoretical principles underlying the doctrine of *harmonia mundi* through a focus both on the instruments used to exemplify those tenets with scientific precision and allegorical figures intended to personify their conceptual authority. This trend spans the medieval period to the late Renaissance. With the purifying ritual associated with the *Joumi* concert, *Touka Gettan* could therefore be said to hark back to both a venerable philosophical tradition and a history of visual representations of its teachings. The intimate bond between music and the visual arts is thus conveyed in an economically effective fashion. The anime's thematic emphasis on music's capacity to integrate and harmonize contrasting energies finds a formal correlative in its employment of a soundtrack wherein traditional and pop melodies are consistently juxtaposed, and their distinctive emotive effects held in a fine balance.

The art of fashion design plays an interesting role throughout the anime, experimenting enthusiastically with styles as varied as demurely fetching maid's outfits, contemporary knitwear, racy cat-girl outfits, cute girl–Santa costumes, full-fledged kimonos and hints at the Gothic Lolita vogue. The anime's school uniforms are particularly memorable and fully confirm the importance of these vestimentary items in Japanese culture and history: a topic to be addressed in greater depth later in this chapter in relation to *La Corda d'Oro*. Whereas the latter, as we shall see, focuses primarily on the uniform's martial connotations, in *Touka Gettan*, stylistic concessions to military fashion, though evident, are modulated by a nostalgically antiquarian fascination with Rococo and Victorian motifs (softened, in the case of the female uniforms, by discreet forays into the province of *kawaii*). One of the most intensely evocative touches in the entire series is undoubtedly the image of Momoka's empty uniform, hanging in her deserted room after her self-sacrificial departure in the wake of the purification ceremony, as a poignant symbol of her absence and of the void she has left both in the Kamitsumihara community generally and in Touka's soul in particular. The garment does not only stand out as a living presence imbued with an individual designer's creative vision but also — and more importantly — as a manifestation of the inherent animateness of seemingly inert entities which economically exemplifies the lessons of animism.

Touka Gettan's pivotal artist is Kikyou: a sort of Shinto priestess devoted to the protection of the three goddesses, who concomitantly acts as the student council president at Touka Academy. The two components of Kikyou's double job may seem quite incongruous with each other in terms of spiritual significance. Yet, their coexistence is entirely consonant with the series' animistic universe to the extent that it both refers explicitly to the spiritual dimension and alludes to the penetration of mundane affairs by the spiritual forces represented by Kikyou on behalf of her divine charges. On the material plane, the character stands out primarily as a dollmaker. She is indeed responsible for the creation — and animation — of the Butterfly Triplets, who start life in the series as *Hina* dolls in Kikyou's workshop; of the formidable Stone Sword, the artifact axial to the drama as a whole and to the prevention of Kamitsumihara's total descent into *shikigami*-infested darkness; and of Touka — a human being described by his sculptor as somewhat unfinished, presumably to suggest a reason for his morosely self-doubting personality, even though he is brought into existence for the heroic purpose of wielding the Stone Sword. Kikyou creates dolls out of nature and returns them to nature by endowing them, magically, with animation. She is an artist engrossed in her materials — and hence in their natural substratum — but she is also a deity and therefore a mythical agency. Thus, her artistic performance offers a unique synthesis of natural and supernatural elements akin to the formula which we will see deployed in *La Corda d'Oro*. With the latter, however, we descend to a more human level despite the undeniable influence of the numinous in the protagonist's artistry. Indeed, the emphasis falls on the performative articulation of a seemingly natural talent even though we are consistently reminded that the heroine's musical skills are almost wholly a result of magical intervention.

Touka Gettan also corroborates the proposition advanced in Chapter 2 regarding the significance of color as a prime constituent of Japan's cultural beauty through a brief but very memorable sequence. This deploys most creatively the technique of color isolation in order to throw the dramatic power of chroma vividly into relief, focusing on touching moment of domestic intimacy. Yumiko here invites Touka and Momoka to play the "princess game" and proceeds to show them the venerable rolls of fabric she has supposedly inherited from her mother. As the fabrics gradually come to cover the entire floor of Yumiko's room, the sense of animateness emitted by their colors proportionately intensifies. The overall atmosphere is enhanced by the depiction of all other aspects of the setting and actors in a monochromatic palette. This technique, it should be noted, is adopted throughout the episode in which this particular sequence is situated, except for moments of special poignancy, so as to mark the series' transition to a hauntingly somber mood. The shift is made most tantalizing by the airing of *Touka Gettan* in a chronologically inverted order, whereby the events presented in the first episode actually mark the end of the story from a strictly logical point of view. The chronological inversion requires the anime's viewers to participate actively in the process of narrativization whereby the story's raw materials actually acquire narrative coherence. It engages their creative energies and requires them to become as absorbed in the process of meaning generation as artists faced with a block of stone or an empty canvas.

All in all, *Touka Gettan*'s approach to the chromatic dimension of art elegantly conveys the idea that colors are animate entities. An analogous message underlies the meticulous representation of the color schemes typical of Heian fashion in *The Tale of Genji*, which captures faithfully that vogue's veritable obsession with the layering of different colour combinations and attribution to each hue of highly evocative poetic names. In both *Touka Gettan* and *The Tale of Genji*, all of the materials are studiously rendered in traditional indigenous patterns and colors, their aura of spirituality being sustained by the fact that many of the intriguing names they bear are untranslatable into other languages and often unknown even to contemporary Japanese audiences. Yumiko's childish yet pithy remark that "the names of the colors are lovely" communicates the impression that such designations have a palpable reality of their own, thus alerting us to the ancestral materiality of language: an attribute of human semiosis embedded in all sign systems but especially essential to the rhythms of an animistic universe wherein all matter is the potential host of spiritual energies and words, qua sound waves or typographic matter, logically share this condition. The emphasis placed by both *Touka Gettan* and *The Tale of Genji* on the materiality of language serves to remind us, in a capsulated visual fashion, of the materiality of absolutely everything in the realm of art and, ultimately, in the cosmos at large.

Japanese architecture's proverbial cultivation of a creative dialogue between a dwelling and its surroundings — and thus between inside and outside — epitomizes the indigenous attitude to the relationship between humanity and nature. This contention is validated by several of the titles under scrutiny through the depiction of the private abodes associated with different characters and their families, friends and colleagues. At the same time, it finds expression in the visions formulated by established professionals in the architectural and design sectors, on the one hand, and by ordinary people in their day-to-day living, on the other. Looking specifically at the anime examined in this chapter, it could be suggested that *La Corda d'Oro* exemplifies the fluid exchange between inside and outside most openly with its meticulous depiction of the school and its grounds. In *Yakitate!! Japan*, *Genshiken* and *Beck: Mongolian Chop Squad*, the same fundamental principle imbues the representation of the various traditional buildings which pepper the shows and colorfully interact with their modern spatial components. In the context of both traditional Japanese architecture and modern interpretations and adaptations of its pivotal principles, nature operates as the designer's and the builder's prime guide and inspirational reservoir. Architect Hirotaro Ota conveys this proposition in his discussion of garden art: "for the Japanese, a building does not resist or subdue nature. While it is built by man, it is no more than a part of the whole view of nature as if it were a tree in the landscape." In corroboration of this vision, Ota pithily adds: "the Japanese garden rearranges the natural landscape in order to create a new beauty from nature" (Ota, p. 23). The closeness to nature fostered by Japanese architecture as its supreme goal often results in the creation of everyday settings capable of engendering sensory experiences of a lyrically refined character by the simplest of means. As long as the desire to establish an intimate connection with the natural environment is prioritized, beautiful impressions and sensations may emerge even in the most mundane or unexceptional of circumstances.

A good example is provided by architect Koji Yagi with his observations regarding a common item of Japanese decor, the "ungathered split curtains made of cloth or hemp" known as *noren*. "Since it flutters in the breeze," the artist explains, "the *noren* enables one to 'see' the wind, and, when used in conjunction with wind chimes than enable one to 'hear' the wind, it is really as though one is 'experiencing' the wind" (Yagi, p. 8). The scenario depicted by Yagi could be regarded as a touching reflection, at the microcosmic domestic level, of the grand mystical macrocosm woven by and through the *kami*, where trees and the wind play especially important roles in the communication of nature's ubiquitous aliveness. As Yoshida maintains, the "awesome grandeur" of Japan's most extensive "forests inspires the sense that they are central and important parts of the world. Huge trees and groves of trees are considered abodes of the spirits under whose care man believed he could live in safety. The forests and great trees, moreover, sway and rustle in the wind, and echo with the cries of birds and insects. People interpret these sounds as conversations among the spirits of the trees of the forest and the flowers of the fields" (Yoshida 1985, p. 11).

Closely following its literary predecessor, the anime version of *The Tale of Genji* emphasizes the relationship between humanity and nature as a vital component of indigenous mentality by industriously proposing close affective correspondences between its characters and the seasons of the year, suggesting that even when the world's afflictions and burdens weigh on them most grievously, they never become so solipsistic or cynical as to grow indifferent to the stupendous changes undergone by the environment when the cherry blossom makes its appearance, the leaves begin to turn red and gold or the first snow flakes can be seen waltzing across the landscape. In foregrounding the emotional web of affinities and sympathies flowing between and across people and their surroundings, *The Tale of Genji* constitutes a particularly poignant instance of contemporary anime's standing as a recent heir to the many generations of artists, aesthetes and scholars who have endeavored to fathom and perpetuate the ongoing collusion of humanity and nature.

The intimacy of the bond between humans and their surroundings is reinforced by the anime's depiction of Heian architecture as an art dominated by the venerable presence of wood, and hence able to let the seasons enter its edifices with the palpable signs of their relentless passing and their forever fascinating rhythms. The spectacle of nature is constantly available and constantly renewed as an unmatched source of pure, though melancholy, delight. In enabling human beings to participate directly in nature's seasonal variations, the anime's organicist architecture therefore draws attention not only to change as such but also to the transience and ephemerality of everything with which its characters commune and everything which permeates their private selves. The unending seasonal drama is rendered especially attractive by the flexibility of the environment's presentation afforded by the sliding panels typical of local architecture as they open onto the environment and frame its bounties to variable degrees. The beholder thus partakes of an experience analogous to the one enjoyed by the viewer of an animated film's concatenated frames. In appreciating the anime's status as a paradigmatic illustration of the collusion of animism and art with a specific emphasis on architecture, it is also important to recognize its broader mythological import. Indeed, given the source text's standing as a venerable lynchpin of Japanese culture, endowed with quasi-mythological significance both locally and internationally, the anime concurrently alludes to the inextricability of the art of storytelling from the phenomenon of mythopoesis.

With *La Corda d'Oro*, we encounter an especially intriguing instance of the dialectical interplay of the old and the new as an ideal terrain for the growth of mythologies. Hence, the anime is deemed worthy of special attention in this context. The series focuses from the start on the intersection of an existing mythology revolving around the history of the school where the bulk of the drama takes place and a new mythology centered on the protagonist's personality, ethics and relationships. The animistic dimension proclaims itself through the anime's supernatural substratum, and especially through the character of the fairy Lili: a being whose mythological credentials are instantly announced by the pivotal positioning of his icon within the school's grounds, and by his physical resemblance to legendary creatures of both Classical and Germanic derivation, including the cupid-like winged kid and the mischievous elf. In *La Corda d'Oro — Primo Passo*, the key setting is Seiso Academy, an establishment vaunting a veritably mythical reputations and distinguished by its strict division into two tracks: a General Studies program for regular students and a Music Department program.

The protagonist is Kahoko Hino, a student enrolled within the non-musical cohorts who, even though she has never touched a musical instrument in her life, is unexpectedly picked as one of the only six contestants due to compete in a prestigious school-wide music competition as a result of her encounter with Lili. Proudly introducing himself as a *fata*, the Latin designation for "fairy" originating in the word *fatum* ("fate," "destiny," "lot" or "doom") and hence suggestive of life-shaping powers, Lili is invisible to all except Kahoko, and instantly proceeds to bestow a magical violin on the girl. The possession of this instrument is central to the accomplishment of Lili's plan, which is to enable the girl to display hitherto unsuspected musical skills and win a place in the contest despite her status as an undistinguished member of the General Studies program. While the heroine is initially reluctant to yield to Lili's proposition, she ends up taking the present and rapidly finds out, as she rehearses her pieces, that as long as she is acquainted with the basic tune and puts her entire soul into the effort, she is able to play virtually anything at all. This marvel, it transpires, is granted by the special bond which the instrument facilitates between the performer and the fairy himself, provided he or she is tuned into the same wavelength as Lili, who has apparently manufactured the violin all alone by preternatural means after years of unflagging dedication. Through its emphasis on the mythical creature's creative skills, the anime draws attention to the art of musical instrument making (and repair) as a pursuit which deserves no less reverence and admiration than the art of music itself.

The Italian word *corda* translates literally as "string," both in the general sense of the term to designate a light cord and in the specifically musical sense to describe the cord of wire or gut used in particular instruments. The literal meaning of the word is therefore directly consonant with the artistic area at the heart of the anime. The metaphorical connotations of the term are also invoked, however, insofar as the titular *corda* is increasingly shown to refer to the special tie connecting Kahoko to Lili, to the magical violin and, by implication, to her concurrently artistic and mythical destiny. From a musical perspective, the string image also evokes a sequence or line of notes and sounds: a thread of vibrations which, in the case of an animated work, can be seen to capture simultaneously the sonic and dynamic properties of action. In addition, the word *corda* is also commonly used with reference to a rope or cable: this available meaning can be taken to allude to the latently coercive nature of the bond connecting the protagonist to the supernatural instrument as an obligation — a duty she is expected to undertake for the benefit of Seiso Academy's tradition and its sustaining mythology. The attribute *d'oro*, "golden," can be taken to refer simply to a material property. Yet, it also holds an auspicious meaning as practically synonymous with "happy" or "pleasing": meanings which are encapsulated, for instance, in expressions of good wishes such as *sogni d'oro*, the equivalent of the English "sweet dreams." Moreover, the anime's title harks back to the Latin etymology of the word "corda." As Alberto Ausoni explains, the Renaissance jurist and writer Andrea Alciato, author of the *Emblemata* (1531), was one of the first to reflect on "the etymological ambiguity between the two Latin terms, *chorda* (string) and *corda* (hearts)" to suggest that "just as it takes only one broken or discordant string to shatter the harmony and interrupt the concert, so, in the political sphere, the loss of just one ally can fracture the alliance necessary for good government" (Ausoni, p. 19). One of the lessons learnt by Kahoko as she negotiates the challenges yielded by her unusual musical ability is precisely that it is enough for one of her peers to doubt her honesty, and thus withdraw his or her support, for the entire network of relationships she has gradually woven to face utter dissolution.

La Corda d'Oro is categorizable as a variation on the typical harem drama based on the simple principle of gender inversion. Thus, the habitual pattern in which a boy is surrounded by a bevy of girls with vastly different personalities, all of whom somewhat inexplicably fall for him no matter what he does, is displaced by one in which a girl is the focus of attention of a bunch of handsome boys who come to develop, each in his own distinctive way, romantic feelings toward the heroine. However, the anime is not only a love-tinged school drama, much as this facet of the story deserves notice for the refreshing originality of its generic perspective. In fact, its kaleidoscopic romance is really a vehicle for the exploration of the multicolored pleasure intrinsic in the art of music. It is this conceptual emphasis that enables the anime to maintain throughout its distinct poetic tone and penchant for highlighting the evolution of the various characters' feelings toward music as a means of engaging with the essence of the art which brings them together. In so doing, it relies all along on a nimble oscillation between cacophony and harmony. As the characters' specifically music-oriented feelings develop, their overall personalities simultaneously mature. The megatalented violinist Len Tsukimori, for example, gradually learns to relinquish his cold and judgmental disposition, thus revealing that behind the customary façade stands a sensitive, charming and vulnerable young man. The dreamy cello player Keiichi Shimizu, in turn, realizes that the achievement of the perfect style is perhaps not quite as paramount as he has grown up to believe, and that human warmth of the kind he senses in Kahoko's notes is far more likely to militate in favor of the genesis of beautiful music than technical excellence. Kahoko operates as a catalyst, in this context, since Len, Keichi and indeed all of the other key members of the cast appear to evolve, more or less explicitly, in response to her music.

At the same time, *La Corda d'Oro* stands out as a contemporary myth about the significance of the past and its bequest. The anime instantly asserts its mythological standing through the once-upon-a-time tenor of its preamble. However, it is with the introduction of Lili that the drama's mythological specificity comes to the fore. The *fata* is portrayed as a creature who, in spite of his obvious otherworldliness, relies critically on Kahoko's acceptance of his magical present. This is because without the willing collaboration of the one student in the entire school who is actually able to see him and communicate with him, the creature would be completely powerless to fulfill his self-appointed mission: the dissemination of the art of music and the awakening of disparate people to its unique properties. The *fata*'s dependence on Kahoko is movingly evoked by the divergence between the girl's response to the gift in the way he projectively imagines it — which is dramatized by means of amusing flashbacks to Lili's visions of Kahoko's enthusiastic reception of the violin — and the unpalatable reality he must deal with when the girl resolutely rejects both him and his gift. It is only when Kahoko finally accepts the magical violin and makes her first forays into the musical realm against the odds that Lili's plan is tentatively blessed by the first hope of realization. nevertheless, the series does not aim in a univocal fashion to underscore a mythical creature's dependence on a human associate, which would render the character of Kahoko no more than a passive instrument and the *fata* a dubious exploiter. In fact, it seeks to fathom the collusion of the otherworldly and the mortal domains — and hence of timeless mythologies and the prosaic here-and-now. It is in this interplay, as the anime consistently and painstakingly reminds us, that authentic creativity resides. Relatedly, *La Corda d'Oro* delves into the processes through which human and non-human species alike may develop as creative agents within a dialectical rapport not so much by recourse to supernatural tools and tricks but also, and far more vitally, through resilience, honesty and perseverance. The story's finale as dramatized in the first season celebrates this message by highlighting its heroine's resolve to learn how to play competently without relying on any magical assistance, and by capitalizing instead on the existential import of everything she has learned along the way about the unparalleled worth of real friendship. Lili himself is finally shown to draw great joy not simply from the achievement of his personal objective but also from his sincere admiration of the kindness and ingenuity fueled by Kahoko into the testing enterprise inaugurated by the advent of the magical violin into her life.

The fantastic/mythical strand of the story gathers substance and momentum as its tune-marked action progresses. It thus transpires that Seiso Academy was established by a man reputed to have rescued a tiny supernatural being and to have been rewarded for his kindness. Furthermore, an ancient romance involving two rival violinists brought together by a fairy appears to constitute one of the students' favorite topics of conversation and a fertile source of spicy gossip. This theme is elaborated in the additional episodes broadcast as a summer special, *La Corda d'Oro — Secondo Passo*, where the former participants in the musical competition are asked to assemble at a training camp during the summer vacation. At this point, one of Kahoko's friends ponders excitedly the possibility of a novel "Summer Violin Romance" developing in the course of the sojourn and thus marking "the start of a new legend." The character's reference to "midsummer" as the ideal time of the year for such an amorous adventure to unfold throws into relief the anime's close relationship with fairy tales and lore, midsummer being a major date in the fairy calendar. The anime's fascination with the academy's past history, and especially its mythical undertones, offers a lore-encrusted and hence potentially subversive redefinition of the mainstream notions of history typically promulgated by the discipline of historiography and its arbitrary, if not downright prejudiced, manipulation of lived events. The concept of history communicated by *La Corda d'Oro* holds the uncanny solidity — discernible yet indefinable — of an afterimage (or ghost image): the unequivocal affirmation of either its reality or its illusiveness can only be a lie.

Kahoko's alternation between moments of intense liveliness and moments of melancholy introspection represents a crucial element in her psychological and emotional development. Of special importance, in this respect, is the episode in which three chords of the magical violin snap and the girl resolves to relinquish the art of music once and for all, thereby engaging in lengthy spells of somber meditation. This period of temporary inactivity functions dramatically as a dark rite of passage indispensable to Kahoko's subsequent maturation, paving the way to her discovery of fresh strength, and hence to her capacity to regain her characteristic energy and enthusiasm. It is at this point that Kahoko becomes able to grasp the full significance of both the challenges and the joys yielded by music as the girl she genuinely is, an unskilled player of a non-magical instrument. It is also at this point, no less importantly, that she begins to develop a more sophisticated understanding of her friends and fellow students, and hence to enter more complex and mutually sustaining relationships.

With the sequel's dramatization of Kahoko's "next step" (the "*secondo passo*" referred to by the title), the heroine's creative path begins to traverse a new zone punctuated by its own distinctive promises and challenges. In the aftermath of the first season's climactic contest, each of Kahoko's former rivals emphasizes, in his or her particular style and vein, the superiority of feeling to mere technical know-how. Therefore, even though these characters acknowledge that the girl's musical performance is as yet technically unrefined, they still believe passionately that it has the capacity to reverberate in the audience's hearts with an intensity to which many highly accomplished musicians could never even begin to aspire. If the titular "*corda*" designates, in strictly etymological terms, a string-like tie, it also alludes, in the context of this ethical message, to Kahoko's unique power to strike a "chord" in her listeners. Moreover, the girl's experiences function as a dramatic lens through which viewers may observe the challenges and pleasures met by someone who is ushered in to the world of classical music without any prior knowledge of the art. Thus, those unfamiliar with that world get a taste of what it might be like for someone like them to explore it for the first time. Those who are already au fait with classical music, in turn, have a chance to revisit the memories of their own initial forays into that realm and its riches.

La Corda d'Oro suggests that unfeigned personal growth is only tenable when we compare ourselves today with ourselves yesterday rather than with other people. Concomitantly, it repeatedly underlines the proposition that no accomplishment can ever be regarded as final, and no resolution as unassailably impervious to infiltration by deceptive diversions and mirages. Fairies and other preternatural entities may at times encourage our efforts, in a figurative or literal manner depending on the individual's stance on their existence. Nonetheless, nothing can be achieved in the absence of a tenacious sense of commitment to the task in hand. The character of Len conveys this message in incontrovertible, if metaphorical, terms when his fellow student Ryoutarou opines that Kahoko "is a Cinderella whose magic wore off" by stating that the girl's own "persistence" is "real" and this is ultimately the only thing which truly matters.

While Kahoko's knack of attuning herself to the magical violin leads to impressive results, she cannot help feeling dishonest, and this motivates her to practise assiduously while also having to confront a slew of hostile music students envious of her achievements, as well as negotiate a bundle of novel emotions triggered by her interaction with five other contestants, grapple with their own complex feelings, and cope with attendant romantic matters. Even after entire days of painstaking practice, Kahoko still senses that her music is "fake" and her talent "deceitful," and that she simply has no "right" to play. Yet, it becomes increasingly obvious, as both ordinary and music students exhibit heartfelt sorrow at her decision to quit the violin, that Lili's supernatural instrument does not ultimately provide Kahoko with a fraudulent mask. Rather, it allows dormant aspects of her personality to surface and evolve: that is to say, to enhance parts of her self which have not previously been allowed any adequate expressive conduits. Concurrently, Kahoko must discover through her own autonomous efforts the actual value of creativity and the immensity of the sacrifices, humiliations and obstacles strewn along the avenue to fulfillment. Neither Lili nor any other magical creature could ever secure her long-term success were she not prepared to embark on a soul-searching quest of unpredictable and disquieting intricacy. Myth, it is thereby implied, can only assist human enterprises as long as the humans themselves are willing to entertain a lively dialogue with the nebulous beyond which is devoid of any prejudice or craving for power.

La Corda d'Oro utilizes the art of music as a means of abetting the collusion of otherwise irreconcilable reality levels, and hence as the quintessence of creative interplay insofar as the ultimate manifestation of creativeness, in the logic of the series, consists precisely of the harmonization of difference and the resolution of conflict. Most crucially, music operates as such a bridge by bringing together not solely the mythical and the mundane spheres but also the two rigidly polarized student categories enrolled at Seiso Academy. While *La Corda d'Oro* prioritizes the arts of music and instrument making to all others, its portrayal of the acutely hierarchical social structure intrinsic in the school's power dynamics also enables it to engage with the art of fashion design. So blatant is the distinction between musical and non-musical streams fostered by Seiso Academy as to find visible expression in the imposition of distinct uniforms for each of the artistically disparate communities. This visual divergence invests what should logically compose a unitary habitat with the semblance of an ambivalent ecosystem in which two mismatched natural orders collide and coalesce by turns. The centrality of uniforms to the maintenance of a rigorously compartmentalized community is best grasped in relation to the broad significance of the uniform in Japan's sartorial history as both a costume and an icon connotative of hierarchy, authority, political expertise and martial discipline. An especially important moment, in this regard, is the Meiji Restoration, when the image of the Emperor was subject to radical restyling in order to emphasize, as Toby Slade argues, "the return of military authority to the monarchy," and vividly communicate "the sophistication of that authority in its grasp of modern military methods." A crucial vestimentary means of furthering this agenda was the Emperor's adoption of a "full-dress French-style uniform" for the purpose of propagandist portrayal. The choice is not surprising when one considers that "in 1868, the French army was still the most powerful in Europe" (Slade, p. 67).

French-style military uniforms were employed on a large scale for some time but "in 1887, around the time when nationalism was on the rise, the army uniforms were changed to the Prussian style, that of the latest victorious power" (p. 68). In examining the infiltration of the academic domain by military fashion, Slade points out that "the Japanese schoolboy started wearing a Westernized uniform, essentially a Prussian military uniform, around 1884, shortly before the upsurge in nationalism." This sartorial ideal has proved so tenacious that "the basic form has always been the same throughout the country, with variations only in small symbols such as the badge, the style of buttons and the number of white lines on the cap differentiating schools.... The Japanese schoolgirl was far behind the boy in wearing a Westernized uniform.... It was well into the Taishou period before some private girls' schools introduced Westernized uniforms" (p. 69). *La Corda d'Oro* throws the uniform's martial connotations sharply into relief in the design of the white outfits created for the musically talented students. Yet, both the white and the black uniforms ultimately partake of an army-inspired conception of social organization latently underpinned by soldierly principles. (As seen earlier in this chapter, uniforms also play a critical role as symbolic cultural markers in *Touka Gettan*.)

With its articulation of a relatively conventional multi-romance yarn and generic situation within the well-tested territory of the high-school drama, *La Corda d'oro* may at first seem wholly preoccupied with volatile occurrences of limited psychological significance. It could hardly be denied, however, that the anime consistently inscribes its more formulaic components in the broader context of an honest and courageous exploration of creative expression — as both a personal accomplishment and the trigger for communal intersubjective achievements which carry potentially mythical resonance due to their latent association with a time-honored ensemble of fascinating rumors and legends. In so doing, the anime is in a position to map universal urges, fears and desires which clearly transcend the boundaries of its localized formal concerns. It is with its subtle take on the topos of creativity — and of its lingering mythological affiliations — that *La Corda d'Oro* is able to rekindle familiar formulae with unique gusto, making that theme the hub of both ephemeral individual experiences and inveterate human drives which are also the classic matter of myths. The show thus presents the dimension of wonder as the activator of an inexhaustible diorama of possibilities. Furthermore, the heroine's preparedness to be awed and enthused by the extraordinary, yet preserve at all times a healthily inquisitive spirit and a tendency to think about what she sees remind us of the double meaning of the verb "to wonder" as connotative of both a passive state of amazement and an active yearning to question, to know. The most talented of the seven competitors, Len, stands at the opposite end of the spectrum. Brought up to put technical perfection above everything else, he has simply forgotten that playing music should never be divorced from enjoyment. In fact, as Lili keeps emphasizing, the Japanese word for music, *ongaku*, is a combination of the words *on* ("sound") and *gaku* ("fun") and the enjoyment factor ought therefore to be regarded as an intrinsic component of the art. It is when he almost accidentally finds himself performing Schubert's "Ave Maria" with Kahoko that he realizes that his style, refined though it is, simply lacks warmth in comparison with hers — and indeed with many of the sounds flowing from his other rivals' instruments.

Keiichi errs in another direction: he knows no form of pleasure other than music but this inevitably isolates him from his fellow students since it is conducive to a purely dual relationship between the boy and his cello with no room for diversion. Moreover, his obsession with discovering the ideal musical style obstructs his achievement of a genuinely personal approach to the art. The character with the clearest understanding of the kinship of music and enjoyment is Ryoutarou Tsuchiura, a marvelously gifted piano player who has deliberately enrolled at Seiso Academy as a regular student insofar as he mistrusts the proprietorial regimentation of music operated by academics as inimical to pleasure. Importantly, Ryoutaru is also good at sports and proficient at the art of cooking — his natural propensity to perceive the kinship of art and fun is confirmed by his commitment to these pursuits alongside music as no less worthy than piano playing. What truly matters, the youth maintains, is the "story your performance is telling"— strictly speaking, this applies to any activity, regardless of the degree of artiness associated with it. The heroine herself gradually comes to appreciate the critical importance of the fun factor as she realizes that even though Lili's instrument can enable her to play well, she must really feel the joy of playing to give life to a beautiful sound. What she feels while she plays, how she feels it, and what particular concatenation of impressions she brings to bear upon those affects are the decisive factors in determining the overall quality of her art.

A significant proportion of the anime's dramatic tension issues directly from the protagonist's uneasy perception of her role as an aspiring artist reliant on magical support. The more accomplished she becomes and the greater the recognition she receives from members of both the regular student body and the musical élite, the more inclined she grows to suspect that she is actually "deceiving everyone." Her predicament is exacerbated by the ambivalent, almost schizoid, conduct exhibited toward her by Azuma Yunoki. The classic golden boy endowed with astounding good looks, academic talent well above average in all areas, and the support of a tremendously affluent family, Azuma also vaunts, among his many skills, an unparalleled ability to project an unflinchingly amiable public image. Left alone with Kahoko, however, he quickly sheds that customary mask to become a hauntingly persistent and prevaricating bully and progressively intensifying his threats, to the girl's utter consternation, with intimations that he knows that she yields a terrible secret.

Paradoxically, just as Kahoko's haunting guilt burgeons, her rivals feel increasingly moved by her notes — Keiichi, in particular, unwittingly proffers an ironical comment on the girl's performance when, with characteristic candor, describes it as "honest music." Kahoko is aware that she has been putting independent effort into her practice instead of relying solely on Lili's fairy skills. Yet, she realizes how unconditionally she has come to "love" the violin only when she discovers that she has indirectly helped people who had no interest in music prior to her participation in the contest to develop deep feelings toward that art. Even Azuma is by and by reformed by Kahoko's frankly human — and not fairy-assisted — magic. Not even these achievements are conclusive, however, as the heroine goes on harboring tormenting doubts about her moral stance toward both her friends and the art of music itself. As these damaging affects escalate, Kahoko learns at her own cost that without a dispassionate commitment to music, she is bound to mar her relationship with the enchanted violin and, by extension, the bonds she has formed with other competitors in the tournament — all of whom have gradually come to feel deeply drawn to the girl in more or less personal terms. At one stage, the sense of frustration Kahoko transmits to the instrument is so potent as to warp its notes until the strings snap beyond repair. Lili's fairy magic is powerless to mend the violin when confronted with such an overwhelming wave of negativity. This aspect of the drama is especially intriguing on two counts. Firstly, it intimates that no otherworldly entity ultimately carries autonomous powers so great as to render it totally independent of its human partners. Secondly, it suggests that magic does not inhabit a transcendental domain sharply at odds with normality but only works properly within the mortal world when it can be harmonized with non-magical human qualities, and thus allowed to interact with them in a constructive alchemical relationship.

Kahoko's fear of the discrepancy between her basic humanity and the preternatural abilities she can display through Lili's violin makes such a dialogue untenable. What the girl must finally learn, therefore, is how to identify her true feelings and how to maximize their creative potentialities as an ordinary human. Magic can no doubt abet this task but cannot undertake the job on her behalf. In this respect, magic could be said to define normality by exposing the limitations of any human being unaided by supernatural agencies. Conversely, normality could be said to define magic by showing that no spell, charm or illusion can work conclusively among mortals without their cooperation and generosity. In this regard, *La Corda d'Oro* offers an engaging metaphorical correlative for the collaborative spirit which, as we have seen, has unfailingly nourished Japanese art over the centuries and abetted both the aesthetic quality of its creations and the spiritual maturation of its practitioners with equal zest. The collaborative ethos is no less central to the protagonist's creative evolution. When Kahoko plays a tune with which she has just familiarized herself by listening to a CD, the melody may be correct but comes across as lifeless, whereas when she plays a piece which she has heard at first hand through a school mate's performance — or, better still, when she plays an improvised duet with another contender in the tournament — her music oozes with vitality and originality. This is because collaborative interaction enables Kahoko to empathize with the other player's own feelings and transfer their creative import to her own practice in an imaginatively adapted guise. For example, it is only after hearing the unwaveringly cheerful and encouraging Kazuki Hihara play the "Gavotte in D" by Gossec on the trumpet that the girl is able to instill her personal interpretation of the tune with the playful enthusiasm conveyed by Kazuki's execution, while remaining faithful to her own emotional disposition, and thus participate in the creation of an inspired melodic synthesis.

On the mythological plane, *La Corda d'Oro* finds some illustrious antecedents in the likes of Dionysus and his retinue, Apollo, Marsyas, Pan, Orpheus, Arion, the Muses, the Nymphs and the Sirens — all of them eminent musical personages attesting to the convergence of musical and visual arts insofar as they have become enshrined in both history and lore mainly through whole centuries of visual representation. Furthermore, *La Corda d'Oro*'s celebration of the fun of music finds a pictorial equivalent in the mock-mythological paintings created by Picasso in the mid–1940s, and primarily in *La Joie de Vivre*, where fauns, satyrs and centaurs (alongside a few new-fangled characters in the same vein) are typically engaged in festive playing and dancing. The sense of joy evoked by these highly personal reinventions of the ancient Bacchanal resonates with the spirit of the Dionysian as conceived of by Friedrich Nietzsche: i.e., as the epitome of nature, irrationality, intemperance, passion and unbridled pleasure in contradistinction with the values of culture, reason, restraint, order and harmony symbolized by the Dionysian principle. The association with the Dionysian conveyed by the overall mood of Picasso's pictures is encapsulated by their iconic integration of wind instruments, and especially the *aulos*, a pipe associated with sensuality or even debauchery. Wind instruments in general have traditionally been regarded as the debasing assets of unruly mythological figures. In countless representations of the contest between the god Apollo and the satyr Marsyas, for example, the tension between reason and excess is captured by the opposition between the satyr's *aulos* and Apollo's *kithara* (a string instrument analogous to the lyre). While Apollo's string instrument alludes to the sublime harmony of the cosmos, Marsyas' wind instrument symbolizes sensory inebriation and hence primordial chaos. If the response invited by the *kithara* is transcendental composure, the reaction elicited by the *aulos*, conversely, is orgiastic frenzy.

Many paintings dramatizing the contest between the same Olympian god and the pastoral divinity Pan encapsulate the conflict between culture and nature by means of the visual opposition between Apollo's flawless mien and Pan's unseemly face, grotesquely distorted by the act of blowing into his syrinx. An analogous, albeit less extreme, tension is evoked by *La Corda d'Oro* through the personality contrast between the exuberant and outgoing trumpet player Kazuki and the haughtily reserved Len. In fact, most of the anime's musicians appear to veer toward either end of the mythological spectrum at some point in the drama. Their allegiances to either the Marsyan or the Apollonian poles tend to result from intrinsic personality traits far more than on the sorts of instruments they play. Moreover, their conduct often evinces both Marsyan and Apollonian characteristics, in keeping with their nuanced portrayal as multifaceted and realistically self-contradictory human beings. The clarinet player Shoko Fuyumi, for instance, comes across as extremely quiet, which may be interpreted as an index of Apollonian proclivities despite her association with a wind instrument. Yet, it soon transpires that beneath the composed façade of the girl's mien there lies a tangle of insecurities and doubts, and that her apparent composure is actually a case of pathological timidity. Ironically, the intensity of Shoko's underlying distress draws her closer to the excess of Marsyan passion than to the moderation of Apollonian self-control. Ryoutarou, by contrast, is a mature and self-reliant individual but often forsakes the Apollonian ideals symbolically attached to the string instrument he plays by indulging in impulsive behavior with scarce concern for the consequences of his actions.

Daniel Albright suggests that the mythical tension centered on Apollo and Marsyas can be extended to the appreciation of particular musicians insofar as "many composers tend either to the Apollonian or the Marsyan model; and the model helps to determine the kind of collaboration that the composer can enjoy with artists in other media" (Albright, p. 19). The Apollonian composer is inclined to defend the art's boundaries by insulating music from all other arts: in this perspective, the sorts of musical-visual relations emphasized throughout this study are regarded as unpardonable transgressions. The Marsyan composer, by contrast, is likely to relish the mutual contamination of disparate arts, and hence to praise the fusion of sound, color and motion as the apotheosis of artistic endeavor. Illustrating this proposition with reference to the example of the scream, Albright contends that "according to Apollonian purism, a scream is a phonic essence," whereas "from the Marsyan perspective," it is not an "essence, but a representation of some peak feeling that might be represented equally well by a great gash of red pigment, or by a dancer's simulation of an epileptic seizure, or by other artistic means.... For a Marsyan composer, a musical scream may be intensified, not diminished, by finding a way of making music, painting, and text disappear into a single devastating convulsion" (p. 21).

Like *La Corda d'Oro*, *Chance Pop Session* articulates a melody-laced tale devoted to the power of music to reach deep into the human spirit and to operate as a binding force of unrivaled vitality. It also shares with the latter drama the penchant for infusing its tuneful yarn with otherworldly tinges in chronicling the artistic journeys experienced by three girls from vastly different backgrounds, brought together by fate, talent and an innate passion for music in the pursuit of a common vision of stardom. Hints at the supernatural gracefully punctuate the action as the girls' voices coalesce in harmony, alluding to the existence of a bond deeper than either ambition or skill, and the Angel of Music observes from above to ascertain whether their dreams deserve fulfillment. Music is likewise pivotal to *The Piano Forest*, a film revolving around a transfer student named Shuhei Amamiya, who moves to Moriwaki Elementary filled with hopes and ambitions but soon becomes the favorite victim of class bullies. Challenged to play the piano mysteriously located in a remote part of the forest and reputed to be broken, Shuhei encounters Kai Ichinose, a kid who appears to be the only one capable of getting any sound out of the peculiar instrument. Though initially reluctant to refine his talent through training despite the encouragement he receives upon exhibiting such a unique ability, Kai eventually relents when he hears Shuhei's music teacher and former master pianist, Sosuke Ajino, play a Chopin piece — an event which fortuitously inaugurates a captivating voyage of self-discovery and self-realization.

In their approach to art, both *Beck: Mongolian Chop Squad* and *Genshiken* take a more radical leap into the contemporary cultural arena, chronicling the progressive development of new mythologies from their protagonists' daring forays into disparate popular arts in the case of the former, and of a musical style capable of generating a whole cult in that of the latter. While the animistic world picture might not seem glaringly obvious in either of these titles, their emphasis falling on decidedly secular and mundane pursuits, its lessons gradually assert themselves as the materials and media on which their characters depend become so pivotal to the drama as to stand out as living entities in their own right. In *Beck*, the employment of an animal as a vital structural catalyst in the instigation of the main drama economically reinforces the anime's animistic disposition. *Genshiken* brings the philosophy of animism into play even more explicitly at an early stage in the series, as one of the key characters draws his friends' attention to this term. Rightly attributing its coinage to the nineteenth-century English anthropologist Edward Burnett Tylor and stressing its etymological root in the Latin word for "soul," *anima*, the character concludes that "animation is the technique of god" with messianic ardor. In the anime itself, the omnipresent aliveness which animism posits as its philosophical mainstay makes itself felt in the guise of an all-embracing creative energy which flows through and between disparate artistic activities, thereby connecting their distinctive values, products and practitioners into a holistic ensemble of unique potency.

The simplest way to convey the essence of *Beck: Mongolian Chop Squad* is to describe the series as a younger and more nonconformist sibling of *La*

Corda d'Oro, keen on displacing the focus on classical music characteristic of the latter with the trials of a bunch of kids struggling to start a rock band. If the familial metaphor is sustained, it could also be suggested that while *La Corda d'Oro* relies on an established body of lore as the backdrop to the creation of its own mythology, *Beck*'s comparatively rebellious disposition largely induces it to discard established belief systems in search of an alternative world picture. The anime is modest enough to concede that such a perspective might not disclose a vision which it could honestly claim as wholly its own but is nonetheless eager to emphasize the unique creative potentialities held by its protagonists' tenacious efforts. Finally, whereas *La Corda d'Oro* adopts a fundamentally optimistic and buoyant attitude, *Beck* exudes a predominantly somber mood, deftly sustained throughout the action by its propensity to play with the darker facets of humanity. This preference is unremittingly bolstered by a shrewd sense of humor, a flair for slice-of-life drama, and a sympathetic grasp of the mercurial fluctuations of young love.

Despite the differences outlined above, *Beck*, like *La Corda d'Oro*, abides in memory as a series about the capacity of music to engineer alchemical interactions among disparate, or even seemingly incompatible, personalities and outlooks. The series follows Koyuki (a.k.a. Yukio), an ordinary kid in junior high school who appears to have already lost his appetite for life even though he is only fourteen. The turning point in Koyuki's tedious and purposeless routine coincides with his rescue of a bizarre-looking patchwork dog, named Beck, from a bunch of abusive children. The animal's owner is the up-and-coming rock musician Ryuusuke Minami, the character responsible for Koyuki's initiation to the art of guitar playing: the first step, as it soon transpires, in a twisty path of self-exploration and self-discovery. The crucial moment in the drama's inceptive phases consists of the dissolution of Ryuusuke's original band, which results in the guitarist's determination to form a new and more accomplished ensemble. This enterprise ought not, in principle, to involve or impact on Koyuki in any way until Ryuusuke's younger sister, Maho, realizes that the kid would make a perfect vocalist for the new band. Focusing on Koyuki's relationships with various members of the new rock group, dubbed *BECK*, and especially with Ryuusuke himself and Maho, the anime dramatizes the growth of the band and its music over time, discreetly drawing attention to its significance both as an artistic venture unto itself and as an allegory for the role played by creativeness in the psychological, emotional and sexual development of its key personae.

The series' authentic novelty does not reside with its use of the motifs of the mediocre kid protagonist, his uninspiring and shapeless existence, his quiescent talent, his encounter with a captivating mentor able to awaken it or the surfacing of his hitherto unknown romantic emotions. Though imaginatively handled, these narrative elements are largely familiar in anime about young people discovering themselves via music, of which several are mentioned in the course of this study. In fact, it is to be found primarily in its thoughtful treatment of the confluence of hidden artistic abilities, perseverance, courage and sheer happenstance whereby Koyuki unexpectedly and awkwardly advances from the dreary rank of a limp nonentity to the status of a devoted and proficient musician. The unassuming fashion in which *Beck* gradually announces its originality, even as it proceeds from uremarkable narrative premises, encapsulates its overall approach, revealing that the anime's objective is not to take its viewers by storm through explosive stunts and twist-laden subplots but rather to encourage serious reflection on the universal power of the art at its core.

The anime's care to record both the protagonist's own perceptions of his changing circumstances and the responses to his metamorphosis evinced by other actors (particularly Ryuusuke) steadily enriches its psychological acuity, eschewing dramatic monocularity in favor of multiperspectivalism. All of its personae are ultimately brought together by their inevitable exposure to the possibility of failure, every goal they achieve ineluctably trailing the phantasmatic vestiges of as many shattered or aborted dreams. The effectiveness of this compositional strategy owes much to the anime's distinctive — and occasionally idiosyncratic — pace. This seeks to capture in as realistic a vein as it is cinematically possible the directionless rhythms and interstitial minutiae of quotidian existence, attentive to the sluggish and meandering fashion in which relationships evolve and resolutely steering clear of decisive dénouements. Hence, the anime allows trivial and momentous occurrences to alternate fluidly within the seamless flow of living instead of laboring to arrange its materials so as to make each event seem obviously meaningful as a step to some major climax or resolution.

Accordingly, the protagonist's reasons for feeling drawn to rock music alter almost capriciously over time, alternately portraying his attraction to that world as an opportunistic means of cultivating his connection with the girl he fancies, as an idle pastime, and as a potential breath of fresh air for an ego smothered by many insipid years of frustration, loneliness and lethargy. *Beck*'s realistic tempo is succinctly encapsulated by the laboriously, almost painfully, clumsy fashion in which Koyuki progresses from the level of an inept beginner to that of a decent musician. The visceral energy issuing from the heaving audiences and dancing crowds which Koyuki witnesses in various clubs enables the viewer to sense personally and palpably the raw magnetic pull exerted on the kid by the rock scene before him. However, the series' realistic attention to the unsensational flow of everyday existence never allows the heady spectacle of rock euphoria to obscure the importance of the simple moments — the quiet reflections, the casual gestures, and the "little, nameless unremembered acts of kindness and of love" (to cite William Wordsworth) which are what finally make life worth living. It is in full consonance with this philosophical stance that *Beck* avoids ostentatious animation and theatrical effects in favor of a meticulously textured drama matched by refined delivery, considerate orchestration and impeccable editing. By the same token, flamboyant portraits are shunned even in the depiction of the trendiest and most eccentric personae in order to make room for an aesthetically pleasing gallery of simple, at times even minimalistic, character designs.

On the aesthetic plane, *Beck* is principally concerned with advancing the supreme value of rhythm as the mainstay of its musical-visual sensibility. In this matter, the anime brings to mind Félix Fénéon's contention that "a picture must first seduce by its rhythm" rather than presume to derive its affective and dramatic force from subject-matter alone. In fact, it is often through the most unassuming content that a visual work succeeds in affecting the viewer most profoundly: "three pears on a tablecloth by Paul Cezanne are moving and sometimes even mystical," while "all the Wagnerian Valhalla" may easily prove "as uninteresting as the Chambre des Députés" when consigned to canvas (Fénéon, p. 131). Rhythm in music is emplaced by *Beck* as the key principle which anime, as an essentially visual medium, should replicate and foster. Relatedly, the visual orchestration of the action is consistently matched to the search for the underlying rhythm connecting disparate musical signs. A particularly versatile strategy consists of the deployment of rising and falling lines, alternately strengthened or mellowed by their association with varied combinations of hues, as an economical means of eliciting diverse emotional responses from the viewer.

Gravitation echoes *Beck* in its sustained emphasis on the myth-making power of music. The anime's protagonist, the aspiring singer Shuichi Shindou, is driven by an all-absorbing desire to become a legendary star. As he tenaciously strives toward his goal, dreaming about the prospect of public recognition and fame, the teenager is virtually blind to anything other than his musical aspirations. Like Koyuki's, Shuichi's creative trajectory evolves courtesy of a totally unexpected turn. In Shuichi's instance, this consists of the incident whereby the lyrics of one of the songs he has composed for the band Bad Luck — a musical duo comprising the boy himself and his best mate, the guitarist Hiroshi Nakano — are accidentally read by the acclaimed romance author Yuki Eiri, who cynically derides Shuichi's lyrical abilities as no more refined than those of a child in elementary school. Resolved to seek out the haughty writer with the ostensible intention of requesting both an apology and an explanation for such unwarranted rudeness, Shuichi does not at first realize that the main reason for which he feels magnetically drawn to Yuki is that he has fallen in love with him at first sight. In this respect, the anime could be said to develop the familiar topos of the captivating guide, seen to play a key role in *Beck* through the character of Ryuusuke, in unusual directions. Although Shuichi and Yuki eventually establish a relatively steady relationship, a barrage of obstacles, chilling experiences and haunting legacies relentlessly threatens to tear them apart even as the twin gravitational forces of love and destiny keep drawing them together.

In consideration of its pointedly capacious perspective on art and creativity as critical to the elaboration of a far-reaching mythology, *Genshiken* deserves special attention in the present context. Dispassionately critical and affectionate by turns, the anime offers an ironical chronicle of the joys and sorrows entailed by being an otaku with a focus on the university club bearing the grandiloquent designation *Gendai Shikaku Bunka Kenkyuukai*, "The Society for the Study of Modern Visual Culture," of which "*Genshiken*" is a comfortably shortened version. In the process, the anime delivers one of the most comprehensive artistic scenarios examined in this study. The series engages with creative practices as diverse as drawing, painting, writing, fashion design, videogame design, and model-making (among others), finally presenting the ongoing creation of a specific lifestyle as an all-inclusive artistic activity unto itself. Few would dispute that *Genshiken* enthrones the otaku regimen itself as an artistic practice in its own right. What is most intriguing, for the purposes of the present discussion, is the remarkable extent to which, with this daring gesture, the anime also succeeds in deploying that cultural phenomenon as the fulcrum of the anime's articulation of an original mythology: a mythology which is no less concerned with the universal ubiquity of art to human civilization than it is with a contemporary popular cult. For this very reason, the concept of otaku and its varied social connotations appear worthy of detailed consideration in the present context. Grasping those aspects of the anime's background is indeed instrumental in appreciating its take on creativity, art and, ultimately, the genesis of cultural identities and roles.

As *Genshiken* gloriously demonstrates with no dearth of detail, otaku has incrementally come to describe a subcultural fandom phenomenon bound up with fetishistically compulsive consumers of anime, manga and videogames. As Lawrence Eng explains, the term "otaku" itself initially meant "'your house,' and more generally it is also a very polite (distancing and non-imposing as opposed to familiar) way of saying 'you' ... The basic idea is that the word is used to explicitly indicate detachedness from who you are speaking to" (Eng). In the influential article entitled "'I'm alone, but not lonely': Japanese Otaku-Kids colonize the Realm of Information and Media — A Tale of Sex and Crime from a Faraway Place," Volker Grassmuck offers an additional definition also worthy of attention in the present context. "The etymology of the word," the critic explains, "is not without black holes." The word derives from "everyday language, and in the original sense means 'your home,' then in a neo-confucian pars pro toto 'your husband,' and more generally it is used as the personal pronoun 'you' (since a Japanese individual cannot be thought of without his connection to his household) ... there are 48 ways to say 'I' in Japanese, and just about as many to say 'you' ... Otaku is a polite way to address someone whose social position towards you do not yet know, and it appears with a higher frequency in the women's language. It keeps distance" [Grassmuck]. The term acquires more problematic connotations when it is used among peers. On such occasions, it is taken to communicate the intention to keep one's friends and acquaintances at arm's length, which can be easily interpreted as an ironical affirmation of superiority on the speaker's part or else as an inability to express oneself adequately due to undeveloped interactive capacities. Idiosyncratic verbal tendencies have often been associated with otaku as people whose interests inexorably lead to their spending a lot of time in isolation, to the development of withdrawn attitudes to the world at large and to a pathological failure to socialize. This idea is reflected in the scene where Saki expresses understandable surprise at Kanji's incongruous use of an excessively formal register in conversation with a peer, and the youth candidly ripostes that this is just the way he speaks.

Although the otaku's seclusion is not in itself a heinous crime, it has often been censured or even, in extreme cases, compared to aberration insofar as it contravenes a leading cultural imperative. As Eng emphasizes, "not unlike American adult society ... Japanese adult society has long had anxieties about its youth culture becoming more individualistic and isolated and less interested in fulfilling mainstream social duty" (Eng). The otaku's dubious reputation, originally unquestioned, has gradually been tempered by more constructive interpretations of their significant cultural role. As Gilles Poitras maintains, "in the early 1990s" the term "began to lose its negative meaning. In fact, it even picked up some positive nuances as the power of the otaku audience (and the vast sums of money it spent on its hobby) made itself known in the entertainment business" (Poitras, p. 71). Intriguingly, Western anime fans have often proved more disposed than their Japanese counterparts to adopt the title of otaku enthusiastically even when in its country of origin it was being used as the equivalent of "nerd" or "geek" at best and "pervert" at worst. This demonstrates that perceptions of fandom are invariably culture-bound: in using the term otaku, a Western consumer is not simply appropriating a facet of Japanese society but also re-encoding it with reference to his or her own social and economic milieu.

The assumption surrounding otaku is that they are self-absorbed and socially dysfunctional individuals who have sought shelter in the illusory promises of satisfaction dished out by ephemeral consumer products in an effort to dodge the harsh realities of their world. One of the aspects of traditional Japanese culture from which many young people have struggled to escape, often in the most tragic of fashions, is the overarching imperative always to do one's best — and succeed — which have been embedded in Japan's philosophy and economic fabric since time immemorial. This contention is notoriously substantiated by the country's high suicide rates among teenagers who fail to meet their academic targets in a fanatically exam-oriented society. As several troubling statistics intimate, self-destructive despair seems to be an endemic reaction to insecurity, loneliness, the fear of failure and a haunting lack of direction or purpose. As David Samuels observes, "from 2003 through 2005, 180 people died in 61 reported cases of Internet-assisted suicide in Japan" (Samuels, p. 1). Interestingly, even though ritualized suicide has featured in Japanese history since at least samurai culture and the attendant ethos of *bushido* ("the way of the warrior") — with kamikaze pilots later providing a sinister anticipation of today's suicide bombers — the "most spectacular manifestation of Japan's exploding suicide culture, Internet group suicide, is unique in that it is rooted in the technologies of the computer age and has no meaningful precedent in traditional Japanese social behaviour" (p. 2).

While it is important to acknowledge otakuism's peculiar idiosyncrasies, it is nonetheless crucial to recognize that addictive fans are not the sole members of postindustrial regimes who lead isolated lives. In fact, atomization is endemic to such societies even though dominant ideologies strive to hide this unsavory truth in order to promote the myths of harmonious sociality and spontaneous gregariousness. What distinguishes otaku from non-otaku, in this respect, is principally the fact that they do not try to conceal their atomized condition but actually declare it — and even embrace it — quite openly. From a historical perspective, this attitude would appear to result from a ubiquitous psychological malaise triggered by unresolved conflicts between regionalism and globalization, traditionalism and modernization. In a sense, otaku are an entirely logical product of a technology-dominated and information-saturated society. Greedily consuming the products meant to embody their consuming passions at the expense of close social intercourse, otaku exhibit little or no concern with either physical fitness or diet. Simultaneously, they are distinguished by an impertinent disdain of fashionable attire even though this stands out as a ubiquitous fetish among Japanese kids at large. Otaku typically nest among the plethora of technological equipment which fills their haunts, which secures not only entertainment pure and simple but also, and perhaps more vitally, constant access to virtual images which fans can identify with and incrementally introject as their own personal self-images.

In this respect, a further phenomenon associated with otakuism which deserves notice from a sociological perspective is the syndrome known by the name of *hikikomori*: the Japanese word used to designate "the phenomenon of reclusive individuals who have chosen to withdraw from social life, often seeking extreme degrees of isolation and confinement because of various personal and social factors in their lives.... Although there are occasions where the *hikikomori* may venture outdoors, usually at night to buy food, the Japanese Ministry of Health, Labour and Welfare defines *hikikomori* as individuals who refuse to leave their parents' house, and isolate themselves from society in their homes for a period exceeding six months.... Often *hikikomori* start out as school refusals, or *toukoukyohi* in Japanese" (Wikipedia, the free encyclopedia—*Hikikomori*). It is also noteworthy, as Poitras notices, that "there's another term in Japan for a dedicated connoisseur of some obscure subject: *maniakku*, or maniac.... Why two terms for the same thing? The difference essentially lies in degrees of obsession. 'Maniacs' can enjoy fairly normal lives while devoting a portion of their energies to their hobby ... otaku ... devote their entire lives to their interest" (Poitras, p. 71). A further concept closely bound up with the otaku mentality is that of "*moe*." As Jonathan Clements and Helen McCarthy point out in their *Anime Encyclopaedia*, "*moe* is a fetishistic obsession with a particular topic or hobby, entering modern parlance as a replacement for otaku ... Toshio Okada has written that a *moe* fan need only be obsessed, while a true otaku actually develops background knowledge. Its etymology here is related to *moeru*, to burn with enthusiastic fervour. Also often associated in anime fandom with one particular kind of *moe*, an intense attraction to cartoon characters, particularly young and innocent girls that need to be nurtured and may be looking for a brotherly protector. Its etymology here is more related to *moederu*, to sprout or bud" (Clements and McCarthy, p. 31). Therefore, it could be argued that "*moe*," at first a way of describing virtually any fixation, by and by came to be equated to the otaku position, and finally gained specifically erotic connotations.

In its anatomy of addictive fandom, *Genshiken* finds an illustrious predecessor in *Otaku no Video*, a witty OVA produced by Studio Gainax in 1991 chronicling the development—or deterioration as the case may be—of its protagonist from a regular college youth into the supreme otaku of all times, the "Otaking." Formally adventurous as well as thematically controversial, *Otaku no Video* alternates the animated footage revolving around its unconventional hero and his absurd ordeal with mockumentary segments analyzing the passions and habits of an astonishingly wide range of fans in disparate areas of the art and entertainment industries. Two less famous instances of fan-centric anime also worthy of mention in this context are the OVA series *Cosplay Complex*, a myth-encrusted show in which fairies produce cosplay outfits out of thin air, and the TV series *Comic Party*, the story of a student's voyage through the universe of *doujinshi*.

While engaging with a variety of artistic practices associated with its personae's hobbies and routines, *Genshiken* grows incrementally committed as the drama unfolds to the assertion of friendship as the most valuable — if also the most demanding and elusive — creative endeavor to which humans could ever aspire. Borne out throughout by *Genshiken*'s emphasis on both the pleasures and the vicissitudes of human interaction, this message conclusively proclaims its ascendancy in the latter part of the series, as the interests which its personae may or may not share eventually take second place to the bonds they have established. The numerous context-specific club activities in which the characters engage, relatedly, often serve as dramatically cogent pretexts for exploring the gradual development of the group's overall chemistry and its advance toward cohesiveness. More than a comical story about otakuism, *Genshiken* is ultimately a psychological anatomy of the alternately funny and poignant moments through which a bunch of people affect and transform each other's lives in often decisive ways. As the club progressively recruits fresh members while its original founders graduate and depart the fictional academic establishment of Shiiou University, Tokyo, old legacies are both preserved and transformed by the newcomers' own visions. This process gives rise to ever-mutating configurations of social interplay and to correspondingly varied approaches to creativity and art. Hence, *Genshiken*'s narrative trajectory emulates metaphorically the accretional rhythm through which mythologies come into being as traditions are by turns integrated and displaced by innovative outlooks and experimental perspectives.

Furthermore, the anime's honest celebration of the value of the group is attested to by its utilization of certain characters at strategically vital points in the drama as ways of introducing particular topics or of occasioning a narrative reorientation. This is evident right from the start, since the character of Kanji Sasahara, one of the principal actors throughout, is clearly employed in the opening episode as a means of ushering in the anime's principal themes, and specifically the notion of otakuism and the lifestyle associated with being an otaku. By portraying Kanji as a timid, inhibited and insecure youth, reluctant to admit to his genuine interests not solely with others but also with himself, *Genshiken* is able to introduce economically and unobtrusively a whole range of mixed emotions associated with the cultural perception of obsessive fans by both themselves and the general (non-otaku) public. Kanji's development throughout the drama suggests that his initial personality is that of a latent otaku whose potential as a full-fledged member of the species, initially inchoate and unrecognized, reaches actualization as he grows up and the Genshiken simultaneously evolves around him. Not only does the boy eventually rise to the status of club president: he is also instrumental in the establishment of a Genshiken *doujinshi* (fan comics) circle, which makes his contribution to the Genshiken a veritable landmark in the club's history — and indeed its mythology.

At times, the drama employs particular characters in order to present and comment on specific activities. Thus, videogaming (especially of the fighting and *hentai*, or sexually explicit, varieties) is introduced mainly through Makoto Kousaka; cosplay through Kanako Ohno and Souichirou Tanaka; plamo (plastic models) through Souichirou; *doujinshi* generally through Mitsunori Kaguyama; and *yaoi doujinshi* (male-male romance narratives) in particular through Chiga Ogiue, the quintessential *fujoshi* (a female fan of *yaoi*). In addition, various personae are linked with precise tastes, resulting in fastidious preferences for certain anime types (e.g., middle-aged men in the case of Kanako, cuties in that of Manabu Kuchiki). With Harunobu Madarame, the most grievously addicted of the club members, *Genshiken* enjoys a precious opportunity, which is imaginatively varied and renewed as the series progresses, to address the extremes to which a potentially healthy interest may grow and hence degenerate into a disabling addiction. This aspect of the drama parallels metaphorically the ordeal of an artist whose creative passion grows so powerful and autonomous as to dominate his or her entire existence, by and by polluting the creative drive and turning creation itself into a destructive act.

Saki Kasukabe, as a non-otaku who actually detests the entire category and range of pursuits but is compelled to mix with members of the club in order to be with her boyfriend Makoto, enables the anime to observe its otaku characters from an external standpoint without having to assume a tiresomely masterful stance of authorial omniscience, which would feasibly put off even the most sympathetic audience. Quite a different version of the otaku-hating modality is embodied by Chiga Ogiue, a girl whose self-professed abhorrence of anything fan-oriented is actually a defensive response to her own otaku nature, of which she feels profoundly ashamed. As the series unfolds, Chiga comes to accept her true disposition, which encourages the audience itself to reassess its initial perceptions of the main characters and their addictive hobbies, and to recognize the creative force unrelentingly at work in their midst. This potent wave of energy bears witness to the otaku's unflinching commitment to their ruling passion. This is an intriguing phenomenon unto itself which Thomas Lamarre has eloquently addressed in his discussion of the otaku movement with specific reference to Studio Gainax and *Otaku no Video*. The following comments on the balance of leisure and labor entailed by being an otaku are particularly relevant to *Genshiken* itself. "Otaku movement — as unofficial work — is at once labor and not labor," argues Lamarre. The two options coexist in the otaku's distinctive "oscillation between discipline and self-cultivation. The statistical information that accompanies each portrait of an otaku, for instance, not only gives the impression that otakudom is far more pervasive than anyone suspects.... It also gives the impression that this is not disciplinisation. Rather, their work as otaku allows these men to know and cultivate themselves. There is, for instance, the self-conscious tone of the otaku telling their stories. They apparently understand their innermost mechanisms of desire. They may not be able to resist the lure of anime.... But they see this passion lucidly, knowingly, and almost rationally" (Lamarre, p. 168).

The variety of creative activities which *Genshiken*'s characters either practice or partake of vicariously, often oscillating between these roles depending on their variable inspiration levels, are consistently complemented by myriad intertextual allusions to both actual and imaginary products in cognate otaku-centric sectors, alongside discussions of specific styles, forms and genres — as borne out, for instance, by the installment in which Harunobu, struggling to think of a valid pretext to strike up a conversation with Saki, having fallen in love with her despite their seemingly insurmountable differences, runs disparate available scenarios through his head in a fashion which suggests a parodic adaptation of the visual novel format. *Genshiken*'s flair for intertextual references alluding to creative works of its own conception reaches an apotheosis with the invention — and attentive employment throughout the drama — of a self-reflexive metastory: the imaginary franchise *Kujibiki Unbalance*— a.k.a. *Kujian* among fans. The opening episode of *Genshiken*'s first season in fact starts with the opening frames of *Kujibiki Unbalance*. This is presented, within the world of the anime itself, as an ongoing manga series in the romantic comedy genre, resulting in numerous games (e.g., "Unbalanced Fighter") and in a 26-episode anime adaptation. Both the manga and the anime versions of the story feature as the subject matter of regular debates engaging *Genshiken*'s main characters. In addition, they serve as the source of inspiration for various *doujinshi* and cosplay initiatives, alongside other spin-offs and tie-ins, and these, in turn, trigger several of the club's activities. In this respect, they are a perfect means of highlighting the characteristic peculiarities and technicalities of ancillary merchandising from an insider's viewpoint.

Kujibiki Unbalance is set in Rikkyuoin High, a high school where all problems are solved by recourse to *kujibiki* ("drawing straws" or "drawing lots") — to the point that even entrance exams are dealt with through such a lottery — and follows various aspiring student council members over the duration of one academic year. The series as a whole comes across as a meticulously assembled compendium of numerous motifs, themes and generic formulae common in various manga and anime series. This makes it ideal as an arena in which seasoned aficionados may test their knowledge of those fields in a lighthearted and noncompetitive fashion, as well as indulge in multiple games of "I-spy." Having attained to special prominence as a cultural product within the world of *Genshiken*, *Kujibiki Unbalance* has hence proceeded to acquire real-world status as an artifact in its own right. It has thus spawned a 3-episode OVA series inspired quite overtly by the materials presented in *Genshiken* (and supposedly including episodes 1, 21 and 25 of the series watched by *Genshiken*'s characters), an independent 12-episode TV series with substantially redesigned actors and a novel storyline, and a manga adaptation of this version.

Another important element of *Genshiken*'s approach to art lies with the creative dialogue it manages to conduct with its manga source throughout its progression. Sensitively adapting the visuals originally executed by Kio Shimoku to the animated format, the series' artwork retains throughout their remarkable charm. Concurrently, it endeavors to adopt the same refreshingly linear crispness which distinguishes the parent text in the portrayal of all of its key personae, from the handsome Makoto to the ungainly Manabu, from the urbane Saki to the grubby Harunobu. The anime's stylistic dialogue with its manga antecedent is paralleled by its productive intercourse with the metafictional series-within-the-series discussed above, placing to great dramatic effect the contrast between its elegantly understated visual discourse and *Kujibiki*'s bold cartoonish style.

The anime's passion for intertextuality is matched by a hearty appetite for self-reflexive commentary on the technical and aesthetic features of the various arts pursued by its cast. Proceeding with unremitting diligence, yet rarely without humor, *Genshiken* raises self-reflexivity to the status of an art by repeatedly calling attention and discussing, often in minute details, legion aspects of the art of anime itself. This is exemplified by the sequence in which Harunobu, Manabu and Souichirou discuss an episode of *Kujibiki Unbalance* (with Kanji in the role of an hesitant novice as yet uninitiated to this kind of intellectual pursuit), and express their contrasting views regarding the effectiveness of the anime version in comparison with its manga source. Opinions are divided as to whether or not the anime's tendency to spell things out is preferable to the manga's penchant for open-ended hints, the former being held to be more dramatic by the pro-anime camp, and the latter to provide greater leeway for the recipient's imagination by the pro-manga camp. This kind of disagreement can often be encountered among real-life consumers of anime and manga, and therefore functions as accurate documentary evidence for interpretative trends characteristic of those two cognate areas of artistic production. The self-reflexive mode is sustained as the sequence seamlessly leads to a scene in which Saki expresses heartfelt shock at the realization that otaku, her beloved Makoto included, find cartoonish drawings of supposedly attractive females sexually arousing.

The hardcore otaku Harunobu instantly launches into an ornate apology of this peculiar taste, regaling Saki with evidence not only of its contemporary prominence but also of its historical standing. He thus traces a bold temporal loop that takes him all the way back to cave painting, and hence to the earliest indications of humanity's primordial representational urge, and then leaps forward to the Edo period and its own passion for specifically erotic images. He also elevates his peroration to the theoretical plane by alluding to the age-old tension between realism and stylization, and elliptically invoking Japanese art's traditional preference for flatness by branding Saki's reaction as a classic instance of the "2D complex." When Saki is forced to admit that her current attraction to Makoto is based entirely on looks and not on actual knowledge of his personality, Harunobu is able to consolidate his argument with disarming integrity, maintaining that if it is the case that fondness of a drawing lacks depth, the same must apply to fondness for a person for purely superficial reasons. Saki's caustic objections to the club members' sexual preferences single her out as an alien presence in their midst. Ironically, however, they soon come to perceive the girl in a radically different light as she recalls her childhood encounter with Makoto, which allows them to visualize her as an anime heroine of precisely the kind one would encounter in a series like *Kujibiki Unbalance*. This also serves to rehabilitate her personality following Harunobu's exposure of her shallow approach to romantic matters.

A great deal of the anime's unique brand of wit emanates from the club members' totally unselfcritical magnification of their trivial aims as valiant missions. The mock-epic tone which characterizes the Genshiken's activities virtually from start to finish is replicated by the absurdly exaggerated flavor of the episode titles used throughout the first season, which include headings such as "Comparative Classification of the Modern Youth Through Consumption and Entertainment," "The Sublimating Effects of the Dissimulation Brought on Through Makeup and Costume," "Limits of Rejection and Receptiveness as Observed in Autonomous Behavior," "Theory of the Individual Outside the Boundaries of the Subculture," "Aspects of Behavioral Selection in Interpersonal Relationships," and "On the Presence of Malicious Intent in Urban Crimes." The anime's penchant for overinflated registers designed to throw into relief its key characters' quirks and foibles is further encapsulated by the occasional use of voiceovers commenting on the action with incongruous levels of pathos.

A paradigmatic example is provided by the installment in which Makoto chivalrously agrees to accompany Saki shopping for clothes in Harajuku, while the other Genshiken members take a trip to the otaku paradise of Akihabara to buy *doujinshi* and sample other new products in the fields of their individual addictions, although it is most likely that he would rather go to Akihabara than to Harajuku. Makoto follows Saki around for the entire day, not once interfering with her schedule. However, just as the girl begins to feel that the object of her desire is almost within her grasp at last, Makoto frustrates her romantic longings by leaving her at the station to go to "Akiba" (i.e., Akihabara) after all and "line up for a midnight release" of "a game with killer content": an event which will allow him to "feel all the users' excitement." The same basic situation is replicated later in the episode as Saki, having come even closer to accomplishing her goal, is once again left behind as Makoto goes off to purchase the new CD of his favorite female voice actor. The first departure is marked by words invested with deliberately inappropriate gnomic density: "in the town of Harajuku, even lovers are sorrowful. They should have been far away from Akihabara. Akihabara was all too near." The second farewell is sealed by a comment which couches the incident in the antiquarian tone of sensationalist melodrama: "the locomotive is departing and the smoke is rising. Her feelings are distant and her wishes are unfulfilled."

It is important to acknowledge, however, that the anime's intertextual leanings do not cause it to indulge in an entirely inward-looking disposition. In fact, *Genshiken* is keen to impart the drama with a realistic feel, interspersing the fiction with accurate references to real-life places — such as Akihabara — and events — such as Comic Festival (Comiket), the massive fair held at Tokyo Big Sight, the Tokyo International Exhibition Center, where *doujinshi* circles gather biannually to showcase their creations. The latter is renamed Comifes in the series. It is at the level of characterization, however, that *Genshiken* proclaims most resonantly its particular brand of realism as the aspect of its style which ultimately distinguishes it from many of its contemporaries. Reluctant to glorify the lifestyles of obsessive fans, let alone depicting nerds and geeks as though they were the harbingers of a superior civilization, the anime is eager to draw attention to its characters' vulnerable humanity—and hence indicate that they are as susceptible to the specters of loneliness, fear, despondency and, above all, boredom as anyone else. Delving beneath the action's comical façade, the series enjoins us to ponder existential issues of global resonance, such as the nature of the boundary separating normality from abnormality, as well as the viability of relationships. Relatedly, *Genshiken* strives to deploy an utterly dispassionate lens in its examination of the myths constructed by otaku around the supposedly legendary fantasies spawned by manga series and anime shows, *doujinshi* and videogames, plastic models and pop idols, tangentially encouraging us to ponder the extent to which cultural fantasies may inhabit and influence our own "normal" lives.

Chapter 4

PERFORMANCE AND VISUALITY

> *Modern Japan is what Michel de Certeau describes as a "recited society" where people walk "all day long through a forest of narratives from journalism, advertising, and television, narratives that still find time as people are getting ready for bed to slip a few final messages under the portals of sleep." Japan is also what Susan Sontag refers to as an "image world," since much of Japanese mass media is involved in producing and consuming images, at a time when they have "extraordinary powers to determine [people's] demands on reality and are themselves coveted substitutes for firsthand experience." ... The animated images that flicker across the screen and all the pages of comic magazines and books are a major source of the stories that not only Japanese, but also an increasingly global audience, consume today.*— Mark W. MacWilliams

As this chapter's opening quotation proposes, the cultural proclivity to frame one's life within the margins of image-laden stories — and, by implication, effectively live through images — is a contemporary phenomenon of global consequence which finds paradigmatic incarnation in the culture of Japan. However, in assessing the role played by visuality in Japanese society, it is important to appreciate the extensive temporal ascendancy of that dimension, which would render its limited equation with contemporariness quite inaccurate. At the same time, it is vital to recognize the significance of visuality as a twofold event which refers at once to the state of being visual (i.e., visualness) and to the dynamic experience of perceiving and interacting with something as visual (i.e., vision).

If the phenomenon of visuality embraces two dialectically interrelated dimensions, performance itself is by no stretch of the imagination to be conceived of as a monolithic reality. In fact, all of the anime discussed in this chapter deal with the relationship between artistic expression and performance by foregrounding simultaneously two distinct aspects of performance: its literal significance as the (normally public) enactment of particular artistic skills, and its aesthetic value as the concretization of a creative ideal. Accordingly, the anime's protagonists engage by turns with the dynamics of spectacle as a communal expression of talents nourished by both technical expertise and personal inspiration, and with the elaboration of forms through which technique and intuition may blend as twin components of a harmonious organic whole.

In all instances, visuality plays a critical role, with differing connotations depending on context and genre, since the performance calls attention to the visual status of the art at stake and to both the performer's and the audience's experience of such performance as a visual occurrence. It thus captures the dimensions of visualness and vision alike. No less crucially, all of the anime seek to highlight the concurrently communicative and kinetic potentialities of their arts by exploring the subtle interplay of performance and performativity. In this context, performance designates the mechanisms entailed in the display of certain capacities as a practical and tangible event, whereas performativity refers to the metaphorical significance of an artistic medium (e.g., sound, motion, color, texture) as an entity which carries the value of a performance even if does not necessarily find overt manifestation through display. Hence, the chosen anime deal not solely with performance per se but also with expressive elements which are not explicitly performance-orientated but are so alive — so pregnant with energy and dynamism — as to function as actions or dynamic gestures, and not just as static images or utterances.

Through their dramatization of arts as disparate as music, fashion design, ballet and calligraphy, the chosen series highlight the status of artistic endeavor as a fluid process involving an ongoing dialogue between the practitioner and the practice, on the one hand, and between the product and its recipient, on the other. At both levels, the performance is underpinned by a shared set of codes and conventions operating as a third party in the performance, and thus tenaciously reminding us that a dialogue is not, de facto, a necessarily dual interaction — that it is not, in other words, to be automatically equated to a duologue — since it actually comprises a much wider spectrum of both realized and potential relations. This proposition is validated by the etymological root of the term dialogue — i.e., the Greek noun *dialogos* ("conversation") and the related verb *dialogesthai* ("to converse"), which in turn combine the prefix *dia-* ("across") and the verb *legein* ("to speak"). The erroneous belief that the word dialogue can only designate a conversation involving two persons results from the confusion of the meanings of *dia-* and *di-* as prefixes.

As Haruo Shirane persuasively argues, dialogism is an intrinsic property of traditional indigenous verse: "Japanese poetry, like many of Japanese traditional arts, usually takes place in a communal context, as a group activity, or as a form of dialogue between two or more people." A classic example is provided by "the thirty-one syllable *waka*" which was first developed in the seventh century within "two types of settings — first, as private exchanges between friends and lovers; and second, in public settings, as what we would call banquet poetry, which could have a highly political or religious function, such as praising the emperor or the high-ranking host or paying respect to the dead or survivors of the deceased" (Shirane, p. 219). A corollary of this cultural perspective was the conception of what constituted a "good poem" as a textual construct which "had open space so that the reader or audience could participate in its production. Linked verse embodied this process since it left each new link to be completed by the next person's verse" (p. 221).

In the anime here explored, both visualness and vision are inextricable from a culturally embedded propensity to conceive of space and time as actors in a kinetic continuum where "change," as Mitsukuni Yoshida puts it, "is the very essence of nature, the basic principle of all life." This notion is so deeply ingrained in the social imaginary of which the anime partake as to entail, as its logical corollary, the belief that "what does not change does not exist" insofar as it is only as a result of incessant transformations and adjustments of variable magnitude that "the value of an entity is established." Just as the temporal dimension is distinguished by inarrestable motion, its spatial partner is likewise engaged in an ongoing process of visual metamorphosis. "Humanity and all the things associated with human life," Yoshida continues, "are subject to constant change. All movement, from static to dynamic, from microcosm to macrocosm, from *hare* [momentous points in a person's life] to *ke* [the uneventful periods between any two *hare* moments], and from natural to artificial, is change" (Yoshida 1982, p. 32).

The performative energy of the visual realm owes much, in all of the artistic ventures dramatized by the anime under scrutiny, to their seemingly spontaneous tendency to trust the faculties of imagination and sensitivity over and above cold intellectualism. When characters like Shinichi in *Nodame Cantabile* fail to give shape to their vision despite their immense talent, this is usually due to excessive reliance on the mind and its supposedly rationalizing capacities. In depending entirely on those powers, they sap their artistic efforts of truly creative verve and ultimately risk sacrificing palpating inspiration and instinctual verve to the dry dictates of technical excellence. People like Megumi (Nodame) and George in *Paradise Kiss*, conversely, often flounder in an amorphous gush of feelings resistant to formalization but eventually succeed in articulating their distinctive creative voices because they honor the energies inherent in the irrational and the inscrutable. They seem to sense instinctively that artworks "are more beautiful," as Soetsu Yanagi maintains, "when they suggest something beyond themselves than when they end up being merely what they are" (Yanagai, Soetsu, p. 150).

In this respect, the anime could be seen as dynamic confirmations of Yanagi's reflections on the contrasting attitudes to beauty and form typically evinced by Western and Eastern cultures: "the ideal of Greek beauty hardly permits irregularity or asymmetry, for it was founded on the symmetry of the human body. By contrast the Oriental found irregular beauty in nature outside the human form.... The scientific thinking of Europe is founded in rational thought. In the East the foundation is in the heart and its inspiration, which to the Western mind, with its emphasis on the intellect, must appear very strange, for Eastern man jumps to his conclusions on wings of intuition, whereas Occidental man arrives at his by a steady progression of intellectual steps" (p. 124). The purity, simplicity, grace and sincere appreciation of natural beauty animating Japanese art ensues from this essentially intuitive and imaginative sensibility.

In traditional Japanese culture, the collusion of performance and visuality is vividly encapsulated by an object of pivotal significance to numerous arts: the mask. As entities endowed with both monstrous and numinous appeal, masks have been accorded important ritual functions over the centuries in milieux as disparate as Buddhist temples, Shinto shrines, aristocratic and military circles, sanctuaries, parades and street festivals. At the same time, they have been adapted to the objectives of diverse practices — including animistic magic, shamanistic seances, esoteric liturgy, propitiatory procedures associated with venatorial and agrarian customs, initiation ceremonies and fertility rites. Masks are also held in high esteem in the context of traditional Japanese theater, being invested with the twofold ability to abet actors in their adoption of stable and symbol-laden expressions, and to assist spectators in their effort to penetrate the alternate universes which the performance evokes. Maskmaking can be traced back to Japan's prehistory, its original aim being the production of tangible icons of gods and spirits to be employed in the practice of either conciliatory rites or exorcisms. In this respect, masks could be seen to issue from an inveterate yearning to bridge the gap between the human and the supernatural realms. This mediating power has been consistently reinforced by the belief that human beings wearing masks could divest themselves of their earthbound subjectivies and take on fresh identities as those masks' own souls, thus becoming the breathing embodiments of arcane preternatural creatures. As Yoshida explains, a mask was initially "a form given a deity, and an expression of its power. A mask hung on a wall meant that the people in the room were constantly under the gaze of the *kami*.... Unlike the human eyes, the eyes of a mask — the *kami*— are never closed but gaze out into eternity" (Yoshida 1985, p. 58). The mask is still profusely utilized in contemporary Japanese culture as a major component of myriad festivals, rituals and dramatic performances. Its seemingly inexhaustible spiritual import has both sustained and renewed its iconic hold over time, to the point that even today, the appearance of a mask on a stage, a catwalk, a museum wall or simply a screen may still carry mystical undertones, reminding us of the entity's original function and influence.

The distinctive significance held by the Japanese mask is typified by the special role it plays in the theatrical realm, and is probably best grasped by comparison with its Western counterpart. As Gian Carlo Calza points out, in the West's dramatic tradition, the mask's chief function is "to conceal, to hide behind another element ... something that is not meant to be seen." In Noh, by contrast, the emphasis is not on the mask's concealing power but rather on its capacity "to evoke, to suggest, even to the point of violently expressing ... specific conditions, both human and divine" (Calza, p. 93). A further difference lies with the contrasting perceptions of a mask's symbolic significance harbored by the two traditions. Western cultures are generally governed by a fundamentally binary mentality disposed to organize reality on the basis of mutually exclusive or antithetical concepts, and with the assistance of supposedly objective and clear-cut categories. They accordingly tend, by and large, to invest masks with symbolic attributes which embody unequivocal principles. In Japanese art and culture, as argued in Chapter 1, ostensibly adversarial concepts coexist quite effortlessly in a pulsating festival of paradoxes and ironies. The mask replicates this proclivity by embodying simultaneously disparate emotions, and by enabling their energies to blend, clash and intersect in often unsettling ways. The multiaccentuality inherent in the Noh mask (*nohmen*) is confirmed by its performative versatility, whereby the actor can make it take on disparate moods simply by playing with how the light is reflected or refracted upon it, or by angling it so as to engineer seamless transitions between conflicting emotions. The actor's body language has the power to enhance with each movement the mask's affective substance insofar as even the least noticeable turn or tilt of the head will cause the artifact's apparently vacuous orbs to brim with pathos, elation or sorrow. In addition, a mask's meaning can alter radically in accordance with the slightest adjustment of its position on the actor's face. Thus, even tough the majority of Noh masks seem to be devoid of any expression whatsoever when inspected outside the performative situation, they actually excel at communicating very specific emotions and atmospheres by means of concentrated abstraction. This is not only a result of performative skill, however, but also depends vitally on the art of maskmaking. The execution of a Noh mask is an extraordinarily complex art governed by strict technical rules for both the sculptural and the chromatic dimensions of the practitioner's task. Minute engravings and barely discernible grooves or indentations, for instance, can be deployed as a means of producing delicate lines able to convey highly refined and unmistakable feelings.

Hence, despite its ability to symbolize relatively constant values, the mask's supreme power resides with its adaptability to the evocation of variable affects, and hence with its capacity to remind us that no unequivocal truths are ultimately available. The only truth to which we may aspire is no less elusive and mercurial than the tiniest shift of a mask on a face or of the play of light and shadow on the mask's surface. As a result, viewers themselves are encouraged not merely to tolerate but also to pursue and embrace their personal inconsistency, vapidity and erraticness, and to regard these attributes neither as crimes nor as sins but rather as inevitable components of humanity. The aversion evinced by Noh theater — and, by extension, by Japanese culture in its entirety — to binary thinking is borne out by the traditional employment of masks as a means of evoking trenchant existential conflicts. Relatedly, the *nohmen* exemplifies Elias Canetti's contention that masks in general have the uncanny power to draw an audience to the sense of menace they embody, and yet simultaneously distance themselves from that audience through the very secret they shield (Canetti).

A notable instance is that of the *hannya*, one of the most formidable mythical figures in Japanese lore — namely, a female demon ruled by intemperate jealousy capable of encapsulating at once extreme malice and incomparable sublimity. In the domain of anime, the *hannya* finds paradigmatic incarnation in one of the principal characters from *The Tale of Genji*, Lady Rokujou. Like the *hannya nohmen*, this charismatic persona combines the contrary forces of attraction and revulsion in a single being. Her uncontainable and eventually devastating yearning to possess the object of desire unnervingly coexists with her horrified awareness of the monstrosity into which she has plunged, caging her within the torment of her own self. In embodying those incompatible affects to baleful extremes, the *hannya* type personified by Lady Rokujou is a symbolic incarnation of the hideous drives which lurk in each and every person, and her self-alienation of the fate awaiting the individual who falls prey to their pull. Rudolf Kassner proposes a poignant metaphorical correlative for that condition by recourse to the forms of the gargoyles punctuating Gothic architecture. These grotesque entities are forever "staring into the abyss: where they look, the abyss opens up. And everything they are trying to seize in their greedy, terrible gaze is swallowed up in this void." Just as the gargoyles lose everything by allowing their passion to possess them entirely, so "a man who harbors great resentment, or is full of envy, loses, in this envy and resentment, one thing after another, both the days of the flowers and the silent nights" (Kassner, p. 56).

A further title worthy of mention in this context is *Ef—A Tale of Melodies*, the sequel to the anime *Ef—A Tale of Melodies* discussed in Chapter 2, where masks feature as a pivotal motif and are accordingly allowed a prominent role right from the beginning of the series. At the same time, they afford numerous opportunities for technical experimentation and for the execution of daring visual effects — stylistic proclivities which the anime shares with its predecessor and occasionally flaunts with even greater verve. On the symbolic plane, the mask as employed in *Ef— A Tale of Melodies* reverberates with echoes of various local traditions associated with Japanese ritual and drama. On the strictly representational plane, however, the styles employed in the depiction of the masks which adorn the home of one of the principal characters — and elliptically allude to various facets of both his and other characters' personalities — overtly recall Western trends, principally of Venetian provenance, in alternately photorealistic and stylized fashions. This aspect of the show is quite consistent with the setting's pointedly European atmosphere. Concurrently, the anime's stylish masks also operate as a vital component of one of its recurrent thematic preoccupations: the clash between reality and illusion. The character of Shuuichi Kuze, an internationally renowned violinist whose whole existence is inextricably intertwined with the art of music, at one point suggests that as people grow older and get accustomed to taking up various roles which may not actually coincide with their genuine selves, masks become more real than the identities they are supposed to shield or conceal. The logical — and deeply unsettling — upshot of this idea is that masks might eventually hide not a presence but an absence, not an authentic identity but rather the vacuum left behind by the self's dissolution into a pageant of imaginary personae.

Thus, both *The Tale of Genji* and *Ef— A Tale of Melodies* could be said to illuminate crucial facets of the dialectical interplay of performance and visuality in their distinctive uses of the mask motif. However, it is in *Glass Mask*, as the anime's very title indicates, that the esteemed artifact's dramatic, symbolic and spiritual connotations proclaim themselves most emphatically. Harking back to the popular Cinderella archetype, *Glass Mask* is based on one of the most cherished *shoujo* manga of all times, produced by Suzue Miuchi for over three decades, and focuses on Maya Kitajima, the thirteen-year-old daughter of an indigent widow. Even as she struggles to make ends meet by working as a part-time waitress in a hectic Chinese restaurant, Maya's true passion lies with the stage. In this instance, the quasi-providential role of the fairy godmother is assumed by a legendary diva, Chigusa Tsukikage, who accidentally discovers Maya's unique acting talent when she hears her recounting tales in a park, instantly feels that she is "the girl with a thousand masks," and hence resolves to maximize her artistic potential. Chigusa's dedication to Maya's advancement grows so intense as to risk degenerating into a full-fledged fixation. At her best, however, the retired celebrity comes across as a benevolent surrogate mother equipped with a healthy fusion of affection and strictness. Maya's real mother, by contrast, is portrayed as a gloomy and narrow-minded woman, adamantly hostile not only to the girl's pursuit of a thespian career but also to her right to harbor any positive aspirations.

Despite her mother's objections, Maya bravely moves from Yokohama to Tokyo to join Chigusa's troupe. Her emancipation from a humble and unrewarding existence does not, however, open up an unproblematic avenue to success and self-fulfillment since the promise of limelight glamor is fraught with hardships, challenges and potentially life-shattering risks. The principal threat to Maya's advancement comes in the person of a rival performer, Ayumi Himenawa: a girl who enjoys the advantages of economic security and a fabulously well-connected family but feels hampered, rather than enabled, by these obvious privileges in her pursuit for unbiased recognition as a gifted player. The two aspiring performers' tortuous paths to dramatic maturity intersect as they find themselves competing for the lead role in *The Scarlet Angel*, a play to which Chigusa owns the rights and will not allow any company to stage until she has discovered the ideal performer for that part. *Glass Mask* acquires the bracing flavor of a chivalric quest of yore — a mood heightened by the anime's deliberately retro look in the handling of its character design, animation style and soundtrack — as Maya and Ayumi face increasingly demanding trials on their way to the ultimate grail. This consists of the achievement not so much of praise and fame, as one might easily expect of the average *shoujou* heroine of their ilk, as of a genuinely personal creative signature capable of demonstrating that they are truly worthy of the boards.

As the series unfolds, the masks presaged by Chigusa will progressively evolve into autonomous performers of tantalizing visual puissance, moving around Maya as the aspiring actress herself seeks out the roles she needs to wear on her way to artistic maturity. The anime's cultural interpretation of the mask — and, by extension, of the performative and visual arts bound up with that image — implicitly reminds us that though masks feature in virtually all known human cultures, they have traditionally played an especially prominent role in the Far East. Relatedly, *Glass Mask* pays homage, with varying degrees of explicitness, to several aspects of indigenous drama embroiled with the conventions of masked performance. Most importantly, *Glass Mask* echoes the aforementioned tradition of Noh theater, and not so much through iconographic allusions to the masks immortalized by that particular kind of theater, which are judiciously interspersed with references to other cultures and trends, as through its compositional employment of the mask as trope. The anime recalls Noh at a deep structural level insofar as it uses the mask as a focal image intended to impart the series as a whole with graphic and diegetic coherence. Thus, despite its extensive breadth, *Glass Mask* is endowed with a potent sense of unity redolent of Noh as defined by Ezra Pound — i.e., a form committed to the constellation of an entire play "about one image ... enforced by movement and music" (Pound 1980, p. 209). Like a Noh play, *Glass Mask* brings together stage performance, plot, dialogue and music into something of an amplified ideogram orchestrated around the semiotic and aesthetic fulcrum provided by the mask. The affinity with Noh can also be perceived in the anime's approach to characterization. *Glass Mask*'s actors tend to come across as deliberately formulaic and two-dimensional but this does not detract from their dramatic effectiveness — in fact, it could be said to enhance it by drawing attention away from the vagaries of individual personality and focusing the viewer's attention on the emblematic and conceptual significance of both the characters and their actions. In this respect, the series embodies the spirit of Noh as described by Daniel Albright: "the Noh theatre ... does not imitate human beings; it imitates signs. The dramatis personae are not rounded, credible characters to whom the audience might react personally — by loving or hating.... They are masks, ideograms carved in wood and outfitted with arms and legs. The proper question is not Who are they? but What do they mean? — for they are incarnations of the transcendental" (Albright, p. 73).

In the anime, the performative and visual energies embedded in the image of the mask are invoked most spectacularly by the emblematic entities which float across the screen as autonomous entities whenever the protagonist becomes so absorbed in her theater-oriented visions as to enter a state of almost mystical rapture. The masks displayed throughout these symbolic sequences reverberate with multiple iconographic echoes of pan–Asian origin. Their designs, colors and textures frequently hark back to the Shishi masks donned in the execution of the *shishi-mai* ("Lion Dance"), traditionally enacted as a means of warding off evil demons and still honored today in various parts of Japan through regular performances. At the same time, they bring to mind the grotesquely satirical Kyogen and Oni masks conventionally designed to capture in emblematic guise the wildest attributes of diverse deities and demons. Chinese opera masks inspired by ancient face-painting techniques and Korean white masks with beak-like noses and black eyes are also alluded to, as indeed are the fanged masks frequently used in Kathakah performances in the context of Indian tradition. Since *Glass Mask*'s perspective on the mask as a cultural concept is prevalently Oriental on the philosophical plane, it is not surprising that many of its masks should be inspired by Oriental models. However, it is not unusual for the visuals to draw on stylistic registers of Western, as well as Eastern, provenance at numerous junctures. Quite a few items showcased by the symbolic scenes indeed exhibit several of the features traditionally associated with Greek and Roman masks of the Classical age, in a stylized vein, while also harking back to masks readily associated in numerous Western cultures with carnivals, popular festivals (such as Halloween) and ritual processions. Since *Glass Mask* often utilizes a pointedly Western repertoire in the dramatization of Maya's exploits, it is entirely logical that it should also transcend the East/West division in its invocation of the mask's symbolic dimension. Simultaneously, the amalgamation and juxtaposition of Eastern and Western elements in the articulation of this seminal constituent of the show as a whole enables *Glass Mask* to attain to cross-cultural standing, and thus exceed the generic limitations of the conventional *shoujo* adventure.

The anime's coming-of-age dimension finds a cogent parallel in the traditional role played by the mask as a major component in various rites of passage, such as initiation ceremonies, performed in countless societies. In such contexts, it is common for ritualized actions to be carried out under the tutelary watch of ancestral masks. Even when the mask element is not as explicit or sensational as it is in the more traditional and more systematically codified of these communities, it is nonetheless perceptible in the emblematic deployment of costumes and accessories, such as the ones worn even in metropolitan milieux for weddings, christenings or funerals. In a sense, the very concept of cultural identity guaranteeing the subject's recognition as a legitimate member of a society is intimately imbricated with masks. This is economically attested to by the Latin word for mask, *persona*: the term which evidently provides the etymological foundation of the very word used to designate a human being.

Finally, it is worth noting that while the mask clearly plays a critical part in the anime's dramatization of the collusion of performance and visuality, the figure of the doll is also notable as a germane iconic entity. As argued in the first chapter, synthetic beings such as dolls, puppets and mechanical automata have traditionally held a special place in Japanese culture as creatures capable of bridging the realms of the animate and the inert by uncannily exuding an aura of sentience despite their obvious artificiality. In Maya's hands, this ontological ambiguity comes superbly to the fore as the young performer devotes her own body and mind to the infusion of the traditional doll figure with vestiges of human sentience while concurrently drawing attention, with tasteful originality, to an elemental divergence between her own pulsating energy and the doll's glass-eyed impassivity.

With *Paradise Kiss*, we witness an inspiring confluence of performance and performativity in the dramatization of fashion's encounter with spectacle: a cultural phenomenon whereby fashion itself comes to be conceived of as a spectacle not only at the literal level of public display but also in the context of private creation. The designing and manufacturing processes stand out as performative events in their own right, and their undertaking accordingly acquires the connotations of a spectacle sui generis. *Paradise Kiss* hinges upon Yukari, an ordinary high-school student with no notable aspirations or goals, who begins to have doubts about the meaning of her lifestyle and daily routine just as a group of fashion design students who associate themselves with the label "Paradise Kiss" choose her as the perfect model to exhibit their collection at the impending school festival. Yukari is at first guarded about this apparently eccentric bunch, unsettled by their palpable divergence from the sorts of people among whom she has grown up and with whom she routinely interacts in the course of her meticulously organized (and tedious) existence. Yet, as Yukari begins to appreciate the utter honesty, patience and self-sacrificial perseverance with which the fashion students pursue their artistic goal, she also learns not only to trust but also to admire their passionate idealism. No less vitally, her new friends provide Yukari with a priceless source of inspiration to explore her own true dreams.

Paradise Kiss is characterized by an unremittingly classy tone: a stylistic trait which informs the anime's visuals and performance with equal intensity. Nevertheless, its axial preoccupation does not lie with the superficial — and falsely joyful — glamor exuded by the fashion dreamland per se but rather with interpersonal dynamics wherein disappointment and fear are no less pervasive than exuberance and hope. Ai Yazawa, the creator of the manga on which Osamu Kobayashi's anime is based, is renowned for her knack of establishing a delicate balance of realism and fantasy. The anime remains loyal to this distinctive aspect of its source text, especially in the depiction of relationships. Fraught with insecurities, anxieties, quarrels and jealousy, these exude a tantalizing cocktail of pleasure and pain. Being as mercurial as the fashion industry itself, moreover, they appear ever-mutating while they last and are almost invariably destined to end. Neither Yazawa's nor Kobayashi's worlds make easy concessions to reparative endings and promises of eternal love, focusing instead on the ineluctable pull of entropy which sooner or later affects all relationships, romantic and familial alike. If human intercourse is capable of delivering any joy at all, this is bound to reside in the fleeting moment.

The philosophical devotion to the concept of ephemerality as a pivotal force in the shaping and endurance of the universe at large, deeply ingrained in Japanese art and culture, repeatedly asserts itself in the anime's emphasis on the transient here-and-now. In this respect, an indirect precedent for the drama orchestrated in *Paradise Kiss* is offered by *Gokinjo Monogatari* with the depiction of a fashion design student, Kouda Mikako, who dreams of becoming a top designer with her own brand. In engaging simultaneously with its protagonist's pursuit of her creative ambition and a web of more or less complex friendships and romantic attachments, the anime foreshadows *Paradise Kiss* not only through its emphasis on the art of fashion design but also in its intelligent portrayal of personal relationships as inevitably awkward, erratic, open-ended and, above all, only likely to yield evanescent pleasure.

It is its treatment of artistic and artisanal production, however, that renders *Paradise Kiss* crucially relevant to the present study. In this area, the series is distinguished primarily by a keen dedication to the ethos of *kazari* as aesthetic delight bound up specifically with decoration. Japanese art, in both its traditional and its modern manifestations, does not regard ornamentation as an ancillary — and ultimately dispensable — supplement to a privileged form but rather as a defining component of the cumulative artifact which contributes vitally to its creative distinctiveness. *Paradise Kiss* promotes this position by foregrounding the worth of a considerable variety of decorative patterns as graphic presences pervaded by perceptible life: that is to say, by performative vigor of a uniquely refined kind. The anime consistently reveres indigenous aesthetics in its devotion to the studious execution of myriad patterns alongside meticulously conceived textures and fabrics. At the same time, its attitude to fashion design also reverberates with traditional values insofar as it is infused with a genuine sense of respect for the materials deployed by designers and an attendant proclivity the evoke the specifically tactile qualities of those materials. In addition, the use not only of materials but also of colors which immediately bring to mind both the four elements and a wide range of organic forms emphasizes art's roots in the natural domain.

The principle of *kazari*, it must be noted, does not underpin exclusively the anime's approach to fashion design. In fact, it is also notable, with shifting degrees of precision or allusiveness, in its plentiful allusions to the design tenets which guide the arts of interior design, packaging, gardening and cuisine. It thus proposes that no ornamental element is ever too lowly or banal for the truly committed craftsman or artist, and that every facet of the creative experience deserves recognition and even veneration. In this matter, the show is overtly indebted to a major lynchpin of the indigenous perspective on design: the concept that "small is beautiful," and that no toil should therefore be spared in the creation of even the tiniest and humblest of items to the highest of specifications. The anime's celebration of *kazari* reaches an apotheosis when George, unable to find a single pattern on the market which he deems suitable for Yukari's festival dress, satisfies his exacting aesthetic palate by drawing an ornamental design of his own conception and by intensifying its impact with the addition of beaded embroidery. Moreover, George's determination to have his pattern embroidered on the material used for Yukari's dress could be seen to issue from a desire to enhance the garment's corporeal presence which is entirely consonant with Japanese design's devotion to the more eminently physical components of creation.

An analogously perfectionistic approach characterizes the design of the various trimmings complementing Yukari's robe. Instead of relying on pre-dyed "fake" flowers, George requires such accessories to employ "real" white roses hand-painted in an appropriate shade of blue — with the use of a substance, George avers, which is nothing other than his own blood. The character of Arashi ungallantly describes the task thereby imposed by George on his co-workers as "last-minute Alice-in-Wonderland shit." In Arashi's pragmatic view, George is just a "stupid prince" but the artist himself unflinchingly maintains that a real designer is a "magical weaver of dreams" and that ultimately, "there isn't a single thing that's impossible when it comes to the world of art." George's designs actually turn out to be too fanciful to stand a chance of emplacing their maker in the fashion realm as a designer of garments congruous with the realities of everyday life for even the most daring fashionista in town. Nevertheless, he remains faithful to his vision to the end, and finally achieve acclaim in the fabulous universe of theatrical costume with the stagy Isabella at his side in the role of a highly proficient pattern maker. The performative dimension of the anime's artistic vision is here enthroned in no uncertain terms.

Paradise Kiss features a subtly nuanced cast of characters whose members never deteriorate into stereotypes even as they embody well-tested anime categories. George is evidently the most challenging of the anime's personae, insofar as he initially bears all the distinctive traits of a licentious and reckless philanderer but is gradually shown to be in fact reliable, sensitive and considerate. The route George chooses to woo Yukari, both as a desirable model and as a potential girlfriend, is so winding and ambiguous, and his determination so haunting, as to cast doubts on the integrity of his purpose. On occasion, George even recalls the legendary type of the demonic lover or suitor. Furthermore, his artistic drive is so engrossing and so obstinate as to evince latently destructive drives. This becomes particularly prominent in the scenes in which George gives in to blinding self-absorption and his attitude toward Yukari grows so proprietorial as to intimate that he is governed by a perverse need to swallow up her whole being into his artwork — to suppress her humanity in order to handle her as a luxurious fabric or a precious stone of the kind which may adorn one of his most accomplished artifacts. George's potential dangerousness is also suggested by his protective maintenance of a secret space reminiscent of Bluebeard's secret chamber in the guise of the cabinet housing all of his favorite creations, which he bestows upon his beloved Yukari as a farewell gift at the close of the series.

The secondary and the supporting personae are also thoughtfully portrayed, and this results in one of those rare casts in which all of the characters turn out to have their own interesting stories to tell. For instance, even though Miwako initially comes across as a fairly formulaic cutie, she does not operate purely as an entertaining prop but is in fact intelligent, mature and rendered all the more endearing by a latent history of emotional turmoil, alongside a complicated case of big-sister complex. The spiky-haired and multipierced punk Arashi exhibits a harsh façade and anarchic temperament congruous with his public image but one quickly discovers that his disdain of conventional conduct and defiance of tradition are not simply a fashion statement but rather an upshot of a frank belief in everybody's right to act of their own free will. Thus, his initial reservations concerning Yukari, whom he first regards as a spoilt kid, gradually give way to respect and to recognition of her courage and autonomy in the face of oppressive notions of decorum. No less complex is the character of Isabella, an imposingly handsome crossdresser typically garbed in period costumes which emanate a palpable sense of stage presence. In spite her statuesque theatricality, Isabella shows a touchingly maternal disposition in her unwavering willingness to offer Yukari comfort in difficult times and to regale her colleagues with magnificent homemade meals at the end of a day's hard work. Even the more marginal and seemingly cardboard characters finally evince considerable psychological complexity. The best example is supplied by the heroine's domineering but innerly troubled mother: a woman who, even though she stands out primarily as a classic embodiment of the *mamagon*, or mama-dragon, is haunted by insecurity and a pathological inability to express her feelings in anything other than a darkly perverted manner.

However, even as the anime devotes ample attention to the portrayal of its multifaceted characters, it is to costume design itself that it accords the role of true protagonist. Virtually every shot devoted to clothes, whether it be in the context of day-to-day apparel or in that of arty fashion photography, is rendered in loving detail. On all of these occasions, *Paradise Kiss* conveys its devotion to the physical dimension of art, a vital component of indigenous aesthetics, and especially in an area with which Japanese fashion design has become proverbially coterminous: the manipulation of fabric. Most importantly, the attitude to sartorial creativity fostered by *Paradise Kiss* underlines that any productive activity holds artistic significance, at least potentially. Fashion design itself is no less respectable an art than painting, architecture or sculpture. Concomitantly, its more overtly functional aspects — such as cutting, sewing and embroidering — are posited as no less imaginative than the abstract processes of conceptualization, visualization and graphic elaboration. The fashion vision communicated by *Paradise Kiss*, concomitantly, encompasses a variety of styles ranging from minimalistic silhouettes to *kawaii*, from stylishly casual citywear to punk, from grand epoch costumes to simple uniforms. What unites all of these vogues across the anime's classy fabric is its enthusiastic experimentation with the idea of the garment as a motile shape — an animated entity with intrinsic performative capacities. Raw materials and final silhouettes are treated as inseparable partners in a dynamic dyad.

The series' vision is both influenced by and interwoven with various other arts, including painting and sculpture, cuisine and architecture. In this regard, it resolutely rejects the hierarchical notion of art as a pyramid wherein fashion is automatically relegated to a lowly position due to its cultural framing as a principally lucrative venture. In fact, fashion is presented — at the levels of both conceptual ideation and manual execution — as the site of a unique synthetic encounter of multiple voices and forms. At the same time, the anime's outlook capitalizes on the interpretation of fashion design as a concurrently sensuous and intellectual enterprise. This mission results in an ironical interplay of continuity and discontinuity — a time-space flow in which tradition endures in a discontinuous manner and, simultaneously, breaks with the past but retains a regard for the organic continuity of its legacy. Change, in this perspective, is not perceived as a one-off moment of demotion — let alone demolition — of established values but rather as a process of incessant re-evaluation. Hence, *Paradise Kiss* never propounds a slavish acceptance of the conventional principles, premises and artifices of couture and tailoring even when it employs highly recognizable formulae. The apotheosis of the anime's aesthetic project lies with the dress created for the climactic competition, which stands out as a performer in its own right overflowing with visual power, and as an incarnation of both the existential and the perceptual sides of the phenomenon of visuality (i.e., visualness and vision). Every facet of the magnificent artifact donned by the heroine for the event reveals studious attention to the relationship between the way fabric hangs and gravitational force, texture and motion, mass and pattern. Simultaneously, it throws into relief the kinetic dalliance of body and dress in such a way that the model's body functions as a part of the costume rather than as its support or content — while the dress, in turn, comes to constitute a vital part of the model's body rather than its shield or container. Body and dress alike, in other words, are above all *performers*.

The bond between performance and performativity is invested with additional significance in *Bartender* and *Antique Bakery*, where the two concepts are linked by their shared and inextricable implication with the phenomenon of interactivity. In both anime, the protagonists' creative visions manifest themselves through their public performance, through their deployment of performative media of distinctive dynamism, and through their ongoing interaction with a motley assortment of customers, friends, relatives and acquaintances. Performance, performativity and interactivity are thus presented as interdependent members of a dramatic triad. The visual dimension concomitantly asserts its ascendancy as neither the fabled cocktails nor the splendid cakes created by the anime's protagonists would abide in memory as poignantly as they do were it not for their aesthetic appeal to the eye.

Bartender revolves around Ryuu, an exceptionally skilled, as well as naturally witty and charming, barman. Ryuu's genius finds expression in the mixing of extraordinary cocktails endowed with the power to revitalize the most miserable, disaffected and despondent of people. This does not mean that from a generic perspective *Bartender* flaunts itself as an anime with a taste for magic, mystery or the supernatural. Nor does it entail that its protagonist goes out of his way to parade his creative talent in search for ideal customers (or patients as the case may be). In fact, the façade of the establishment where Ryuu works blends so fluidly and discreetly with its urban surroundings as to be barely noticeable to casual observers or to persons walking by on their daily business. The barman himself, quite fittingly, invariably comes across as a tactfully sympathetic and sensitive individual who only ever proffers comfort or advice in the subtlest of manners. This remains true even as his actions have a life-transforming impact on his establishment's hapless patrons. Relatedly, while Ryuu somehow manages to touch and influence the lives of all his customers, whether or not they explicitly invoke his assistance, his conduct never appears insolent or inquisitive. It is only too easy, given its unassuming premise, to overlook *Bartender* as an excessively mellow, sluggish and possibly monotonous animation. This impression may be reinforced by the show's adoption of a sedate visual style appropriate to its dramatic mood, which typically results in the use of pale and soothing hues and gentle dynamic rhythms, matched by a relaxing soundtrack. Yet, most people who have at least sampled *Bartender* on an experimental basis would find it hard to deny that its stories carry universal appeal. Ryuu's performance, the reservoir of performative energy inherent in his art, and the skills he deploys to interact with his troubled customers do not presume to fathom intricate alternate worlds but touch us all, at least potentially, by addressing common problems and anxieties to which most people can relate.

Upon first encountering *Antique Bakery*, it is tempting to compartmentalize (and perhaps even dismiss) it as a farcical romance verging on parodic melodrama. This is certainly the feeling generated by the initial shenanigans centered on Keiichirou Tachibana, the grandson of an affluent entrepreneur who decides to open an exclusive café-cum-pâtisserie even though he detests cakes of all kinds, and his first new employee, Yuusuke Ono, an esteemed pastry master endowed with a "Demonic Charm" which inexorably causes any man to whom he feels attracted to become besotted with him in return, regardless of his customary sexual preferences. This dubious gift has been a cause of endless problems for the talented pâtissier insofar as it has led several of his former colleagues to fight over his favors, as a result of which Yuusuke himself has time and again been given the boot in spite of his exceptional artistic abilities. However, we soon discover that there is more to the show than meets the eye in the course of superficial sampling. Indeed, even though its initial tone may seem clownishly over-the-top or tacky (especially if compared with a series as unobtrusively classy as *Bartender*), *Antique Bakery* rapidly steers its course in the direction of genuine drama, devoting sufficient time and attention to all of its characters, secondary ones included, and making the most of its atypical setting to avoid obvious stereotypes and engage instead with carefully nuanced psychologies. The thriller mystery element is also admirably handled in that it transcends the familiar narrative formulae associated with the motif of the character haunted by traumatic experiences. For one thing, it is unusual to say the least for the victim of an abduction to be tormented with the injunction to eat cakes all the time.

Antique Bakery honors indigenous aesthetics most explicitly in its emphasis on the primacy of the artifacts and the materials entailed in a creative practice over and above conventional hierarchies and economic considerations. This idea is tersely encapsulated by the scene in which Eiji Kanda, Ono's apprentice, insistently requests employment at the bakery and, inspired by his inordinately sweet tooth, claims that the owner is bound to hold an ancillary position in the business because "the only god here is the one who makes the cakes." In this scene, the anime also declares by the most economical of means its specialist dedication to a particular facet of gastronomic artistry. Yet, *Antique Bakery*'s purview stretches well beyond the boundaries of cake-making by proffering an adventurous commentary on the enduring hold of two-dimensional graphics in Japan's aesthetic sensibility at large and, more specifically, on the impact of this legacy on contemporary anime and its integration of traditional cel animation and computer-generated images. This aspect of the series finds memorable expression in its stark juxtaposition of hyperrealistic 3D visuals, most notably in the rendition of settings and backgrounds, and overtly flat character designs whose blatant artificiality is insistently intensified by the use of caricatural effects and both anatomical and affective distortion. The visuals matched to the series' opening theme paradigmatically encapsulate its passion for stylistic contrasts of this kind by situating cardboard cutouts of various characters in highly photorealistic scenarios of the titular venue.

Among the various directors behind the anime explored in this study, Kenichi Kasai stands out as a creator endowed with an exceptionally commodious perception of creative endeavor. This proposition is incontrovertibly borne out by *Honey and Clover* and *Bakuman* (here examined in Chapter 2) through their mature insights into diverse artistic practices. With *Nodame Cantabile*, as will be argued in detail later in this chapter, Kasai continues to promote a wide-ranging approach to creativity even as he concentrates specifically on the art of music. The spectrum of arts encompassed by *Honey and*

4 — Performance and Visuality 173

Clover, Nodame Cantabile and *Bakuman* gains a further illustrious member in *Kimikiss Pure Rouge* with Kasai's engaging treatment of a distinctive *ars amatoria*. One of the series' most memorable components clearly consists of some of its key actors' progressive articulation of a nuanced art of loving through a trial-and-error methodology redolent of mock-scientific research. The crucial events indeed pivot on the performance of specific romantic actions in accordance with a code of gestures, postures, props and verbal devices. However, it is also important to recognize that like the other anime titles examined in this book with Kasai at the helm, *Kimikiss Pure Rouge* does not limit its aesthetic vision to the treatment of a single art. In fact, it is keen on exploring both obvious and latent interactions among various artistic practices and media. Thus, even as it foregrounds the distinctive operations, codes and conventions of the amatory art, *Kimikiss Pure Rouge* simultaneously harnesses its graphic inventiveness and chromatic sensitivity to the communication of a broad spectrum of visuality. Special prominence is here accorded to gastronomy and music but cameo appearances of exquisite subtlety are also granted to the arts of fashion design, interior decoration, flower arrangement and garden design.

A major quality which *Kimikiss Pure Rouge* shares specifically with *Nodame Cantabile* is its emphasis on the closeness of the tie binding performance and performativity. Performance, in this particular instance, refers to the strategies deployed by characters in the enactment of concrete movements and ritualized gestures, while performativity pertains to the figurative value of the tools at their disposal as entities which harbor performance-oriented powers in a potential form. As the actors literally engage in their *ars amatoria* charades, or else allude to their possession and incremental refinement of the relevant skills, we are invited to feel that performance and performativity are virtually interdependent and reciprocally defining. Crucial to the anime's dramatization of the interplay of performance and performativity is its inspired take on the conventional trope of the romantic triangle. Evidently dissatisfied with the existing ensemble of anime strategies typically governing that ploy, *Kimikiss Pure Rouge* proposes a deftly diversified triangulation of desire, enhanced by the employment of multiperspectival vision. In so doing, the anime is able to yield nuanced variations on its pivotal concerns by relying on the characters themselves to present different interpretations of those issues instead of having to resort to the cumbersome agency of an omniscient author to steer the action over alternate scenarios.

Looking in more detail at the anime's integration of its *ars amatoria* and its triangular relationships, it appears that *Kimikiss Pure Rouge* essentially revolves around two performative events: an ensemble of love experiments and a romantic movie. Each of these is deployed as a structural device in order to frame a triangular relationship. The plot itself unfolds across two arcs. One of these chronicles the vicissitudes unleashed by a single triangle comprising the characters of Eriko Futami, Asuka Sakino and Kazuki Aihara. The other arc encompasses two interrelated triangles, both of which feature the characters of Mao Mizusawa and Kouichi Sanada, the third corner being occupied by Eiji Kai in one case and by Yuumi Hoshino in the other. In order to appreciate the exact bearing of the anime's orchestration of a distinctive art of loving, it is vital to grasp the significance of the romantic gestures sustaining each of its structuring devices as elements in a rhetorical system rather than as literal acts assessable according to the criteria of classic realism. This proposition is paradigmatically exemplified by the image of the kiss: a performative sign which asks to be read precisely as that — as an image, figurative unit or trope. In both arcs, the kiss is deployed as a rhetorical device in an attempt to establish the extent to which, within a coherent amatory syntax, the same strategy may be used as a means of either nourishing or thwarting a relationship. The arc centered on the Eriko-Asuka-Kazuki triangle illustrates the former option utilizing the image in the scene where Eriko kisses Kazuki not because she feels especially drawn to him but simply because he happens to be available as an appropriate test subject in her ongoing research into the nature of love. In the Mao-Kouichi-Kai triangle comprised in the other arc, the same trope is deployed to explore the opposite outcome as Mao is initially shocked and even repelled by Eiji's unexpected kiss.

The use of same basic image in both arcs as a means of exploring alternate outcomes points to the anime's overall identity as an integrated ensemble romance constellated around a set of independent yet ultimately interlocking stories. This remains the case to the end, even as the Eriko-Asuka-Kazuki arc increasingly veers toward the happy end of the romance spectrum despite its undeniable share of drama, while the other arc proceeds in the opposite direction by underscoring the motifs of pain, conflict and separation and even touching, at times, some authentically tragic peaks. Like the kiss, the structuring device provided by the romantic movie must be approached primarily as a rhetorical construct. Its dramatic effectiveness within the anime as a whole cannot be overestimated as it offers a resplendent instance of one of the most baffling aesthetic phenomena which many artists and theoreticians alike have in vain struggled to negotiated: that of life imitating art. Yuumi, unable to act in the movie and increasingly alienated from her beloved, feels spontaneously inclined to take on the role of a star-crossed tragic heroine in concordance with her natural generic preferences. Mao, conversely, assumes the part left vacant by Yuumi and her bond with Kouichi, rooted in childhood experiences, grows more and more potent.

In examining the anime's handling of *ars amatoria* in the context of the romantic triangle as a narrative and dramatic trope, it seems appropriate to take into consideration René Girard's speculations on the mimetic nature of desire in *Deceit, Desire, and the Novel*. Girard focuses on a classic staple of Western literature: the type of text which encourages the reader to identify so thoroughly with its protagonist as to elect that fictional persona both as a role model and as a mediator whose desires have the power to shape the reader's own desires. According to Girard, human beings typically borrow their desires from others. Their yearning for a certain person or object, therefore, is not an autonomous drive. In fact, it is inevitably sparked off by the longing of another person — the model or mediator — for that same person or object. This entails that relationships orchestrated around the shifty dynamics of desire are fundamentally triangular insofar as they do not consist of a direct line of communication between a desiring subject and a desired object but rather involve the constant interaction of a subject, a model/mediator and an object. Girard's parable comes with an intriguing twist as it gradually transpires that in this triangle, what the subject really seeks is not the object as such but rather the model or mediator as the ultimate signifier of authority and supreme guarantor of meaning.

Kimikiss Pure Rouge draws on the matrix of mimetic desire delineated by Girard, albeit in a modified guise, by implying it in the dramatization of its intradiegetic relationships. By extension, it might also induce its replication at the level of the extradiegetic interaction between the audience and the characters implicated in its polygons — or rather, *erogons*. While the extradiegetic dimension is purely a matter of speculation and it is therefore up to individual spectators to evaluate the likelihood of its occurrence (and potential implications), the latter is traceable within the performative weave of the story itself. It does not, however, manifest itself overtly but is rather hinted at whenever a character deliberately chooses to act in a certain way, to exhibit certain proclivities or, most critically, to elect particular people as their supreme objects of desire. Thus, although the anime's personae may not explicitly adopt one another as models or mediators, one senses the ascendancy of affective undercurrents predicated precisely upon the tricky rhythms of imitation and idealization.

In the musical realm, a particularly intriguing articulation of the relationship between performance and performativity is supplied by *Princess Tutu* through a close focus on the performative dimension of language itself. On both the thematic and the structural planes, this phenomenon is thrown into relief by the interplay of two manifestations of language: the art of writing as a literal ensemble of words, and ballet as a nonverbal sign system. Within the anime's sui generis universe, writing and ballet both sustain and mutually define each other as alternately colluding and colliding forms of language-as-performance. They collude when aspects of a written text and parts of a ballet number strive to convey a shared story. They collide when they fight for supremacy over the characters' lives through the imposition of incompatible narrative options. Thus, the interaction of writing and ballet as performative arts becomes the pivotal means by which the anime's protagonists endeavor to oppose the sinister stories imposed upon them by an external agency through the creation of their own rival yarns, on the one hand, and to consolidate the positive import of their divergent visions, on the other. The protagonist herself, forced to transcend words by the knowledge that were she to declare openly her love she would vanish, learns to rely on the quintessentially nonverbal language of dance not only as a tool for artistic expression but also, in a visceral sense, as a survival mechanism. The drama's creative stance on nonverbal communication parallels the tendency to prioritize musical and visual forms of expression which are not automatically amenable to investigation on the basis of linguistic models: a proclivity, as suggested later in this discussion, inherent in *Nodame Cantabile*.

Before embarking on a detailed discussion of *Princess Tutu*, the transcultural significance of nonverbal language requires some attention insofar as this multifarious semiotic system has played an important part in some of the most inspired and inspiring animated works produced not merely within the sphere of anime but also in the history of Western animation. In this context, one of the most memorable manifestations of the immense performative power inherent in nonverbal language can be found in the works of Yuri Norstein. Profoundly influenced by the compositional conventions of classical music, by pantomime style gestures and postures, and by the highly stylized visual codes of Japanese Kabuki theater, Norstein's cinema communicates a highly distinctive sense of rhythm. This relies crucially, for its overall efficacy, on the punctilious harmonization of motion and timing with the unique expressive powers indigenous solely to the language of silence. The artist's genius is exhaustively documented by the movie anthology *The Complete Works of Yuri Norstein* released in 2006. A particularly touching example of Norstein's creative vision is offered by the short film *Hedgehog in the Fog* (1975), where Norstein is able to communicate simultaneously and with no hint at personal bias the modest beauty of everyday rituals and the sublime beauty of nature's deepest mysteries.

A more recent manifestation of the effectiveness of nonverbal language as a communicational vehicle of great performative and visual puissance is offered by Sylvain Chomet's *The Illusionist* (2010). Chronicling the bittersweet plight of an old-fashioned music-hall conjuror as the lonesome champion of an obsolete art, the film is virtually silent except for a few mumbled snippets of dialogue, choosing to speak to the viewer essentially by means of hand-drawn pencil lines and visual gags. In the process, performance and performativity alike are posited as the essence of a wordless art of visions which paradoxically gains palpability and verisimilitude in inverse proportion to the attenuation of reality as an empirical given. Both visualness and vision are concurrently presented as effects of the visionary powers of a performer and of an audience willing to participate in the parallel world of illusionism — i.e., something more than a mere web of mirages. Chomet's handling of non-verbal language ensures that everything feels intensely present — which may seem ironical when one considers that the film's visuals are predominantly stylized ad dreamlike. In fact, the terse simplicity of the visuals turns out to be precisely what enable the audience to engage directly with the alternate world summoned by the performer.

Princess Tutu foregrounds from the start its dependence on intertwined, nested and traversing performances by recourse to the technique of *mise-en-abyme* (the containment of an image within an image in a fashion that is virtually repeatable ad infinitum). Accordingly, *Princess Tutu* abides in memory as an elaborate story-within-a-story framed by a story which is in turn situated within a ballet nested within a story. Such a description, vertiginous though it might seem, only approximates to the full complexity of the anime's structure and patterning method. These aspects of its dramatic identity are methodically disclosed as the story unfolds. Their exact import cannot be fully appreciated, therefore, until one has reached a relatively advanced stage in the drama. They are, however, ushered in from the start by the drama's key setting: a city shaped by a mechanism which effectively traps it within a story. This tantalizing — though undeniably ominous — contraption is the creation of the powerful mage Drosselmeyer, an author renowned for his power to make fictional yarns come to life. The artificer of the baleful mechanism, though effectively dead, still manages to control it attentively from the heart of its cradle of grinding cogwheels and gears. The character of Drosselmeyer is obviously named after the clockmaker, toymaker and inventor from Hoffmann's "The Nutcracker and the Mouse King," the story on which Tchaikovsky's ballet "The Nutcracker" is based. The intertextual dimension serves to reinforce the anime's overriding preoccupation with the vagaries, joys and mysteries of textuality at large. Stories, in the logic of *Princess Tutu*, are both omnipresent and never-ending. This proposition is economically captured by Drosselmeyer's climactic reflections — "what if I'm a character in someone's story, too"— and eventual decision to leave the scene not in order simply to disappear but rather to "go to another story."

The metafictional aspect, consistently thrown into relief by the strategies of multiple encasement described above, is bolstered by the anime's treatment of its terpsichorean dimension. Whenever the titular character makes an appearance, the standard anime-style backgrounds are superseded by scenarios which are overtly indebted to the spatial priorities of proscenium theater, while the characters themselves are encircled by spotlights intended to emphasize their performative roles. In all of these scenes, the music is meticulously integrated with the flow of the action, and serves to sharpen both our perception of the actors' dynamism and the energy of the colors and shapes, bringing out their own performative worth though an emphasis on the synesthetic resonance of light and line. At the level of the onscreen performance, the action replicates the plot's metafictional thrust by recourse to the ethos and techniques of metatheater in the pure sense of the term — i.e., a type of performance marked by the proclivity to comment on itself, the circumstances of its own production, and its unfolding in the presence of an audience.

This aesthetic choice is encouraged by the eminently stylized nature of the artistic influences which the anime brings to bear on its visuals and on its approach to performance, while striving to choreograph their characteristic tropes with impeccable gusto and a discerning use of suspenseful sequences: namely, ballet and the fairy tale. Both of these forms are so consummately and self-consciously constructed in accordance with well-established visual and performative codes as to preclude all temptations to regard their images as mimetic reflections of the real. In fact, they compel us not only to recognize their artificiality but also, and more critically, to realize that their creative power is inseverable from such artificiality. Extreme stylization, in this context, should never be dismissed as a corollary of unimaginative and stolidly formulaic reliance on convention. It is actually the primary means by which both the anime itself and the art forms which inspire it are able to celebrate their craft and to communicate the distinctiveness of their visions. It is by alerting us to their dependence on time-honored images and motifs that both ballet and the fairy tale are also able to sensitize us to their ability to reconceptualize those elements from within. This is a skill which they consistently demonstrate by juggling their materials as though they were figurative orbs, and hence giving rise to ever-changing cascades, fountains, showers and mills-mess tricks.

Princess Tutu revolves around the proposition that entire lives can be made and unmade through stories, emphasizing the value of language — the vehicle through which those stories are woven and divulged — as an incomparable creative power. Words, the anime incessantly reminds us, do not serve a reportorial function by merely providing an account of an existing state of affairs. Nor do they play a straightforwardly descriptive role by explaining, illustrating or evoking the subtexts which course nonverbal language at all times. In actual fact, they actively construct reality and, by extension, the meanings we choose to attach to particular portions of the real at any one juncture in history and in the service of distinct cultural dicta. By encoding the world we inhabit in virtually all of its expressible manifestations, words define it for us both by naming its components and by circumscribing its compass, thereby creating shifting notions of truth and untruth. Reality, in this regard, constitutes first and foremost a malleable artifact crafted by an artist called language. Most crucially, for the purposes of the present discussion, this artist plays an eminently performative part in the achievement of its creative enterprise, infiltrating everyday activities and remote fantasies alike with dynamism and energy even when it is apparently still, inert and invisible. The worldbuilding flair of the art of writing as a performative endeavor gains special prominence as we discover that each string of words holds a latent capacity to spawn a sprawling semiotic galaxy. Not only are stories posited as animate organisms teeming with unpredictable possibilities and outcomes, multibranching ramifications and prismatic repercussions: in effect, practically each and every line dwelling inside a story — including its seemingly peripheral details and accidental detours — is an embryonic reality pregnant with creative potentialities. As such, it is capable of unleashing a proliferation of further, both actual and hypothetical, developments, convolutions and complications. This expansive perspective on creativity entails that in principle, even a character who originally occupies only a minimal portion of a fiction may unexpectedly obtain not merely a new lease of life but totally novel significance when it is appropriated by another author, rewritten, fleshed out, and by and by turned from a relatively unimportant narrative function into a pivotal presence.

    The key story on which the entire anime's narrative premise is founded is the one held to have been left unfinished by Drosselmeyer when he was killed by people who feared his power to transform fictions into realities. The tale's protagonists, a prince and an evil raven, have found themselves locked in an unending battle as a result of Drosselmeyer's failure to supply them with a satisfying closure. Unhappy with this unresolved state of affairs, the raven extricates himself from the unsuccessful yarn and the prince, in order to contain the enemy again within its designated fictional compass, shatters his own heart into myriad shards. Drosselmeyer, exploiting his ability to go on steering events even after his demise, enables the story to develop a life of its own when he sees a duck observing the prince, whose name is Mytho, as he dances on the water, and decides to transform the bird into a human girl — Ahiru — so that she may help the unfortunate prince regain his heart's scattered fragments. Ahiru finds out about Mytho's shattered heart while attending ballet classes at the school for ordinary humans in which she has enrolled following her portentous transformation, and resolves to help him out by morphing into the formidable superheroine Princess Tutu with the assistance of a magical ovoid pendant which glows red whenever it senses the proximity of one of the lost heart shards. These are lodged within people affected by powerful emotions, which they fuel and amplify with their own affective vigor to noxious effects. To heal the victims of this peculiar predicament, Princess Tutu fathoms their tormented souls by inviting them to dance and by relying on the wordless language of dance as a means of communicating to them a way to overcome it. Once the shards have been thus removed from their unwitting hosts, Princess Tutu can return them to Mytho and gradually abet the reconstitution of his broken heart.

While exploring the performative significance of language, *Princess Tutu* presents identity itself as an effect of performance and performativity. This contention is substantiated by the anime's portrayal of its protagonist as a tripartite being, and as each of Ahiru's three recurrent incarnations as roles rather than as manifestations of some esoteric essence. The duck, the ordinary human girl and the superheroine coexist as parts in a play, fluidly replacing one another according to the drama's circumstances and demands. As the heroine's three roles fluidly alternate throughout the drama, two further characters attempt to shape its course by adopting performative identities of their own which operate by turns as antagonistic and supportive forces within Ahiru's personal quest. One of them is Mytho's girlfriend Rue, who seeks to oppose Princess Tutu's mission for fear that the eventual possession of a whole heart might cause the prince to fall in love with somebody else. Unleashing her own superpowers to morph into Princess Kraehe, Rue is keen not only to prevent Princess Tutu from returning the shards to Mytho but also to gather those precious entities for the sake of the raven, whom she believes to be her father, to help him escape once again. The other key character is Mytho's childhood friend Fakir, a descendant of Drosselmeyer who is also able to shape reality through fictions. Fakir initially strives to hinder Princess Tutu's quest lest the restoration of Mytho's pristine self should enable the old story to unfold once again — which would require the prince to destroy his own heart one more time in order to block the fiendish raven. Despite Rue's and Fakir's fierce antagonism, the heroine persists in pursuing her goal against all odds.

The power of writing as an unrivalled creative force gains fresh prominence as Ahiru comes to realize that Mytho could be conclusively healed with the assistance of one of Fakir's stories. Fakir, however, resolutely resists deploying his gift, which he has perceived as nefarious, and indeed regarded as the trigger of unspeakable horrors, since he was a child. It thus transpires that the reality produced out of one of his stories culminated in the violent death of his own parents even though it had been inspired by benevolent intentions. Aware that his willingness to write again is critical to Mytho's redemption, Fakir eventually yields to the heroine's request, thus enabling Princess Tutu to retrieve the final fragment of the prince's heart and then disappear forever.

At this point, the performative identity revolving around the superheroine's magical feats gives way to an intensely human persona—and, concurrently, to a performance imbued with pure human pathos. This coincides with Ahiru's realization that the restoration of Mytho's heart is not unproblematically conducive to a happy ending and begins to dance, putting her whole being into the performance. This gem of selfless conduct paves the way to further outcomes. Thus, even as Drosselmeyer's notorious preference for tragedy threatens to dominate the climax, Fakir manages to wrest control of the narrative and crowns it with an inspirational finale in which a little duck, though repeatedly assaulted by an army of vicious raven mutants, tenaciously goes on dancing supported by everlasting hope. The heroine's guiding intention, in the climax, is to transcend words by communicating even the most convoluted and troubling of emotions through dance. In their development toward this uplifting culmination, all of the principal characters gradually transcend their archetypal meanings to acquire the function of interpreters of an intricate skein of dark existential issues. These gravitate around a battle against determinism which requires selfless commitment to the recovery of dormant emotions, and a dispassionate exploration of the feasibility of distinguishing lived experience from fiction and, by extension, living from storytelling.

All of the protagonist's roles are intrinsically gendered insofar as each draws attention in its own stylish manner to Ahiru's femininity as a duck, as a human girl, and as a magical creature. Accordingly, they are instrumental in the advancement of the metafiction's romantic strand and of the heroine's efforts to grapple with the broader implications of her multifaceted selfhood, progressively bolstering her resolve to accept her nonhuman origins, and hence embrace the duck persona and its destiny as her most appropriate options. Ahiru's mature resignation to her fundamental nature draws attention to her irreducible otherness, thus reminding us of the character's latent association with the charismatic figure of the swan maiden, here discussed in Chapter 2 vis-à-vis the movie *Swan Lake*. *Princess Tutu*'s protagonist may not overtly conform with the classic type, since it does not exhibit its legendary amalgam of innocence and seductiveness, and its simultaneous resemblance to a standard fairy tale orphan, on the one hand, and to a treacherous femme fatale, on the other. Yet, Ahiru's metamorphic powers and multiple performative identity ultimately serve to emplace her as a member of that hybrid progeny, albeit an unusual and uniquely endearing one. Rue's and Fakir's roles are also carefully defined with reference to gender to the extent that the girl's quest proceeds from Eros-dominated imperatives, while the youth's gradual development of contrasting feelings toward Ahiru—ranging from scorn through tolerance to affection and respect—are themselves tinged with romantic connotations.

Princess Tutu's emphasis on the performance-related character of identity, and specifically of gendered identity, brings to mind Judith Butler's analysis of the concept of gender itself as a fundamentally performative phenomenon. Gender, Butler contends in *Gender Trouble* (1990), is not only a cultural construct but also a type of performance revolving around the adoption and display of distinctive signs and on the ritualized repetition of a particular repertoire of conventional acts. Any sense of coherence or continuity which the self might presume to realize can only ever be a corollary of the reiteration of given forms of role-playing. "There is no gender identity behind the expressions of gender," Butler maintains, because "identity is performatively constituted by the very 'expressions' that are said to be its results" (Butler, J., 1990, p. 25). This daring reversal of traditional causality mirrors the anime's tendency to question many of the unexamined assumptions on which classical logic thrives, and hence release a dizzying web of metafictions and metarealities. Since all gender categories imply the possibility of disparate kinds of performance, it is preposterous to champion the essentialist approach to identity as an ontological immutability. Far more fruitful, according to Butler, is the notion of identity as "a history of identifications, parts of which can be brought into play in given contexts and which, precisely because they encode the contingencies of personal history, do not always point back to an internal coherence of any kind" (p. 331).

In *Bodies That Matter* (1993), Butler both extends and redefines her original views on performativity in ways which strike even more resonant chords with the self-reflexive drama articulated in *Princess Tutu*. This text focuses on the practices through which dominant conventions come to determine the very matter of which our bodies consist. Reflecting on the work, Butler has described her aims as follows: "one of the interpretations that has been made of *Gender Trouble* is that ... if gender is performative it must be radically free. And it has seemed to many that the materiality of the body is vacated or ignored or negated here — disavowed, even.... So what became important to me in writing *Bodies that Matter* was to go back to the category of sex, and to the problem of materiality, and to ask how it is that sex itself might be construed as a norm ... I wanted to work out how a norm actually materialises a body, how we might understand the materiality of the body to be not only invested with a norm, but in some sense animated by a norm, or contoured by a norm" (Butler, J., 1994). The visible metamorphoses undergone by Ahiru as she switches identities and attendant appearances, accordingly adopting different roles within her personal relationships, could be seen as stages in a fluid history of the kind which Butler presents as pivotal to the construction of identity in the later book.

Princess Tutu consistently underscores the mutability of the linguistic parameters brought to bear on the construction of reality in keeping with specific circumstances and with their contingent requirements. It thus throws into relief the sheer performative fluidity of all identities fashioned by language. This message finds a particularly compelling formulation in the anime's climactic episodes. While the baleful storyline traced by the evil Drosselmeyer is ultimately displaced by a more optimistic narrative pathway, it is never altogether elided or suppressed. In other words, even as the anime pays homage to a widespread (albeit far from universal) fairy tale formula in granting us a happy ending, it does not encourage us to forget the possibility of bleak alternatives. In fact, it allows those unchosen narrative options to maintain a phantasmatic presence within the drama as persistent and shadowy vestiges. The realized story is allowed to assert its contingent dominance at the syntagmatic level, and hence to hold credence and performative primacy within an identifiable stretch of time and space. Nevertheless, the vast paradigm of unaccomplished potential alternatives vibrantly announces its aliveness both in the interstices of the anime's finale and beyond its closing frame. The vision disclosed by *Princess Tutu* is that of a quantum theory universe in which seemingly irreconcilable realities must be seen to coexist, and any one concept or action must therefore be grasped not according to the binary logic of opposition and mutual exclusion but rather in terms of its accommodation of incalculable and discordant multiplicities.

The series' adventurous take on the art of writing finds a direct generic correlative in its own authors' innovative approach to a popular anime modality: namely, the magical girl (*mahou shoujo*) show. Few directors could ever be expected to be more intimately familiar with this kind of anime than Junichi Sato, the creative talent responsible for helming the TV series with which the magical girl show is instantly associated even outside anime circles, *Sailor Moon*. *Princess Tutu* appears to comply with the standard set of codes and conventions associated with that format in its opening episodes, and continues to leave their overall validity unquestioned until roughly the half-way mark. From that point onward, however, virtually all expectations commonly surrounding the *mahou shoujo* typology are systematically dislodged and subverted. Accordingly, it is in the second half of the series that the boundary between reality and fiction is obfuscated virtually beyond recognition. *Swan Lake*, as shown in Chapter 2, endeavored to match its settings to the emotional range evoked by Tchaikovsky's music, allowing the music itself to guide its visual flow. *Princess Tutu*'s score also relies heavily on the Russian composer's oeuvre — especially *The Nutcracker* but also *Swan Lake* and *Sleeping Beauty* — even though it also incorporates pieces by other classical composers, including Mendelssohn, Prokofiev, Ravel, Mussorgsky, Schumann, Bizet, Saint-Saens, Wagner, Beethoven, Strauss, Satie, Mozart, Chopin, Rimsky-Korsakov, and

Kaoru Wada. In its approach to Tchaikovsky's music, *Princess Tutu* expands considerably the landscape of musical-visual correspondences suggested by *Swan Lake*. While the 1981 movie aims for allusive conciseness, which is entirely appropriate to its feature-length format and capsulated narrative disposition, the 2002 series capitalizes on its substantial dramatic breadth (38 installments) in order to elaborate the immense potentialities of figurative landscape as a metaphor for music. It hence creates a resonant environment in which the terrain, vegetation, water and atmosphere coalesce in an incessantly shifting architecture of rhythms and forms. As it sensitively registers the diurnal and seasonal cycles, *Princess Tutu*'s landscape manages to capture the spirit of music in a veritably symphonic fashion.

Nodame Cantabile stands out as one of the most original and thought-provoking anime in which music plays a pivotal dramatic role to have been produced not only in recent decades but also in the history of the form at large. The show's musical emphasis is instantly announced by its very title: *cantabile* is indeed a musical term of Italian provenance which literally translates as "singable" or "songlike" but has also, by extension, come to designate a smooth, flowing and tuneful style. Shinichi, the male lead, defines the heroine's own performing style as *cantabile* (as well as *capriccioso*, i.e., "whimsical") early in the first season, instinctively recognizing that term as the most apposite epithet for the free-spirited and seemingly unrestrained manner in which she plays the piano: an approach which the accomplished musician's traditionalist and perfectionist disposition logically ought to abhor, yet carries enticing connotations even for such a punctilious performer.

Nodame Cantabile is an anime to be remembered not only for its unique juxtaposition of effervescent comedy and poignant drama — undeniable and commendable though this is — but also for its special capacity to establish a dynamically symbiotic relationship between performance and performativity. The anime assiduously endeavors to emphasize the significance of performance as the enactment, both public and private, of specific artistic gifts (including extempore inspiration) and technical abilities. At the same time, it foregrounds with equal dedication and consistency the aesthetic import of performance as the realization of abstract ideals through the conception of forms which are capable of concretizing — and even visualizing — the impalpable and the invisible. These twin aspects of the show's aesthetic are vitally important in determining its distinctive flavor. However, *Nodame Cantabile* does not concentrate singlemindedly on the phenomenon of performance as a concrete physical occurrence. In fact, it concurrently seeks to underscore the intrinsic performativity of the medium it brings into play as an entity which holds potential value as performance even when it is not physically harnessed to tangible presentation. At this level of the drama, *Nodame Cantabile* focuses on those expressive elements of the art of music which are not overtly performance-driven and yet are so energetic, so palpably charged with animateness, as to stand out as actions rather than as inert notions. Eager to highlight the interaction of performance and performativity from the very start of the first season, *Nodame Cantabile* progressively elaborates the complexity of the bond over the two following seasons.

The drama pivots on Megumi Noda, a.k.a. "Nodame," as she adamantly insists on being called: a talented second-year piano student at Momogaoka College of Music. The anime's comic dimension, evinced throughout by its zestful humor and rippling energy, is instantly announced by its heroine's portrayal as a careless, indolent and voracious girl who will exploit any pretext to play by ear rather than in accordance with orthodox notation. Pivotal to the entire drama over its three-season unfolding is Nodame's romantic attraction to the portentously gifted third-year student Shinichi Chiaki. A snobbish and arrogant polyglot born into a musical family and brought up in several European countries, the youth is equally accomplished at the piano and the violin but secretly aspires to become a conductor and trains himself to this effect while majoring in the piano. At the same time, Shinichi is haunted by a pathologically severe fear of flying which prevents him from going abroad to study and to pursue his dream of becoming a renowned conductor. The youth's entrapment in this psychological deadlock initially supplies the series with a perfect excuse for some exuberant comic moments but gradually gains depth as the phobia's origin in a traumatic juvenile experience is revealed. Concurrently, Nodame's loathing of traditional musical instruction is incrementally shown to emanate from her childhood subjection to an abusive piano teacher.

Compared to an "imp" when she behaves in a wayward or devious fashion, the heroine is nonetheless also depicted as a benevolent presence, capable of operating as a catalyst among hostile or incompatible forces, and thus bringing them together or even paving the way to their hoped-for reconciliation. This power is both eloquently and touchingly confirmed by Nodame's ability to revive the latent artistic leanings of Shinichi's family, long repressed in the service of economic achievement and philistine utilitarianism. The flair for spiritual healing evinced by the girl at several critical junctures — without, it must be stressed, deteriorating into New Age mysticism — is beautifully captured by the assessment of her character proffered by one of the key judges in a competition joined by Nodame in the first season's climactic episodes. At one stage, he explicitly equates the girl to an "*onibi* [demon fire] trying to bewitch travelers." Interestingly, this evaluation is put forward in the course of Nodame's performance of Franz Liszt's Transcendental Etude No. 5 in B-flat *Feux Follets* (i.e., Will o' the Wisp). It is noteworthy, in this regard, that the anime does not limit the development of its fantastic strand to the portrayal of the heroine, which could easily have come across as a single-minded insistence on her specialness at the expense of the realistically multi-faceted representation of a comprehensive character gallery. This is succinctly borne out, later in the same contest, by the description of Nodame's dreaded rival as "a little demon wandering the streets late at night, when people seldom walk," redolent of "the phantom Scarbo"—a character, as the judge's assistant emphasizes, traditionally regarded as "a fairy." The piece being performed in this instance is indeed Maurice Ravel's *Gaspard de la Nuit*, Third Movement, "Scarbo," where this being is presented as something of a ghostly goblin.

In its elaboration of the bond between performance and performativity, *Nodame Cantabile* reveals rare sensitivity to the interplay of music and the emotions, which sets it clearly apart from many other anime concerned with the art of music in more literal ways. In the process, it brings into play three types of the emotions: those of the music per se, those of the players and listeners involved in the story itself, and those of the anime's audience. Focusing throughout, with varied degrees of emphasis and explicitness, on how music can express emotions at all, *Nodame Cantabile* thus engages simultaneously with how players and listeners, both intradiegetic and extradiegetic, develop and articulate their emotional responses to music. The anime's exploration of such elemental phenomena invites us to reflect not only on why people react affectively to music and on the mechanisms through which they manifest their feelings but also on the aesthetic significance of their experiences. A particularly intriguing question, in this context, concerns the ambiguous relationship between pleasure and unease—an issue thrown into relief by the realization that music may be able to induce melancholy or sadness, for example, even at its most vivacious, or else inspire elating emotions while emitting the softest and most pensive of notes. In addressing this topos, the anime alludes to the theory of associationism, which proposes that certain emotional states are conventionally associated with particular musical elements or strategies. Through its attentive presentation of its intradiegetic listeners' reactions to diverse compositions, techniques and styles, the show repeatedly suggests that this approach is simply inadequate to account for the subjective fluctuations to which any one listener's responses to any one passage of music are susceptible. A slow tempo is not mechanically conducive to a somber or reflective mood any more that a sparkling one automatically unleashes exhilaration or euphoria.

Music's ability to appeal to emotions both more directly and more intensely than any other art has often been adduced as one of the key reasons for electing it as an exemplary model for the visual arts to emulate. Relatedly, as Peter Vergo argues, visual painters have been drawn to the "seemingly vague, imprecise character" of this art, which seems to afford "more room for inspiration and for the irrational aspect of creativity" while also allowing "listeners to invent 'meanings' of their own" (Vergo, p. 8). Even more importantly, music has attracted visual artists for its eminently "non-imitative character" (p. 9). The non-representational nature of the art of music has time and again been highlighted by visual artists eager to absorb its lessons into their own practice. Eugène Delacroix, for example, commended the ostensibly imprecise character of music, which allows it to transcend the limitations of verbal language, as an ideal to be emulated by painting through the pursuit of a poetics of vagueness and imprecision. In a similar vein, the painter Paul Gaugin states that the art painting should "seek suggestion rather than description, as in fact does music" (cited in Junod, p. 30). This vision echoes Japanese art's proverbial cultivation of imprecision and allusiveness as crucial aesthetic tenets. James Abbott McNeill Whistler, a painter also discussed in Chapter 1, likewise posits imprecision as the primary objective of the art of painting, championing a visual style which could provide "the exact correlative of music, as vague, as purely emotional, as released from all functions of representation" (cited in Vergo, p. 72). In addition, Whistler was eager to establish visual harmonies which would integrate not solely the shapes and colors on the canvas, wood or paper but also the frame by devoting no less care to the ornamentation of this portion of the artifact than to the execution of the painting itself. In this regard, Whistler's approach bears a direct resemblance to the Japanese tendency to emphasize the artistic status of decoration as no less respectable an art form than painting or sculpture themselves.

The philosophical complexity of music's emotional substance is underscored by *Nodame Cantabile*'s subtle differentiation between expression and expressivity. The former refers to a person's overt demonstration of his or her affective state, whereas the latter designates a more elusive propensity inherent in the artwork itself: an affective current which a piece of music or musical performance as such ought not, strictly speaking, to be capable of releasing insofar as it is not in itself a psychological agent, or performer, in the way a person is, and yet has the power to evoke in more poignant a fashion than either description or representation could ever aspire to accomplish. The anime delicately prompts us to contemplate the possibility that this conundrum might actually constitute one of the deepest — and most bewitching — of the mysteries to which music owes a considerable proportion of its beauty. The relationship between expression and expressivity forms a dyad which complements the performance/performativity pair. Indeed, just as performativity differs from performance per se insofar as it embraces the potential for enactment intrinsic in a medium rather than its contingent manifestations as spectacle, so expressivity encompasses the emotional import which animates a piece of music as a latent energy regardless of its perceptible constellation as a semiotic ensemble. Music, *Nodame Cantabile* persistently intimates, is expressive independently of the specific emotions which a composer channels into its creation or a player into its performance. Besides, its fluid character is reinforced by the variability of the receiver's responses, which can logically be expected to alter over time and even from one hearing to the next.

The emotional import of musical performance is foregrounded in the climactic installment in which Nodame plays a piano concerto in London with Stresemann as conductor. The anime's audience, like the audiences whose hearts are captured by Nodame's art not only within the auditorium but across the globe, is temporarily transposed to a dimension in which the passage of time seems to have come to a halt and everyday perceptions to be bathed in an atmosphere of unreal, suspended elegance. Yet, the anime does not totally relinquish its sense of humor even on this poignant occasion. In fact, it still endeavors to strike comical chords by setting up a strident discrepancy between the theater's magical mood and the almost crudely corporeal sense of presence evoked by Nodame's motion and grim mien as she walks onto the stage despite the otherworldly appeal of her gown. In this sequence, director Kasai appears to be relying to a significant degree on the principle of incongruity as a mainstay of his characterization techniques, in much the same way as he did in the portrayal of Hagumi in *Honey and Clover*, here examined in depth in Chapter 2. Most importantly, the conservatively traditional setting in which Nodame's performance takes place is infused with novel vitality by its underlying performativity: that is to say, by a virtually boundless reservoir of creative and expressive potentialities. At the same time, the visuality of the sequence is irreducible to its elemental status as a visual event within the conventional space of the performance, and enters the realm of vision as an effort to ideate the invisible energies which course the performer's art.

Nodame herself is instinctively inclined to envision the emotional substance of the pieces she plays throughout the series in terms of either snippets of memories of mundane occurrences or fantasy scenarios bursting with imaginary actors and magical settings, regularly punctuated by cameo appearances by the characters in her favorite anime and multimedia franchise, *Puri-Gorota*. Despite Nodame's overactive imagination and attraction to childlike pursuits, her overall grasp of fantastic matters never indulges in romantic soppiness. In fact, some of the most arresting scenes she visualizes in accordance with fantasy formulae of a conventional stamp tend to feature ill-fated figures and tragic dénouements. This contention is emblematically validated by Nodame's visual and performative interpretation of the "pitiful end" suffered by the eponymous clown puppet Petrouchka from Igor Stravinsky's ballet, which she sees as comparable to her own failure when a malicious opponent (the "Scarbo" performer himself) teases her with incapacitating reminders of her juvenile tribulations. In addition, Nodame gives vent to her passion for fantastic characters through costume design and, relatedly, cosplay. This is borne out by the charmingly bizarre mongoose outfit she dons to perform a harmonica solo when "Orchestra S" makes its daring appearance at the school festival. In the Paris-based arc, the heroine enjoys a unique opportunity to indulge her impersonation fetish when she is invited to perform at the grand abode of a "Mozart maniac," and her gown's accidental tearing gives her a perfect pretext for wearing one of the original Mozart child outfits treasured by her patron.

Nodame's inclination to ideate the passages she plays with reference to visual images and animations serves as an elliptical commentary on the relationship between music and language as concurrently syntactical and semantic formations. The preference for visualization over verbalization underscores the irreducibility of music to a sign system equivalent to verbal language, and therefore graspable according to linguistic criteria. *Nodame Cantabile* thus reminds us that music is not about emotions in the way language is insofar as it has the expressive power to embody emotions rather than simply describe them. In other words, music is capable of harboring and feeding emotions within its very texture instead of simply stating their existence from an external standpoint. Nodame's visualizing flair reaches an apotheosis in the sequence where she communicates the visions she associates with an eminently juvenile *kawaii* piece of her own invention to her new piano teacher, the formidable Kouzou Etou, drawing him into the song's fantasy world and its population of dancing animals. At this point, the heroine's power acquires veritably world-building magnitude. Notable in itself as evidence for the strength of Nodame's infectious enthusiasm, this occurrence is rendered all the more remarkable by the nature of the person on whom she spontaneously works her magic. Etou is indeed widely renowned as an exceptionally influential but no less strict instructor. His severity is proverbially encapsulated by his dubious habit of carrying a *harisen* (the "slapping fan" used in traditional comedy shows) to his lessons — a weapon he deploys to chastize the pupils he deems negligent at the slightest infraction. The teacher's nickname is indeed "*Harisen sensei*." Etou has only agreed to listen to Nodame's compositions in exchange for her promise to accept him as a tutor thereafter. Yet, in the presence of her ostensibly inane melodic creations, even *Harisen sensei* is so deeply affected by the vitality of the images which her music is intended to convey as to become quite absorbed in the exercise, and to start ideating his own alternative versions of the scenarios suggested by Nodame's performance.

The protagonist's visualizing propensity should also be understood as a key facet of a broader stylistic proclivity which pervades the fabric of the franchise as a whole: an unflinching dedication to the drama's visual dimension. While the show's musical dimension is indubitably prominent, it is vital to acknowledge that *Nodame Cantabile* owes much of its dramatic verve to its beautifully animated drawings and ample, yet never gratuitously formulaic, range of character designs: in other words, to its more eminently visual components. Attentively harmonized with the anime's stunning soundtrack, the visuals both contribute to the music's dramatic impact and draw energy from its invisible forms. What imparts the show's visual aspect with a distinctive aesthetic identity is its ability to assert its originality not by laying it out before its viewers as a complete spectacle which they have no choice but to observe and absorb in a fundamentally passive fashion but rather as a process requiring their active participation in the actualization of potential messages. Thus, *Nodame Cantabile*'s visuals could be said to corroborate the contention, advanced earlier in this chapter, that visuality is not coterminous with visualness as the mere state of being visual but actually entails a perceiver's imaginative involvement and interaction with the image — that is to say, the preparedness, ability and desire to entertain a vision. Therefore, as the same time as it eagerly highlights the collusion of performance and performativity, *Nodame Cantabile* is also keen to alert us to the twofoldness inherent in the phenomenon of visuality.

Although the heroine is the character who most persistently evinces an instinctive proclivity to visualize musical passages in both vivid and dynamic terms, other actors concurrently reinforce this aspect of the anime through their visualizing instinct. The endearingly quirky violin student Ryutarou Mine, for example, has a natural tendency to translate the sentiments which he perceives within a piece of music into visual images. On occasion, he even goes as far as giving vent to this passion through the conception of costumes for the orchestra members. The youth also pictures his own style as the offspring of a profoundly personal vision, even though others (and especially the perfectionist Shinichi) are more inclined to regard it as simply sloppy and unrefined. In order to express the energy and passion inherent in Beethoven's Symphony No. 3 ("Eroica"), Ryutarou encourages his fellow players in the violin section of the orchestra to perform a bold flourish intended to emulate Jimi Hendrix's style and infuse a touch of "rock" in the composition. Other characters consolidate the drama's visualizing thrust as a result of their symbolic association with particular images or even disembodied waves of color. A memorable example is provided by the installment in which Nodame discovers that Shinichi has decided to conduct Mozart's Oboe Concerto in C Major with the character of the highly gifted oboe player Yasunori Kuroki in the capacity of soloist. Nodame finds this decision most amusing, insofar as she instinctively perceives Mozart's music as "pink-colored" and therefore incongruous with Shinichi's stern personality. Yasunori is silently associated by the conductor himself with the austere image of a "warrior," while the notes exuded by his instrument are compared to a "dull silver." When Yasunori falls in love with Nodame at first sight and, oblivious to her true nature and horribly shoddy habits, instantly proceeds to idealize her as an angelically pure and ethereal being, his music suddenly acquires emotive nuances which Shinichi visualizes as indeed "pink." Love, incidentally, also appears to have a softening — and comparably color-coded — impact on the character of the prodigiously talented violin player Kyora Miki as soon as she begins to develop feelings for Ryutarou.

The Russian piano student Tatiana ("Tanya") Vishneva, who lives in the same apartment block as Shinichi and Nodame in Paris, later describes Yasunori as "glauque"— by which she means dark and depressing, even though the term also translates as "blue-green" or "sea-green." This point deserves expansion, in this context, insofar as the contrasting interpretations of this color centered on the character of the apparently dour oboe player actually carry broader cultural implications. Equated in many cultures with spirituality, sincerity, inspiration, calm and moderation, blue also holds an unmatched capacity to convey the impression of distance, and has thus served an eminently technical purpose in several pictorial traditions as a means of conveying the illusion of perspective and depth. In conjunction with green, and especially in the shade of blue tinged with green known as turquoise, the properties conventionally associated with blue are combined with feelings of refreshing energy, fervor and motivation. The feelings of detachment and gravity which Yasunori characteristically, though unselfconsciously, tends to communicate to his peers explains Tanya's choice of the term "glauque" as an apt personality marker. However, the vibrant energy which typically flows though Yasunori's performance tinges his blue-hued aloofness with invigorating emotions for which green provides an apposite chromatic correlative. As seen in Chapter 2, blue holds special significance in the Japanese color spectrum and related symbolic code, being associated not only with the conventional property of coolness which so may cultures accord it but also with mystical and lyrical connotations of metaphysical magnitude. An even wider range of interesting associations comes into play when blue merges with or approximates to green, the classic Japanese emblem of immortality and life-giving sap. It is also important to appreciate that the modern Japanese noun *ao* (adjective: *aoi*) encompasses what Anglophone speakers would think of as both blue and green at once. Although the Japanese language does contain a distinct word for green, *midori*, its connotations are by no means identical to those carried by "green" in English. Introduced in the Heian period, when (as noted in Chapter 1 in relation to the art of fashion) Japan's chromatic sensibility feasibly reached its apotheosis, the term would undoubtedly capture a gamut of aesthetic and affective nuanced inconceivable today.

Colors do not only serve as character-specific symbolic markers in *Nodame Cantabile*. In fact, they constitute a major component of the anime's visual identity, pervading the fabric of its musical performance both at the level of realized events and at the level of performativity: that is to say, of implied, recalled or anticipated enactments. Thus, at the same time as it experiments with the dramatic potentialities inherent in its hues by alternating between vivid palettes and melodious watercolor effects, *Nodame Cantabile* concurrently focuses on the tone color characteristic of each of the instruments it brings into play, and on the orchestral colors generated by the encounter of diverse instruments within a performance. While drawing attention to the musical properties of color, or the chromatic connotations of music as the case may be, the anime also proposes intriguing affinities between the art of music and other aspects of pictorial composition. At times, it cultivates the integration of musical and pictorial elements so passionately as to bring to mind the nineteenth-century Neoclassical French painter Jean August Dominique Ingres' advice to his students: "if I could make musicians of you all, it would be to your advantage as painters. All is harmony in nature, a little too much, or a little less, disturbs the scale and strikes a discordant note. One has to learn to sing true with the pencil or brush, just as with the voice; correct form is like correct sound" (cited in "The Jackson Symphony").

Another intriguing manifestation of the intersection of painting and music in the cultural climate outlined above is offered by the works of the Neo-Impressionist painter Paul Signac. This artist indeed regarded his pictorial creations, and especially the riverscapes and seascapes which featured prevalently in his work throughout the late 1880s and the early 1890s, as akin to music. The series titled *La Mer*, in particular, is best approached as an attempt to paint a symphony. Signac underscores this analogy by comparing the Neo-Impressionist artist to a composer: "the painter has played on his keyboard of colors in the same way that a composer handles the diverse instruments to orchestrate a symphony" (Signac, p. 126). In Signac's musical sceneries, mood, harmony and thoroughly calculated rhythmic arrangements are consistently given priority over any considerations of mimetic verisimilitude. While Signac sought to capture the boundless drama of water in paintings capable of embodying the energy of music, the composer Claude Debussy, conversely, strove to translate music into a painting by evoking a visual image of the sea with his own *La Mer*, a symphony produced in 1905. The French composer drew inspiration from Claude Monet's Impressionist works, from William Turner's glowing seascapes and, above all, from the painting *The Wave* by Japanese *ukiyo-e* artist Katsushika Hokusai — the terrifying, yet strangely elegant, harbinger of a potential *tsunami*. (The composer was indeed fascinated with Japanese woodblock prints and Eastern art at large.) Debussy's painterly imagination no doubt ensues from his instinctive attraction to the visual image, a passion to which he overtly draws attention in a letter to Edgar Varèse of 1911: "I love pictures almost as much as music" (Debussy, p. 1389). In Debussy's hands, the fundamentally acoustic medium at his disposal acquires visual qualities so pronounced as to render it akin to a palette of notes. Camille Mauclair has explicitly compared the musician to a painter and his compositions to Monet's landscapes in his vivid assessment of Debussy's music, describing it as "based not on a succession of themes but on the relative values of sounds themselves.... It is Impressionism consisting of sonorous patches" (cited in Lockspeiser, p. 18). Debussy himself appears to have been naturally inclined to perceive direct affinities between the musical and the pictorial realms, as exemplified by his comments on the works of the sixteenth-century composers Orlando di Lasso and Giovanni Pierluigi da Palestrina: "the melodic lines unfold in a way that reminds you of illuminated manuscripts and ancient missals" (Debussy, pp. 44–45).

In the region of line, *Nodame Cantabile* suggests subtle parallels between the musical meaning of the term as the series of notes defining the shape or contour of a melody, and its visual significance as the elemental principle on the basis of which animation creates the impression of motion, and from which varied dynamic configurations accordingly ensue. Linear arrangements, like music, can be said to have a certain tempo, the impressions of speed and slowness, of acceleration and deceleration, depending on a line's length, thickness and coloration. The emotional significance of the line as an entity capable of impacting on the perceiver's mind and senses is beautifully highlighted by Moses Mendelssohn (the composer Felix Mendelssohn's grandfather) in the treatise *On Sensations*: "a line, if suddenly interrupted, could to some extent serve to depict fright, while a succession of rapidly intersecting lines might represent anger, in the same way that the artless prolonging of a gently undulating line represents a kind of mental absorption.... Could one not insert an admixture of melodious colours into the play of one another of these lines? Could one not, in order better to please the eye, combine various kinds of undulating lines with those shaped like tongues of fire?" (cited in Stelzer, p. 132). These observations, noteworthy as they are in anticipating certain aesthetic developments characteristic of abstract painting, are also astoundingly relevant to anime as an art form whose emotive impact results to a significant extent on linear strategies of the very kind which Moses Mendelssohn envisages.

Moreover, the anime extends the geometrical analogy connecting drawn and musical lines into the realm of solids through Tanya's lyrical description on the sensations unleashed by Nodame's performance as "beautiful and perfectly spherical beads of sound." At the same time, the action consistently matches the acoustic alternation of the ascending and descending lines in a melodic structure to the visual juxtaposition of the ascending and descending lines of its graphics. In both areas, intervals of varying magnitude are deployed to generate either gliding or angular patterns, and thus impart both sounds and images with different degrees of harmony and energy, smoothness and bounciness, quietude and urgency. It is from these sensory impressions that the overall form of both a piece of music and a constellation of drawn images ensues, and the processes through which their building blocks are assembled may be progressively grasped. In the pursuit of formal balance, the anime assiduously translates the quintessentially musical property of rhythm into the visual property pivotal to the effectiveness of the composition *qua* animation. This typically manifests itself as the tempo or beat according to which the illusion of movement is created by alternately inviting the eye to skip swiftly and glide quietly from one frame to the next.

Moreover, the linear energy of both musical performance and drawn animation is enhanced by the anime's deft handling of texture. Thus, the visuals strive to suggest the specific feel of its objects though the pictorial simulation of smooth and rough surfaces at the same time as the music weaves its fabric of horizontal elements, which form the melody, and vertical elements, which form the harmony. The principle of contrast is particularly useful in abetting the emergence of these concurrently graphic and auditory effects in the areas of line, form, rhythm and texture. Numerous pieces performed either as protracted components of the action (e.g., Rachmaninov's Piano Concerto No. 2 in C minor, Gershwin's *Rhapsody in Blue* "Piano and Harmonica Version"], Mozart's Sonata for Two Pianos in D major, Brahms' Symphony No. 1 in C minor) or as fleeting cameo citations, rely to a crucial extent on contrasts produced through dynamic oppositions of loud and quiet sections, through stylistic alternations of smooth songlike passages and choppy rhythmical passages, and through orchestration strategies which juxtapose sections played by string, percussion and wind instruments. These musical contrasts are studiously accompanied by visual contrasts conceived by highlighting the kinetic divergences between various elements of a frame or sequences of frames. Colors again assert their technical ascendancy, in this context, insofar as the anime's chromatic oppositions of bright and soft hues drawn from both the cool and the warm ends of the spectrum (and combined or contrasted with angular and rounded shapes) are an especially efficient means of accomplishing that ruse.

Performance and visuality come together most vibrantly, from a strictly dramatic point of view, in the portrayal of personal relationships as forever evolving clusters of multiple performances and cognate visual symbols. The protagonists and their artistic gifts are obviously pivotal to this crucial aspect of the story. While Shinichi is slow to recognize Nodame's authentic worth, the two characters laboriously progress toward the establishment of a reciprocally enriching relationship—a bond which transcends the boundaries of mere romantic infatuation and actually enables them to learn some precious lessons about both themselves and their peers, friends, relatives, tutors and sponsors. Nodame learns from Shinichi the necessity of confronting her most inveterate fears and taking risks, when appropriate, as the prerequisite of her artistic development. Concomitantly, Shinichi begins to rise above his self-centered superciliousness, to appreciate other people's distinctive gifts and aspirations, and to respect with equal poise both their virtues and their foibles when Nodame first encourages him to lead a student orchestra. Sharp-tongued, cynical and undemonstrative though he may be, the youth is ultimately as vulnerable as anyone of his less skillful or privileged peers and, therefore, no less touchingly human. If anything, Shinichi's mask (to invoke again one this chapter's main motifs) serves to augment his underlying weakness as one discovers that it is essentially an obvious, albeit elaborate, defensive mechanism. Shinichi's inherent ability to transcend his arrogance evolves slowly and the audience, accordingly, discovers its existence and potentialities at the same pace as the youth himself does. Particularly significant are the installments in which he gradually and tentatively learns to interact with people who, though far less gifted than him, have the capacity to teach him the supreme worth of collaborative effort and unselfish inventiveness. In this regard, Shinichi learns more from the eccentric members of "Orchestra S" than he could ever hope to learn either from the highfliers of "Orchestra A" or from any well-established and globally acclaimed maestro.

The chief architect of the challenges met by Shinichi in his quest to become a conductor—the greatest trials he has thus far had to face in his relatively charmed existence—is Stresemann, the internationally renowned conductor who visits Momogaoka College as a guest instructor. Firstly, the maestro opposes Shinichi's ambition by tersely rejecting each of his repeated applications to major in conducting. Secondly, he exposes his shortcomings as a would-be conductor by forcing him to recognize his inadequate understanding of interpersonal dynamics and resulting failure to communicate constructively with his colleagues. Stresemann himself, conversely, is someone who spontaneously "nurtures" other people and thus enables them to "flourish" even if their talent is not remarkable and their performative appeal not obvious—a reality which Shinichi rapidly discovers by observing the maestro in action. According to the voiceover closing the relevant episode, the youth will later acknowledge that this revelation caused his personal evolution—not just as an aspiring conductor but also as a human being—to undergo a "one hundred and eighty degrees" reorientation even though at the time he had no conscious idea that this was the case. Thirdly, even after he has eventually resolved to appoint Shinichi to the status of his personal conducting assistant, Stresemann goes on challenging the boy by requiring him to confront incrementally arduous tests. An especially formative moment, in this regard, consists of Shinichi's performance of Rachmaninoff's Piano Concerto No. 2 in C minor with the main school orchestra as Stresemann himself acts as the conductor. This event contributes significantly both to the youth's personal maturation and to the consolidation of the anime's philosophical message. This is pithily communicated by the quirky maestro himself in the scene immediately preceding his and Shinichi's public appearance, where he goads his apprentice on with these words: "let's go have some fun by playing some music."

The refreshing thing about Stresemann's portrayal is that he is never posited as a perfect mentor or idealized as a paragon of virtue. In fact, he is depicted as a signally undignified lecher who would rather spend his time dating young girls and patronizing host clubs and night clubs than attending rehearsals or instructing his pupils. Even the maestro's stubborn refusal to accept Shinichi as his conducting student is triggered entirely by a grudge of an amorous nature which he bears against Sebastiano Viella — the great conductor whom Shinichi met in childhood and instantly began to idealize as his future instructor. Stresemann, moreover, does not deem it necessary to conceal his vindictiveness behind a façade of loftier (or at least more rational) motives. In fact, he snubs the youth's pleas most unceremoniously and, in response to Shinichi's request for the reason behind his rejection, he simply states: "I hate you" and "you piss me off"— such feelings, he adds as an afterthought as though to seal the finality of his pronouncement, should just be accepted as a "common occurrence" in human intercourse. Even after befriending the aspiring conductor, Stresemann goes on resenting most fiercely his good looks, natural charisma and popularity among ladies of all ages. Moreover, Stresemann's professional decisions often appear so arbitrary as to verge on the fascistic, and his overall conduct so demanding as to make his sheer presence in a room quite overwhelming. As the series progresses and Stresemann gradually exhibits degrees of compassion, solidarity and paternal benevolence of which one would not initially have held him capable, his personality retains a mischievous edge. Thus, in the late installment where he urges Nodame to make her debut with the performance of a piano concerto at a prestigious event in which he will personally feature as the conductor, the anime's use of visual imagery imbued with Faustian undertones serves to present him as something of a latter-day Mephistopheles.

Nodame Cantabile is keen to emphasize that without pleasure, music is powerless to affect either the performer or the listener. The anime's rich character gallery attests to this proposition with prismatic diversity, indicating that all of its members — both in spite and because of their personal quirks, talents and fantasies — share one fundamental drive: the desire to play out of a sheer love of music. They know full well that only a handful of music students ever manage to rise to professional status, yet make huge efforts to realize their aspirations, if not for the sake of a lifelong career, at least for the limited time available to them within the academic milieu. In developing this thread of its nimble narrative, the anime consistently suggests that accomplished musicians who care solely about the refinement of technique and theoretical knowledge cannot, therefore, expect to recognize — let alone benefit from — music's capacity to bring out the dynamic essence not only of its notes but also, ultimately, of life itself. By implication, *Nodame Cantabile* invites us to ponder the extent to which any creative enterprise may endeavor to make the progressive revelation of performative dynamism a priority. It is in its studious commitment to this component of creativity that the series, despite its frequent forays into jocularity, is able to penetrate the metaphysical import of the concept.

On the narrative level, *Nodame Cantabile* often exhibits a passion for unpredictability. This is characteristically demonstrated by the events surrounding Shinichi's earnest efforts to establish an orthodox orchestra comprising first-class students with good chances of becoming professionals after graduation. As Shinichi faces the prospect of a public début in a large and well-known hall, he is aware that several students in his orchestra are also scheduled to participate in a major competition, and is concerned that their anxiety (combined, in some instances, with the unsettling experience of first love) might unfavorably influence their performance. Therefore, the aspiring conductor decides to defer all rehearsals until after the contest is over so as to lessen the pressure. Things take an unforeseen turn as two of the most capable musicians perform appallingly in the challenge due to their emotional troubles and related mishaps, and thus resolve to make a durable impression by pulling off an excellent performance at the imminent concert — which accidentally happens to advance Shinichi's personal ambitions. Accident, chance and contingency are thus posited as far more determining agents in the shaping of a situation's outcome than any amount of rigorous planning and calculation. At the same time *Nodame Cantabile* evinces a preference for non-linear storytelling which allows for a seemingly spontaneous coral-reef accretion of events and the gradual revelation of personality traits.

Concomitantly, potentially momentous occurrences are deftly juxtaposed, with scarce or no concern for formal hierarchies of any kind, with loving representations of everyday actions of the most prosaic kind imaginable such as cooking and eating. In so doing, the franchise throws into relief the latently artistic worth of many of these activities. This is especially true of Shinichi's displays of culinary flair, a talent which has undoubtedly been refined by years of exposure to diverse gastronomic traditions but ultimately strikes its roots in the youth's instinctive, modest and dedicated attitude to the art of cooking itself and to each of the tools and ingredients it brings into play. On two major occasions, *Nodame Cantabile* employs the supporting character of Rui Son and her uninspiring attitude to food as a pretext to expound its gastronomy-oriented philosophy. A globally acclaimed Chinese pianist endowed with remarkable good looks and urbane manners, Rui has managed to persuade her fame-obsessed mother to cancel her public performances and let her study in Paris for a year, in the hope of making the friends whom her packed professional schedule has never allowed her to have and, ideally, even to fall in love. Despite her impressive achievements and striking appearance, Rui is actually a lonely, anxious and fundamentally unhappy young woman. In the course of her Parisian sojourn, she grows hell-bent on receiving private tuition from Professor Charles Auclair, the highly esteemed piano teacher who has offered Nodame the opportunity to pursue her studies at the conservatoire where he works, and decided to help her maximize her unique potential by selecting her as one of his personal pupils — much to the envy of more conventionally trained piano students. Initially rejected, Rui worms her way into the tutor's schedule through bribery, taking advantage of the elderly man's exuberant appetite for choice chocolate treats. However, she soon finds that Professor Auclair is not especially interested in her performance and therefore hardly takes the trouble to comment on the pieces she plays as part of her private lessons, not hesitating to cut a session short if he feels hungry.

On one such occasion, Rui indeed discovers that her recalcitrant mentor is far more fastidious about the cooking and serving of food — activities which she personally regards as "a hassle"— than about her style and execution. Having tersely instructed the girl to "get the meat out of the pot and cut it" in preparation for dinner, Professor Auclair instantly loses his normally suave temper when he sees her hacking away at the meat with no inkling of the appropriate carving techniques. At this point, he spews out a string of peremptory commands in a fashion reminiscent of the sternest of teachers: "cut the string first, and lay the meat sideways! Hold the knife by the top! Keep your back straight! Keep your arms and elbows next to your body! Turn your wrist! With confidence and elegance!" The clueless Rui, alas, is totally flustered and only manages to wreck the succulent hunk beyond recognition. When the obviously incompatible pair eventually sits down to eat their dinner, Professor Auclair is obviously displeased with the look of the meat, and sarcastically remarks: "I can't believe your artistic skill." While Rui protests she has carved the meat "so it's easy to eat," the esteemed pianist remains unimpressed. Keen to awaken Rui to an aesthetic value to which she has thus far been wholly oblivious, he point outs: "you know how we call a conductor 'chef' in France? Harmony is an integral part of cooking, just like in music." The implication carried by this cautionary statement is that if Rui is devoid of culinary sensitivity, she is unlikely to truly understand the value of harmony in *any* art. In a later scene, Shinichi discusses eating and cooking habits with Rui in an analogous vein while eating out at a picturesque Parisian restaurant, thereby confirming his natural dedication to the culinary arts as a vital trait of his personality. Rui once again shows little or no respect for either food or the rituals surrounding its preparation and display, and finds it irritating to discover that the young conductor, like Professor Auclair, likes cooking and eating. As Shinichi comments on the excellence of the "polenta" he is eating, wondering whether it might have been flavored with "juniper berries," Rui does even not seem to know that polenta is a dish made with "boiled cornmeal."

Rui rapidly takes a liking to Shinichi and initially teases him about his liaison with Nodame. Yet, she eventually realizes that despite her reputation, her approach lacks the vibrance of Nodame's own style. The epiphany occurs when Professor Auclair allows her to observe one of his lessons with Nodame and Rui is stunned by the sheer suppleness of Nodame's fingers as they dance over the keys. Rui's lack of interest in food and relative lack of performative vitality in comparison with Nodame are thus implicitly equated as two flaws she needs to overcome if she is to become a genuinely accomplished artist. Interestingly, Nodame herself is distinguished from the start by an almost excessive interest in food.

Nodame Cantabile's catholic grasp of art is also discernible in its interpretation of the relationship between music and the visual arts. Without being blatantly audacious in the purely technical sense, the anime does experiment assiduously with multifarious variations on this tie. This appetite for experiment plays a significant part in the anime's endeavor to bring out the performative import of the medium to which it is thematically committed without ever losing touch with the question of visuality to which it is also, and no less studiously, dedicated. The visual dimension is thrown into relief both by the nature of the show as a fundamentally image-centered experience unto itself, and by the story's propensity to explore the ascendancy of the visual image in its protagonist's perception of music, emotions, relationships and indeed reality itself. An important facet of *Nodame Cantabile*'s experimentative project, in this respect, consists of its effort to grasp the interplay of the visual arts and music as a historically situated phenomenon: that is to say, a constellation of performative events which can be related, more or less directly, to particular moments of human culture. This is not to say that the anime presumes to deliver a potted history of the collusion of the visual arts and music over the ages. Rather, it means that *Nodame Cantabile* is both sensitive to, and able to convey in a stylized fashion, some thought-provoking interpretations of that relationship as a historical framework which tangentially impacts on modern perceptions of both fields of creative endeavor. Such interpretations make themselves felt as underlying dramatic linkages even if they are not consciously grasped by the individual performers on which the story revolves. The history is implied, not sketched out or explained, in the same way as emotions in music tend to be viscerally embodied rather than rationally enunciated.

In weaving an interstitial tapestry of historical allusions, *Nodame Cantabile* does not simply invoke the aesthetic attitudes which have developed in the wake of Modernism and its tendency to explore many diverse ramifications of the confluence of the visual arts and music — which could be feasibly expected of a contemporary work. In fact, it also addresses elliptically a range of pre-modern and early modern trends paving the way to that synergy to invite us to reflect on its evolution over the centuries. A good example is provided by Shinichi's obsession with technical accuracy: a compulsion comparable to the approach to the same art evinced by the character of Len Tsukimori in *La Corda d'Oro*, here discussed in Chapter 3. Springing as it does from a staunch belief in the essentially scientific nature of music, Shinichi's attitude brings to mind the tendency, inherited by the Christian West from the lessons of antiquity, to categorize music as one of the seven *artes liberales* ("liberal arts") alongside arithmetic, geometry and astrology (*quadrivium*) and grammar, rhetoric and logic (*trivium*). Initially inspired by the teachings of the Greek philosopher Pythagoras, and especially by his theorization of music in terms of mathematical principles, music's privileged status gained specifically cosmological connotations in the Middle Ages. With the other three members of the *quadrivium*, music was indeed held by medieval philosophers and academics to enclose the crucial scientific laws which regulated the relationship between the microcosm and the macrocosm. The fine arts, in this system, were relegated to the lowly status of artisanal activities.

Nodame Cantabile also hints at a later development in the consolidation of the partnership between music and the visual arts associated with the codification of Christian liturgy. In this context, the very structure of the edifices designed to host the celebration of the mass underscores simultaneously the importance of both the visual arts and music in the ritual process by decorating the altar with carefully selected imagery, and by placing the choir next to that pivotal component of the church as a whole. In *Nodame Cantabile*, ecclesiastical architecture is first introduced as a major performative component in the setting of the Paris-based installment in which a fellow student asks

Nodame and Yasunori to play the role of the donkey in a children's Nativity Play as a result of the regular actors' sudden illness. While the kid is not at the time aware of Nodame's passion for cosplay, his request turns an otherwise formulaic performance into a novelty and a sensational success as the substitute donkey unexpectedly performs a hilarious dance inspired by one of Japan's most traditional performances, the aforecited *shishi-mai* ("lion dance"). The church itself stands out as a distillation of French Gothic architecture of the kind prevalent between the early twelfth century and 1500. In addition, this episode brings to mind the medieval tradition of the Mystery Play, a genre which first emerged in Europe in the twelfth century, as a further performative event inviting the coalescence of visual and musical elements in the guise of popular spectacle.

Practically the entire action span covered by the second and third seasons is more or less explicitly influenced by Western attitudes to the relationship between traditional solemn architecture and both music and the visual arts. This is most notable in the segment of the Paris arc in which Nodame is invited to perform her first recital by the aristocratic Benoit family, whose current head is the obsessive Mozart fan mentioned earlier, in the medieval city of St. Malo, Bretagne — the semilegendary "Corsair City." The old walled town, with its picturesque streets and shops, and the magnificent castle where the Benoit family resides, with its ramparts, monumental gates and gorgeously maintained Gothic interiors and decor, are depicted with painstaking attention to the minutest detail. So are the city's surroundings, and especially the harbor, the beach offering access to a fairytalish isle, and the cliffs overlooking a glittering sea pregnant with echoes of ancient history and pirate lore. At the same time, the employment of watercolor effects in the handling of color and light ensures that such descriptive and environmental elements do not become so imposing a presence as to weigh upon the eye, helping the setting retain an airy and dreamlike atmosphere. Ecclesiastical architecture is again accorded a prominent performative position by the setting in which the actual recital is staged. While this is supposed to be a church adjacent to the Benoits' château, its architecture is influenced by the more conspicuous edifice of St. Malo Cathedral (i.e., St. Vincent Cathedral): a Gothic masterpiece built in the twelfth century (though not actually completed until 1987), and renowned the world over for its mesmerizingly beautiful violet stained glass.

Moving on to a later epoch to which *Nodame Cantabile* also alludes beyond the Gothic era, the Renaissance, it is worth noting that at this point in history, painters sculptors and architects began to be accorded a higher status within the creative hierarchy. Yet, several eminent artists were still keen to found their practices upon scientific principles. A prime example is the pioneering architect Leon Battista Alberti, who insisted on applying strictly calculated mathematical proportions to his construction designs. Likewise, the designs for Andrea Palladio's famous villas sought to incorporate musical harmonies of Pythagorean derivation. Their height-width-depth relations, accordingly, were supposed to replicate the harmonic proportions commended by fifteenth-century musical theory inspired by Pythagoras via Neo-Platonism. At the same time, however, fine art practitioners were also beginning to assert the excellence of the visual arts with unprecedented confidence and vigor, and hence to demand their elevation to a rank no lower than the one conventionally granted to the art of music. Leonardo da Vinci, in particular, argued that music should not be regarded as superior to painting but rather as its sibling. *Nodame Cantabile* mirrors these developments in its commitment to the elaboration of a synthetic semiotic ensemble which is able to integrate the musical dimension with a comprehensive structure of visuality. This is a quest which the anime tirelessly pursues both through its inspired handling of the animated image per se and through its protagonist's unique knack of visualization.

Nodame Cantabile also engages with Baroque aesthetics. While paying sustained homage to Baroque music, it concomitantly harks back to the symbiotic relationship between music and the visual arts characteristic of the period. This manifests itself paradigmatically in the pictorial emphasis on music as a source of sensuous delight: a topos to be found in all manner of mythological, allegorical and still-life paintings of the seventeenth century. *Nodame Cantabile* appears to take this motif as the Baroque's chief lesson, seeking to throw into relief the sheer joy of music — regardless of the contingent affects presumed to course a piece of music — as a physical rather than purely intellectual experience. In this respect, the anime evinces a major point of contact with *La Corda d'Oro*. Concurrently, *Nodame Cantabile*'s vision finds a partial antecedent in the film *Gauche the Cellist*. This chronicles a collaborative artistic enterprise engaging a keen but inept cellist whose aspiration is to equal Beethoven and a team of small creatures comprising a cat, a cuckoo, a badger and a mouse. Night after night, the animals painstakingly endeavor to inculcate in the young musician the values of perseverance and rigor, and to help him grasp the unsurpassed importance of a performer's honest desire to communicate his passion to the audience as the prerequisite of performative beauty.

Music's interrelation with the visual arts is overtly dramatized in the installment in which Shinichi and Nodame visit a Parisian museum, and the highly educated youth is keen to remind his companion that "music is not the only form of art" and that she therefore "should expose" herself to "other forms of art, too" in order to achieve a comprehensive grasp of creative endeavor. Nodame herself is intrigued with the idea that Romanticism and

Impressionism in the visual arts bear correspondences with analogous movements in music. Impressionism is an artistic movement which deserves special attention, in the present context, on two important counts. Firstly, the anime's visual style evinces an Impressionistic approach to color and light in the use of backgrounds and settings characterized by distinctive watercolor qualities. Both J. C. STAFF, the animation studio behind the series, and Kasai are renowned for their ingeniously evocative handling of this technique. Secondly, it marks a uniquely important chapter in the history of synergistic relationship between music and painting. The emergence of Impressionism in the visual domain was indeed rapidly followed by the development of a comparable trend in music. Its most prominent representatives are two composers, both of whom have already been mentioned in the course of this discussion, to whom *Nodame Cantabile* devotes significant moments in the series: Ravel and Debussy (though it must be noted that the latter was not keen on being overtly associated with the Impressionist label). The key pieces, in this regard, are Ravel's *Miroirs—Alborada del Gracioso, Gaspard de la Nuit, Les entretiens de la belle et de la bête* from *Ma mère l'oye, Bolero, Jeux d'eau* and Piano Concerto in G major, and Debussy's *L'Isle Joyeuse, Prélude à l'après-midi d'un faune* and *Images*.

Furthermore, Shinichi makes explicit reference to Debussy's oeuvre in the museum sequence mentioned above, explaining that this musician's "early compositions are similar to Impressionist art," insofar as the desire to "express complex colors using only primary ones" animating Impressionist painters is echoed by Debussy's endeavor to do "something similar with his music." Significantly, the paintings which Shinichi is observing as he voices this idea are appropriately adapted versions of Monet's "Boats at Argenteuil" and Édouard Manet's "Déjeuner sur l'herbe." Shinichi's comment is quite accurate when one considers that Debussy, drawing inspiration from his encounter with Impressionism in painting, indeed strove to create the musical equivalent of the subtle nuances of color and light which had instantly, and even scandalously, singled out that pictorial style as a revolutionary phenomenon. It is with *Prélude à l'après-midi d'un faune* that Debussy's experimental flair announces itself as a likewise groundbreaking creative gesture, thriving on unprecedented orchestrating strategies in the treatment of lines and harmonies and concurrently defying the rules of conventional tonality. At the same time, the composer was profoundly influenced by Symbolist poetry, and specifically by the works of Paul Verlaine and Stéphane Mallarmé, the author of the poem *L'après-midi d'un faune* whence Debussy's famous composition derives its designation. Debussy's extension of the collusion of music and painting into a virtually boundless realm of synesthetic correspondences fully validates Shinichi's commendation of the mind's openness to diverse art forms. Symbolist poetry is also worthy of notice, in the present context, due to its implicit affinities with Japanese aesthetics. Like the latter, that literary movement typically exhibits a preference for allusiveness, vagueness and imprecision to direct statement and explicit description. Debussy's music reveals these same qualities in its predilection for unresolved and incomplete passages. This is a stylistic choice on which *Nodame Cantabile*'s dénouement capitalizes to great dramatic and visual effect, providing a satisfying finale, yet steering clear of any conclusive assertions or resolutions in order to accomplish a remarkable equilibrium of motion and color, emotions and textures, language and light.

Shinichi also draws attention to the chromatic dimension of Impressionist music in his silent reflections on the beauties and challenges intrinsic in Ravel's *Bolero*. This orchestral piece "uses a Spanish dance rhythm from beginning to end," Shinichi observes. "Each time the melody is played by a different instrument. The same melody ... presented with a variety of colors." A further example of the coalescence of musical and pictorial sensibilities in modern art is supplied by the character of the painter who lives in the attic of the building where Nodame and Shinichi lodge as exchange students in Paris, who recalls the days when he would draw inspiration for his art and translate his vision onto canvas while listening to the music played by Shinichi's father, an acclaimed pianist in his own right. With its sensitivity to the atmosphere of the present moment and its random emotive variables, Nodame's own musical style echoes the Impressionist approach to vision. Thus, even though this work is not explicitly referred to in the show, it is tempting to visualize the heroine's piano playing with reference to František Kupka's *The Piano Keys* (a.k.a. *The Lake*). The highly dynamic pattern formed by the diatonic and chromatic keys as envisioned by the painter — so lively as to animate the lakeside setting of which they constitute the foreground — resembles the motion of Nodame's fingers on the keyboard, so elegantly agile as to be at one point compared by Rui to "ballet." Nodame's association with Impressionism is further consolidated by Rui's suggestion that her personality is akin to Ravel's music, and specifically to the Piano Concerto in G major, a composition pervaded by jazz harmonies which both Rui herself and Yasunori the oboist describe as "cute." The Impressionist elements intrinsic in both Ravel's and Debussy's music — and, by implication, its correlatives in the domains of painting and literature — represent an intriguing aspect of *Nodame Cantabile*'s speculative range which serves to illuminate emblematically the anime's philosophical depth. This constitutes a facet of its performative identity which may occasionally seem overpowered by its comical and romantic strands but should never be underestimated in the study of its interdisciplinary import.

In its constellation of the interplay of art and anime, *Nodame Cantabile* brings to fruition a project launched by Kasai with *Honey and Clover*: namely, the exploration of artistic production as a simultaneously intellectual and emotional exercise requiring the achievement of a fine balance between reason and intuition, between technique and inspiration. In the earlier anime, Kasai elaborated this topos by underscoring the inseparability of imagination and expressiveness from a process of direct physical involvement with the creative act as an intensely material phenomenon. With *Nodame Cantabile*, he takes it to fresh levels of aesthetic refinement by engaging, albeit obliquely and not without a fair dose of humor, with one of the most profound and most baffling questions which have faced both Eastern and Western thinkers for centuries: the relationship between meaning and truth. Thus, the anime urges us to ponder whether there might be more meaning, at the level of emotive response, in a performance which appears to lack truth in the sense that it is not submissively true to the aims of its source but rather reinvents them at the prompt of the elan of the moment. Alternately, it asks us to consider the possibility of there being greater truth — i.e., intuitive honesty — in a performance which defies the original meaning of the abstract codes it translates into embodied action. In the process, *Nodame Cantabile* intimates that neither meaning nor truth can ultimately be posited as immutable givens and should rather be grasped as variable effects of the perception of significant beauty. Such an insight consists of an instinctive, yet mindful, awareness of a loveliness which is meaningful only insofar as it is allowed to flow in the always rescindable here-and-now. Hence, it entails a commodious understanding of one's art which the perfection of technical skills can no doubt enhance and refine but cannot obtain in the absence of a creative urge grounded at least partly in intuition rather than sheer expertise.

Shinichi is confronted with this challenging lesson when he participates in the prestigious "Platini Conducting Competition" early in the Paris arc. Faced with the prospect of humiliating failure as a result of an unexpectedly poor performance at a crucial stage in the context, the aspiring maestro succeeds in snatching a triumph from the jaws of defeat upon realizing that he must embrace the music from the bottom of his heart and enjoy the experience while it lasts — transient though the pleasure it yields necessarily is. This epiphany owes much to Nodame's words of encouragement on the eve of the final round, which alert him to the importance of enjoying oneself to the fullest when the opportunity arises. This is not to say, however, that Nodame herself has fully internalized that vital lesson. In fact, she is also often prone to a solipsistic tendency to project her own emotions onto the pieces she plays so unrestrainedly as to foreclose the possibility of a fruitful dialogue with their melodies. As Stresemann points out, this indicates that she is not yet genuinely prepared to "face" the music, and that her unique talent is therefore not afforded any proper chance to evolve. Trusting spur-of-the-moment intuition to the exclusion of a more thorough understanding of the music, she therefore frequently fails to open her own soul to its loveliness. Thus, both nit-picking perfectionists like Shinichi and instinctive improvisers like Nodame have something to learn. The former must develop the ability to temper academic knowledge with emotion, while the latter must appreciate the importance of processing their feelings through the filter of conscious reflection. Only then will their respective gifts truly shine forth.

Time and again, the anime urges us to consider whether the desire to play freely rather than in strict accordance with orthodox parameters and technical strictures is legitimate or even tenable in the universe of classical performance. On the one hand, the anime commends the principles of proficiency, precision and loyal observance of a composer's intentions as preconditions of a pleasing performance. On the other, however, it is keen to remind us that those qualities are not in and by themselves sufficient to generate the waves of sheer elation which music guided by instinct is sometimes capable of evoking despite its technical idiosyncrasies and apparent carelessness. Hence, it is in the synthesis of technical expertise and affective inspiration that the most beautiful music finds inception, striking unforgettable chords despite — or perhaps because of — its inexorable ephemerality. The anime's philosophical dimension delicately pervades its entire yarn as a constant yet unobtrusive actor in its own right, and thus fulfills a performative function of considerable importance. Indeed, it can be regarded as an explicit invitation for the viewer to reflect on a variety of ways in which the musical world has colluded with the history of art at large and, by metaphorical extension, with the history of human civilization itself. We are thereby alerted to the interplay of the visual arts and music as a phenomenon which has assumed many different guises in diverse epochs and cultures. Musical symbols, sounds and allegories have consistently accompanied mythological, religious and didactic themes, provided documentary evidence for the evolution both of specific instruments, materials, accessories and styles and of the performative codes and conventions pertinent to each.

Nodame Cantabile simultaneously underscores the importance of performativity, as opposed to actual performance, with the intimation that the theoretical import of music has provided the foundation of influential philosophical perspectives which have gained prominence and evolved over the centuries quite independently of musical performance per se. A classic case in point is the scene in which Shinichi comments on the mission he faces as a consequence of having been put in charge of the "Roux-Marlet" orchestra, a long-standing institution currently undergoing a major identity crisis caused by the departure of many of his members, disenchanted with their managers' modus operandi, and resulting in increasingly poor performances and attendant drop in attendance. In this scene, the young conductor makes explicit reference to the concept of *harmonia mundi* (the harmony of the spheres) as he states: "about 1,500 years ago, there were studies done in order to understand the harmony of the world." The disciplines harnessed to this ambitious goal, he explains, were "astronomy, geometry, number theory and music." The concept is pertinent to his present task, Shinichi reckons, insofar as "for this orchestra" he has "to find the harmony among them all." Nodame will recall this scene at a vital turning point in her own creative development. At this juncture, the content of the girl's recollections is symbolically visualized, with impeccable iconographic aptness, by the image of a Renaissance-style Celestial Globe of the kind used by astronomers and mathematicians of bygone ages to capture the harmony of the spheres as a 3D model of a universe governed by musical relationships and correspondences.

The harmony of the spheres, as explained in some detail in Chapter 3 vis-à-vis *Touka Gettan*, is a seminal notion in Western thought of the medieval era which strikes its roots in antiquity. Its central proposition is the idea that the heavenly bodies emit sounds which express the numerical relationships defining cosmic equilibrium. In Shinichi's instance, the notion of *harmonia mundi* is implicitly associated with a germane concept of Platonic derivation: the principle of Good Government. This proposes that the promoter of fair governance is allegorically akin to a musician. Just as the latter has the ability to produce peace-inducing harmonies though his art, so the just ruler must be able to inculcate the values of temperance, tolerance and cooperation by balancing discordant energies within society. At the same time, *Nodame Cantabile* offers a tangential commentary on the interaction of music and the visual arts in the articulation of themes and motifs which bring into relief the rhythms of human existence, and hence illuminate perennial human preoccupations with the vicissitudes of love, power, self-fulfillment and sheer desire. In making these topoi central to the progression of the drama over three seasons, the anime assiduously seeks to constellate them as both graphic and melodic events, establishing alternately overt and subtextual correspondences between the two dimensions in such a way that each visual experience echoes and is echoed by a parallel musical experience. Those existential concerns are also often highlighted by means of voiceovers which register the silent reflections formulated by particular characters, and mainly Shinichi, as actual compositions are being performed.

Nodame Cantabile occasionally focuses on specific instruments — e.g., the piano, the violin, the viola, the drums, the oboe, the cello, the harmonica, the bassoon, the celesta — and seeks to draw attention to the most salient qualities of each. The frames devoted to such instruments do not concentrate exclusively on the objects' musical identity. In fact, they also foreground their fundamentally visual features as aesthetic realities in their own right. In so doing, they present them as something much more significant and alive than mere props. The use of CGI to enhance the photorealistic accuracy of those images enables them to stand out against the pervasively hand-drawn quality which characterizes the anime's prevalent style. In the realm of painting, frames such as these find an honored correlative in the tradition of still-life pictures intended to express the concept of *vanitas*: the corruption and dissolution awaiting all life forms. This idea is also pivotal, as recurrently emphasized in this study, to specifically Japanese art and aesthetic theory. Furthermore, in staging musical performance in a wide range of settings — i.e., not only in concert halls and theaters but also in school auditoriums, family homes, student digs, churches, castles and private salons — *Nodame Cantabile* serves an additional documentary function by reminding us of a simple, yet crucially important, cultural reality: the ubiquity of music in human society. This message is reinforced by the anime's endeavor to allude to the cultural and historical meaning of events such as music lessons, concerts, recitals, rehearsals and public performances, alongside institutions such as the orchestra, the conservatoire and the patronage system. At the same time, we are tangentially reminded that events and institutions of this kind have repeatedly provided thematic inspiration for painters, consolidating the synergy of music and the visual arts to unique effect.

Nodame Cantabile's ending marks the triumph of its foremost philosophical message, incontrovertibly upholding the idea that without enjoyment, music is bound to remain inert. No amount of either training or technical excellence can replace the supreme value of this experience. Having been invited again by the Benoit family to perform at St. Malo, Nodame addresses the audience prior to her concert with the same invitation she proffered in the previous occasion: an exhortation to *enjoy* what they are about to hear. As the frame portraying her in her Mozart outfit gives way to the closing screen, the word embroidered upon it in elegant cord-like script is in fact the word "fun"— and not, as one might expect at such a juncture, the customary "The End." This time around, the global reputation gained by the heroine in the wake of her London début has attracted a huge crowd of fans, and Nodame could be pardoned if she were to adopt a more assertive or self-congratulatory attitude. However, much as she may have grown in both stature and skills since her first St. Malo performance, Nodame has neither forgotten nor relinquished her constitutional dedication to the joy and pleasure of music above all other values to which the art may aspire. The heroine's abiding playfulness, demonstrated by an unabated fondness of cosplay, corroborates this idea with both visual immediacy and performative gusto.

As argued throughout this study, the art of music holds special significance in the context of anime's multi-artistic exploration of creativity. Music's dialogue with visual drama frequently serves to bolster the elaboration of coming-of-age trajectories and personal journeys of self-discovery and self-realization. This proposition is confirmed by several anime here employed as primary case studies — i.e., *Piano: The Story of a Young Girl's Heart* (Chapter 2), *Beck* and *La Corda d'Oro* (Chapter 3), *Nodame Cantabile* (Chapter 4). Among the titles enlisted as secondary or ancillary references, an analogous trend can be witnessed in *NANA* and *Skip Beat!* (Chapter 2), *Gravitation* (Chapter 3), *Gauche the Cellist* and *The Piano Forest* (Chapter 4). At times, the bildungsroman element is couched specifically in terms of a healing process enabling the negotiation of traumatic events: *Myself; Yourself* and *Full Moon O Sagashite* (Chapter 2) illustrate this proposition. Not seldom, the synergy of music and animated images gains mystical and supernatural colorations, as exemplified by both primary titles such as *Swan Lake* (Chapter 2), *Touka Gettan* (Chapter 3) and *Princess Tutu* (Chapter 4), and supplementary productions such as *Shinkyoku Soukai Polyphonica* and *The Melody of Oblivion* (Chapter 2) and *Chance Pop Session* (Chapter 3). However, the interplay of anime and music does not result solely in a considerable number of productions explicitly utilizing music as their pivotal theme with reference to a variety of styles and genres. In fact, the anime here studied also point consistently to a wide-ranging aesthetic phenomenon of confluence of music and other arts, especially of a visual orientation, which carries deeper philosophical implications. This contention is corroborated by the role ascribed to music in anime which do not actually posit this art as a theme in the way the titles cited above clearly do but rather integrate it in their worldview and diegesis as a structural mainstay.

In order to illustrate some of the principal modalities in which this idea has communicated itself in modern anime, the ensuing paragraphs look at three titles released over the decade spanning the mid–1990s to the mid–2000s. *Neon Genesis Evangelion* is arguably the first anime to have integrated Western classical music into its diegesis and overarching symbolism as a structural lynchpin, and could therefore be said to constitute a groundbreaking contribution to the history of visual-musical relations in its medium. In the 26-episode series released in 1995 and 1996, Western classical music is not used with conspicuous frequency but whenever it does come into play, its dramatic impact is awe-inspiring — this is paradigmatically exemplified by the show's employment of Handel's *Messiah* and of the fourth movement of Beethoven's Ninth Symphony, commonly referred to as "Ode to Joy," toward the end of the series. *Evangelion*'s adventurous interpretation of the synergy of graphic and sonoric discourses announces itself with uncontestable vigor in the two movies released in 1997, *Neon Genesis Evangelion: Death & Rebirth* and *Neon Genesis Evangelion: End of Evangelion*, where Western classical music rises to the status of a major player.

In *Death & Rebirth*, the scenes in which Western classical music plays its most prominent part are the four melodic interludes dramatizing the String Quartet rehearsal set in the school gymnasium in which the characters of Shinji, Asuka, Rei and Touji tune and play their musical instruments. Even though these sequences do not overtly contribute to the development of the action, they offer welcome pauses for reflection which illuminate the characters' relationships with one another and different perspectives on their roles within the band — and, by extension, their social and professional milieux. Vital aspects of their personalities are thus thrown into relief. The characteristically perturbed Shinji, specifically, comes across as more serene and composed in these scenes than anywhere else in *Evangelion*. This is not entirely surprising when one considers that learning to play the cello is the sole activity from which the kid has ever derived any hassle-free solace, and in which he has therefore persevered by choice rather than as a result of external pressure. In this instance, Shinji performs Johann Sebastian Bach's Cello Suite No. 1 in G major, "Prelude." Asuka, a likewise tormented character, is constitutionally hell-bent on affirming her superiority in a desperate effort to exorcize the demons of insecurity and loneliness. In keeping with this fundamental aspect of her personality, she approaches music itself as a means of showing off her skills: hence, she exalts her role as a violinist while disparaging Shinji as performer of mere "arpeggios." Asuka's piece is the Partita for Violin No. 3 in E major, "Gavotte in Rondo." Rei, a habitually compliant and withdrawn girl who never questions the meaning of the task laid before her, simply gets on with the job in hand as is her wont and tunes her viola as appropriate. Her performance, accordingly, consists simply of the third string tuning of the instrument. The character of Touji plays a purely ancillary part in *Death*'s String Quartet interludes but the scene in which he features is nonetheless instrumental in imparting the film's musical armature with overall coherence insofar as it enables a collective performance to take place at last. The piece here performed is Johann Pachelbel's *Canon* in D major. The directors' adoption of this particular composition is itself worthy of notice insofar as the chosen piece serves a symbolic function as a harmonizing and unifying force. This crucial attribute of the canon as a distinctive composition is paradigmatically borne out by the anime series *Kanon*, as shown later in this discussion.

The second film's inspired approach of Western classical music is testified by its use "Air on the G String," an adaptation by August Wilhelmj of "Air," the second movement from Bach's Orchestral Suite No. 3 in D major, as the background to raging battles of epic proportions intercut with confrontations of a personal nature supposed to be unfolding simultaneously. No less memorable is *End of Evangelion*'s employment of Bach's *Jesu bleibet meine freude* (*Jesus, Joy of Man's Desiring*), the tenth movement of the cantata *Herz und Mund und Tat und Leben*, for the sequence in which the footage abruptly switches to live-action mode to regale the eye with a stream of images of shapeless crowds, dreary buildings, pylons and street signs which ought to look quite uninspiring but actually translate the urban environment into sheer poetry through the camera's agile interaction with the soundtrack. Music also plays a structurally defining role in the four new films comprised in the *Rebuild of Evangelion* series (two of which have already been released), offering an alternate version of the events presented in the TV series and incorporating new scenes, characters and settings. In this case, music is overtly foregrounded by the films' four titles: *Evangelion Shin Gekijouban: Jo — Evangelion: 1.0 — You Are (Not) Alone*; *Evangelion Shin Gekijouban: Ha — Evangelion: 2:0 — You Can (Not) Advance*; *Evangelion Shin Gekijouban: Kyuu*; *Evangelion Shin Gekijouban: Final*. According to the relevant *Wikipedia* entry, "the concept of *jo-ha-kyuu*, which roughly corresponds to 'beginning,' 'middle,' and 'end,' originated in classical *gagaku* music and is best known to describe the acts of a noh play" (*Rebuild of Evangelion*).

Evangelion's innovative take on the role of music in anime tallies with its bold interpretation of the medium's most popular and well-tested formulae — an aspect of its identity so marked as to have triggered ongoing controversies among anime experts and casual audiences alike ever since its original release. On both the technical and the thematic planes, *Evangelion* continues to stand the test of time as an elaborate process of rule-bending and genre-straddling capable of redefining the anime canon at large. Where techniques are concerned, both the TV series and the feature films are distinguished by their unprecedented handling of montages, collages and cut-ins, as well as live-action footage interspersed with snippets of newspaper clippings and graffiti, and for their integration into the action of drawings, sketches, impressionistic flecks and patches of color, minimalist animation emphasizing the aliveness of the line itself, elements of calligraphy and typography in numerous fonts. While these features of its makeup have established *Evangelion* as a pioneering gesture, it is with its themes that the anime has sparked off some of the most heated arguments in the history of anime. While embracing the *mecha* subgenre as its superficial plot trigger, *Evangelion* is actually a multilayered psychological thriller of unrivaled intricacy and unpredictability. Engaging in the dispassionate anatomy of a varied gallery of tormented personalities, the anime manages to penetrate many of the least palatable facets of existence, and thus yields a vision of humanity which feels estranging and yet disquietingly familiar at one and the same time.

As an anime unwaveringly committed to a unique aesthetic of refinement, it is quite logical that *Kanon* should adopt music — the most aerial of arts — as a structural core. This formal principle is paralleled by the show's utilization of musical vocabulary in its episode titles, which include the terms overture, introit, partita, caprice, serenade, divertimento, fugue, fantasia, berçeuse, requiem, intermezzo, waltz, trio, concerto, sonatina, oratorio, nocturne. On both the diegetic and the symbolic planes, *Kanon*'s most inspired use of music consists of its adoption of Pachelbel's *Canon* in D major (also employed, as noted earlier, in the *Death* component of *Neon Genesis Evangelion: Death & Rebirth*). In *Kanon*, the piece provides the accompaniment for markedly poignant moments punctuating the series from its opening installment onward. The philosophical importance of the canon as a musical composition is highlighted by the character of Sayuri as she explains that a canon repeats the same melody a number of times, allowing the beauty of its harmony to emerge gradually and unobtrusively. The canon indeed relies on a contrapuntal structure in which a dominant melody (*dux*) leads to one or more imitations of that melody (*followers*) played in a different voice. The canon, therefore, constitutes a fitting musical correlative for the experiences and relationships explored by the anime itself: namely, quotidian events inspired throughout by a courageous — yet laboriously unfolding — struggle toward harmony. Just as each repetition in a canon echoes the melody at its basis, so the series' characters constantly return to the past as the springboard for any positive change. The formal organization of the canon as a piece whose cumulative effect pivots on the promotion of incremental change through the repetition of a fundamental motif has an equivalent in the process of anime production carried out by the superb studio behind *Kanon*, Kyoto Animation (KyoAni). Just as the reiterated musical components coalesce in the pinnacle of the composition, so the visual elements ideated over the production process harmoniously dovetail in the photography/CG stage.

The TV series *Gilgamesh* provides a further instance of anime in which visuality enters a collaborative project with music so as to weave a transdisciplinary tapestry of images, sounds, words and gestures. Like *Kanon*, *Gilgamesh* draws attention to the structural significance of its musical theme through the titles of some of its most pivotal installments: e.g., 1. "Les Préludes," 7. "Dissonance," 12. "Die Lustige Witwe," 16. "Nessun Dorma," and 17. "Hammerklavier." The anime's soundtrack bolsters the drama's affiliation with classical music, featuring as recurrent pieces the second movement of Beethoven's Piano Concerto #5 in E-flat major, commonly known as the "Emperor Concerto," and "Love Unspoken," the Waltz from Franz Lehar's *Merry Widow*, as well as Robert Lowry's hymn "Shall We Gather at the River?" The character of Kiyoko is central to the series' treatment of music. The girl's real talent is her almost intuitive grasp of the art of music down to the most delicate gradations: she is even able to perceive the distinct notes emitted by each raindrop as this comes into contact with the ground. As the drama unfolds and Kiyoko's dark destiny presses on toward its tragic climax, the few pleasurable moments in her life are afforded by the broken piano she lovingly refurbishes and nurtures as though it were an animate entity even though it will never regain its voice. Even though the instrument is mute, Kiyoko can hear the notes in her own head and when Novem (a member of the preternatural Gilgamesh race) follows her to the desolate spot in which she keeps the piano, he tells her that she has brought the instrument back to life and that he, too, can hear the soundless tunes she elicits from its keys.

In the handling of musical-visual relations, *Gilgamesh* deploys its visual style to stunning effect, demonstrating that musical impressions can emanate from visuality — and thus intimating that visual impressions, conversely, can be acoustically induced. It is often through its graphic constellation of line, color and mass that the anime communicates most tersely its sonoric message. *Gilgamesh* never allows the gentler and smoother aspects of its medium's stylistic range to blotch or soften the stark outlines of its distinctive visuals. In fact, it consistently embraces an approach to design centered on the amplification of the intrinsic properties of its geometric and chromatic components as corporeal realities. The anime's character designs, in particular, have no match in modern anime, capitalizing as they do on boldly drawn physiques and penetrating eyes, vividly defined features and chunky locks. Concomitantly, the affective power of the characters' colors — vibrant yet never jolly — are highlighted by their juxtaposition with dusky or dappled backgrounds. Most crucially, *Gilgamesh* evinces a pervasive preference for desaturated palettes, verging on the colorless as often and as much as a show in color can realistically approximate such an effect.

The use of white in many key sequences abets this overall effect, bringing to mind Wassily Kandinsky's observations on that mysteriously fascinating color. In Kandinsky's subtle reading of the sonoric connotations of white, this is described as "a symbol of a world from which all colour as a definite attribute has disappeared.... A great silence, like an impenetrable wall, shrouds its life from our understanding. White, therefore, has this harmony of silence ... like many pauses in music that break temporarily the melody. It is not a dead silence, but one pregnant with possibilities. White has the appeal of the nothingness that is before birth, of the world in the ice age." This is a somewhat unusual reading of the color (or rather non-color, as some would regard it) when one considers the more common association of black with the pre-natal condition (as noted in Chapter 2). Assessing the emblematic significance of black, Kandinsky argues that this color, by contrast, signifies "a totally dead silence" which finds a musical equivalent in "one of those profound and final pauses, after which any continuation of the melody seems the dawn of another world.... The silence of black is the silence of death" (Kandinsky 1977, p. 39).

Silence is an important aspect of *Gilgamesh* whose metaphorical function is to invite us to assess the artistic significance of this dimension in both the specifically musical and the broadly artistic sense. Insofar as the most distinctive type of silence articulated in the anime is that associated with a mute musical instrument, it is a silence produced — paradoxical though this may seem — by musical means. It is also, however, a multi-artistic silence to the extent that the negation of music which the mute piano automatically invokes is not presented as an isolated phenomenon but rather as a component of a prismatic visual and performative event coursed by multifarious sounds — in other words, an artistic gesture of great dramatic vibrance and undeniable auditory density. *Gilgamesh* thus alerts us to the importance of grasping and expressing the acoustic qualities of silence as artistic materials worthy of care and respect. In recent decades, a groundbreaking attempt to demonstrate the sonoric capacities of silence has emanated from the experiments of the composer, philosopher, poet and artist John Cage and especially from his controversial *4'33"*, a supposedly musical composition in three movements performed without a single note being played, and yet intended to be perceived not as four minutes and thirty-three seconds of silence but rather as the ensemble of sounds produced by the audience's environment.

Although Cage was repeatedly accused of being no more than an opportunistic charlatan, his work has undeniably made a unique contribution to ongoing debates surrounding the import and status of art in contemporary cultures. It urges us to appraise dispassionately what we mean by art as individuals and as sentient entities instead of merely swallowing the doxastic definitions of art which have been passed down from generation to generation as eternal givens when they are, in fact, ideologically determined and context-bound constructs. Relatedly, Cage's work encourages us to question the validity of the boundaries traditionally held to separate various art practices and art forms, and hence contemplate the visual and performative qualities of music as no less integral to its being than notes, harmonies and melodies. Addressing the relationship between music and the everyday world in the context of a lecture delivered in 1957 at the Music Teachers' National Association in Chicago, Cage stated that he deemed it crucial not to lose sight of an elementary but often neglected reality: the fact that "we have eyes as well as ears, and it is our business while we are alive to use them" (cited in Vergo, p. 350). Cage's works aspire to the ideal of a total work of art redolent of the Wagnerian concept of *Gesamtkunstwerk* but in an inverted form insofar as the vision they pursue is not that of a unitary whole. On the contrary, they aim to evoke a mobile constellation of coexisting, yet fundamentally disparate, creative codes which defy hierarchical organization. As Simon Shaw-Miller maintains, in this instance, "the concern is with silence over amplification, coexistence over synthesis; music does not sublimate the other arts.... Volume does not drown out the other arts' voices. Rather, it is through Cage's aesthetic of silence that the other arts can be *seen* to be part of the discourse of music — textual, visual, and theatrical" (Shaw-Miller, p. xii).

Imbued by allusions to Shinto mythology, the TV series *RahXephon* consistently supports this worldview and its perception of the interconnectedness of all things by means of allusions to music as a mystical energy whose ultimate goal is "tuning the world": that is to say, transforming the planet into a more harmonious and balanced environment. The musical motif is also notable, once again, in the show's episode titles, where the term "Movement" is repeatedly used, and in the names assigned to the "Dolem," *mecha*-like entities deployed as weapons: e.g., Allegretto, Fortissimo, Grave, Ritardando, Larghetto, Sforzando, Vivace, Falsetto, Arpeggio, Metronome, Forzando, Obbligato, Brillante and Vibrato. Each Dolem is bound to a specific melody, and different sound waves correspond to distinctive martial strategies. Furthermore, the facial expressions evinced by both the Dolem and the person responsible for controlling it (the "Mulian") show that singing is instrumental in abetting the interaction between the clay giants and their manipulators. While asserting its privileged role by permeating the series' indigenous lexis and figurative repertoire, music also informs the fabric of *RahXephon*'s kaleidoscopic settings. Throughout the action, these are indeed pervaded alternately by melodious arias and sinister vibrations, comforting echoes and raucous chants, idyllic harmonies and portentous whispers prophesying discord. Most crucially, music proffers the invisible thread which ultimately enables the anime's beleaguered protagonists, Ayato and Haruka, to retain memories of each other despite enforced separation and mnemonic reprogramming. This is movingly demonstrated by the sequence in which Haruka's singing voice brings Ayato back from his hallucinatory journey through the alternate reality he has accidentally entered by accessing an enchanted shrine. The scene's importance is confirmed by a later sequence in which Ayato suddenly recognizes the tune sung by Haruka at that vital moment, and although he has no lucid recollection of when or how he might have heard it before, he recognizes instinctively that it fills him with an unprecedented feeling of security and warmth.

In their exploration of the collusion of art and anime both as a thematic reservoir and as an arena for self-reflexive speculation, the productions addressed in this study assiduously highlight the inextricability of the interdependent concepts of imagination and creativity from a distinctive aesthetic perspective of quintessentially Japanese orientation. Within this outlook, the process of creation is typically accorded greater significance than the object created. This principle is axial to any artist's quest both for novel expressive codes and for bold syntheses of fresh ideas and time-honored traditions. In both instances, the pursuit of a harmonious relationship between humanity and the environment is indefatigably promulgated. At the same time, quotidian actions and rituals are revered, while even the humblest of materials are attributed social value. Rescued from the fate of amorphous and monotonous anonymity to which repetitiveness would otherwise condemn them, such actions, rituals and materials are in fact recognized as the contingent correlatives of the cyclical patterns through which nature goes on renewing itself and the *ki*, the energy inhabiting all things, accordingly reveals itself as a forever dazzling, albeit discreetly understated, life current. Working in tandem, the incorporeal ideals and the concrete practices fostered by this world picture yield a spellbinding portrait of art — the vision of a dance of signs through which illusions intermesh with reality, fluid worlds are conjured, and life stories themselves are relentlessly made and unmade in images.

Filmography

Primary Titles

Bakuman (2010–11)

Original Title: *Bakuman*. **Status**: TV series (25 episodes). **Episode Length**: 24 minutes. **Directors**: Kenichi Kasai, Noriaki Akitaya. **Series Composition**: Reiko Yoshida. **Script**: Reiko Yoshida, Seishi Minakami, Tsutomu Kamishiro, Yuniko Ayana. **Music**: Audio Highs. **Original Creators**: Takeshi Obata (art), Tsugumi Ohba (story). **Character Designer**: Tomoyuki Shitaya. **Art Director**: Chikako Shibata. **Chief Animation Director**: Tomoyuki Shitaya. **Animation Directors**: Sachiko Kotani, Tomoyuki Shitaya. **Sound Director**: Jun Watanabe. **Director of Photography**: Kazuya Iwai. **Color Designers**: Hiromi Okamoto, Mayumi Tanahashi. **Digital Paint**: Haruka Yoshida, Kana Tabe, Michiko Watanabe, Mika Funabashi, Syouko Mori, Yuka Kojima. **Editing**: Masahiro Goto. **Sound Effects**: Kaori Yamada. **Animation Production**: J.C. Staff. **Production**: NHK Enterprises, Shogakukan Productions Co., Ltd.

Beck: Mongolian Chop Squad (2004–2005)

Original Title: *Beck*. **Status**: TV series (26 episodes). **Episode Length**: 25 minutes. **Director**: Osamu Kobayashi. **Series Composition**: Osamu Kobayashi. **Original Manga**: Harold Sakuishi. **Character Designer**: Motonobu Hori, Kobayashi. **Art Director**: Shinichi Uehara. **Music Coordination Producer**: Toru Hidaka. **Music Director**: Yukio Nagasaki. **Sound Effects**: Hidekuni Satou. **Director of Photography**: Masayuki Narai. **Composite Director**: Takaharu Ozaki. **Editing**: Kashiko Kimura, Satoshi Terauchi. **Color Designer**: Yoshimi Koshikawa. **CG**: Ayumu Mochimaru, Hiroshi Sakamoto, Nobuyuki Suchi, Osamu Sasaki. **CGI Director**: Hiromi Hayashi. **Animation Production**: Madhouse Studios. **Music Production**: DefSTAR RECORDS. **Recording Studio**: KSS Recording Studio.

La Corda d'Oro — Primo Passo (2005–2006)

Original Title: *Kin-iro no Corda — primo passo*. **Status**: TV series (26 episodes). **Episode Length**: 25 minutes. **Director**: Koujin Ochi. **Series Composition**: Reiko Yoshida. **Music**: Mitsutaka Tajiri. **Original Manga**: Yuki Kure. **Character Designer**: Maki Fujioka. **Art Director**: Chikako Shibata. **Chief Animation Director**: Fujioka. **Sound Director**: Hiromi Kikuta. **Director of Photography**: Shinya Matsuzaki. **Apparel**

Designer: Rie Nishimura. **Color Setting**: Rieko Sakai, Yukiko Ario, Yuuko Satou. **Editing**: Seiji Morita, Yuri Tamura. **Photography**: Satoshi Shimizu, Tetsuya Enomoto, Tomoyuki Shimizu. **Special Effects**: Tomomi Ishihara. **Animation Production**: Yumeta Company.

La Corda d'Oro — Secondo Passo (2009)

Original Title: *Kin-iro no Corda — secondo passo*. **Status**: Special (2 episodes). **Episode Length**: 25 minutes. **Director**: Ochi. **Screenplay**: Reiko Yoshida. **Original Manga**: Yuki Kure. **Character Design**: Maki Fujioka. **Chief Animation Director**: Fujioka. **Production**: Aniplex.

Genshiken (2004)

Original Title: *The Society for the Study of Modern Visual Culture Genshiken*. **Status**: TV series (12 episodes). **Episode Length**: 25 minutes. **Director**: Takashi Ikehata. **Series Composition**: Michiko Yokote. **Music**: Masanori Takumi. **Original Manga**: Shimoku Kio. **Character Designer**: Hirotaka Kinoshita. **Art Director**: Shin Okui. **Chief Animation Director**: Hirotaka Kinoshita. **Sound Director**: Jin Aketagawa. **Director of Photography**: Eiji Tsuchida. **Color Designer**: Kayoko Nishi. **Editing**: Jun Takuma. **Animation Production**: Palm Studio. **Music Production**: Lantis. **Production**: GENCO, KIDS STATION, Media Factory, Tora no Ana, Toshiba Entertainment.

Genshiken (2006)

Original Title: *The Society for the Study of Modern Visual Culture Genshiken*. **Status**: OVA series (3 episodes). **Episode Length**: 24 minutes. **Director**: Tsutomu Mizushima. **Series Composition**: Michiko Yokote. **Screenplay**: Michiko Yokote. **Music**: Tomoki Hasegawa. **Original Creator**: Shimoku Kio. **Character Designer**: Yoshiaki Yanagida. **Art Director**: Shin Okui. **Chief Animation Director**: Yoshiaki Yanagida. **Art Designer**: Hiro Izumi. **Sound Director**: Jin Aketagawa. **Director of Photography**: Akio Saitou. **Editing**: Yukie Oikawa, Yuri Tamura. **Animation Production**: Asiadou.

Genshiken 2 (2007)

Original Title: *The Society for the Study of Modern Visual Culture Genshiken 2*. **Status**: TV series (12 episodes). **Episode Length**: 24 minutes. **Director**: Kinji Yoshimoto. **Series Composition**: Michiko Yokote **Script**: Michiko Yokote, Shimoku Kio. **Screenplay**: Michiko Yokote, Shimoku Kio. **Music**: Masaya Koike (4-EVER), Shun Okazaki (4-EVER). **Original Creator**: Shimoku Kio. **Character Designer**: Yoshiaki Yanagida. **Chief Animation Directors**: Takayuki Noguchi. Yoshiaki Yanagida, Yukiko Ishibashi. **Animation Directors**: Satoshi Urushihara, Takayuki Noguchi, Yukiko Ishibashi. **Sound Director**: Jin Aketagawa. **Director of Photography**: Kazuhiro Sasaki. **Editing**: Jun Takuma. **Animation Production**: ARMS. **Music Production**: Lantis. **Recording Studio**: Procen Studio. **Sound Effects**: Sound Box. **Sound Production**: Magic Capsule.

Glass Mask (2005–2006)

Original Title: *Gurasu no Kamen*. **Status**: TV series (51 episodes). **Episode Length**: 30 minutes. **Director**: Mamoru Hamatsu. **Series Composition**: Toshimichi Saeki. **Music**:

Tamiya Terashima. **Original Manga**: Suzue Miuchi. **Character Designer**: Satoshi Hirayama. **Art Director**: Shunichiro Yoshihara. **Sound Director**: Toru Nakano. **Director of Photography**: Eiji Tsuchida. **Editing**: Tomoki Nagasaka. **Music Production**: Masaaki Fujita. **Sound Effects**: Aki Yokoyama, Masakazu Yokoyama. **Animation Production**: Tokyo Movie. **Production**: TMS Entertainment, TV Tokyo Media Net.

Honey and Clover (2005)

Original Title: *Hachimitsu to Clover*. **Status**: TV series (26 episodes). **Episode Length**: 25 minutes. **Director**: Ken'ichi Kasai. **Script**: Yousuke Kuroda. **Music**: Yuzo Hayashi. **Original Manga**: Chika Umino. **Character Designer**: Shuichi Shimamura. **Art Director**: Chikako Shibata. **Chief Animation Director**: Takahiko Yoshida. **Sound Director**: Jin Aketagawa. **Director of Photography**: Yutaka Kurosawa. **Producers**: Atsuya Takase, Hiroaki Nakane, Masarou Toyoshima, Nobuhiro Osawa. **Clothing Supervision**: Kazuki Kuraishi. **Editing**: Shigeru Nishiyama. **Food Designer**: Mitsuyo Sakuma. **Sound Effects**: Katsuhiro Nakano. **Animation Production**: J.C. Staff.

Honey and Clover II (2006)

Original Title: *Hachikuro II*. **Status**: TV series (12 episodes). **Episode Length**: 25 minutes. **Director**: Tatsuyuki Nagai. **Series Composition**: Yousuke Kuroda. **Script**: Yousuke Kuroda. **Music**: DEPAPEPE, Yuzo Hayashi. **Original Manga**: Umino. **Character Designer**: Shuichi Shimamura. **Art Director**: Chikako Shibata. **Chief Animation Director**: Takahiko Yoshida. **Sound Director**: Jin Aketagawa. **Color Setting**: Miyuki Ishida, Noboru Yoneda. **Editing**: Shigeru Nishiyama. **Sound Effects**: Masahiro Nakano. **Visual Art**: Ryusuke Shiino. **Animation**: J.C. Staff. **Music Production**: SME Records. **Sound Production**: Magic Capsule.

Kimikiss Pure Rouge (2007–2008)

Original Title: *Kimikiss Pure Rouge*. **Status**: TV series (24 episodes). **Episode Length**: 25 minutes. **Director**: Kenichi Kasai. **Series Composition**: Michihiro Tsuchiya. **Music**: Hikaru Nanase, Masaru Yokoyama, Noriyuki Iwadare. **Original Character Designer**: Kisai Takayama. **Character Design**: Kazunori Iwakura. **Art Director**: Shichiro Kobayashi. **Chief Animation Directors**: Masaru Hyodo Tomoyuki Shitaya, Tsuyoshi Kawada **Sound Director**: Jin Aketagawa. **Director of Photography**: Yutaka Kurosawa. **CG Designer**: Yoshihide Mukai. **Color Designer**: Tomomi Andou. **Color Setting**: Ayako Suenaga, Maya Muranaga. **Editing**: Shigeru Nishiyama. **Animation Production**: J.C. Staff. **Sound Effects**: Katsuhiro Nakano (Sound Box). **Sound Production**: Rie Tanaka. **Music Production**: Lantis. **Production**: Bandai Visual, Enterbrain, Inc. Hakuhodo DY Media Partners, J.C. Staff, Kimikiss Production Team.

Nodame Cantabile (2007)

Original Title: *Nodame Cantabile*. **Status**: TV series (23 episodes). **Episode Length**: 25 minutes. **Director**: Ken'ichi Kasai. **Series Composition**: Tomoko Konparu. **Music**: Suguru Matsutani. **Original Creator**: Tomoko Ninomiya. **Character Designer**: Shuichi Shimamura. **Art Director**: Shichiro Kobayashi. **Sound Director**: Jin Aketagawa. **Director of Photography**: Yoshio Ookouchi. **Producers**: Atsuya Takase, Kouji Yamamoto, Nobuhiro Osawa, Yukihiro Ito. **Color Designer**: Mayumi Tanahashi. **Digital**

Special Effects: Atsushi Sato. **Editing**: Shigeru Nishiyama. **Sound Effects**: Katsuhiro Nakano, Masafumi Watanabe, Masahiro Nakano. **Sound Production**: Rie Tanaka. **Animation Production**: J.C. Staff.

Nodame Cantabile: Finale (2010)

Original Title: *Nodame Cantabile: Finale*. **Status**: TV series (12 episodes). **Episode Length**: 24 minutes. **Director**: Chiaki Kon. **Series Composition**: Kazuki Nakashima. **Music**: Suguru Matsutani. **Original Creator**: Tomoko Ninomiya. **Character Designer**: Shuichi Shimamura. **Art Director**: Shichiro Kobayashi. **Chief Animation Director**: Yukako Tsuzuki. **Sound Director**: Jin Aketagawa. **Director of Photography**: Yoshio Ookouchi. **Producers**: Kouji Yamamoto (Fuji TV), Makoto Seino (Fuji TV), Nobuhiro Osawa. **Animation Producers**: Masao Ohashi, Yuji Matsukura. **CG Production**: Shinji Imai. **Classical Music Supervisor**: Daisuke Mogi. **Color Designer**: Mayumi Tanahashi. **Digital Special Effects**: Atsushi Sato. **Editing**: Shigeru Nishiyama. **French Language Supervision**: Erika Sudou. **Location Assistance**: Fumio Araki. **Music Production**: Haruki Tahara (WARP), Hiroaki Sano, Noritaka Suzuki, Satoshi Aoki, Takatomo Baba. **Music Supervision Assistance**: Erika Numamitsu. **Okawa Dialect Supervision**: Megumi Noda. **Animation Production**: GENCO, J.C. Staff. **Music Production**: Epic Records Japan. **Sound Effects**: Sound Box. **Sound Production**: Magic Capsule.

Nodame Cantabile: Paris (2008)

Original Title: *Nodame Cantabile: Paris*. **Status**: TV series (12 episodes). **Episode Length**: 23 minutes. **Director**: Chiaki Kon. **Series Composition**: Yoji Enokido. **Music**: Suguru Matsutani. **Original Creator**: Tomoko Ninomiya. **Character Designer**: Shuichi Shimamura. **Art Director**: Shichiro Kobayashi. **Chief Animation Directors**: Shuichi Shimamura, Yukako Tsuzuki. **Sound Director**: Jin Aketagawa. **Director of Photography**: Yoshio Ookouchi. **Producers**: Kouji Yamamoto (Fuji TV), Makoto Seino (Fuji TV), Nobuhiro Osawa. **CG Production**: Norikazu Kamibayashi. **Classical Music Supervisor**: Daisuke Mogi. **Color Designer**: Mayumi Tanahashi. **Digital Special Effects**: Atsushi Sato. **Editing**: Shigeru Nishiyama. **French Language Supervision**: Erika Sudou, Vincent Giry. **Location Assistance**: Fumio Araki. **Music Production**: Haruki Tahara (WARP), Hiroaki Sano, Noritaka Suzuki, Satoshi Aoki, Takatomo Baba. **Okawa Dialect Supervision**: Megumi Noda. **Orchestra Direction Supervisor**: Toshiaki Umeda. **Setting Production**: Atsushi Fujishiro. **Sound Effects**: Katsuhiro Nakano (Sound Box). **Animation Production**: GENCO, J.C. Staff. **Music Production**: Epic Records Japan, Sony Music Entertainment. **Sound Effects**: Sound Box. **Sound Production**: Magic Capsule.

Paradise Kiss (2005)

Original Title: *Paradise Kiss*. **Status**: TV series (12 episodes). **Episode Length**: 23 minutes. **Director**: Osamu Kobayashi. **Series Composition**: Kobayashi. **Script**: Kobayashi. **Music**: NARASAKI from COALTAR OF DEEPERS, THE BABYS. **Original Manga**: Ai Yazawa. **Character Designer**: Nobuteru Yuki. **Art Directors**: Asami Kiyokawa, Shinichi Uehara. **Sound Director**: Masafumi Mima. **Director of Photography**: Seiichi Morishita. **Producers**: Kouji Yamamoto, Masao Maruyama, Ryo Oyama, Tetsuya Watanabe, Yoko Matsusaki, Yukihiro Ito. **Chief Editor**: Yoshiko Kimura. **Clothing Designer**: Atsuro Tayama. **Color Designer**: Yoshinori Horikawa. **Digital Art**: Rei

Kawano. **Digital Effects**: Shinichi Igarashi. **Sound Effects**: Shizuo Kurahashi. **Special Effects**: Ayumi Arahata, Kumiko Taniguchi, Tomoe Ikeda, Toyohiko Sakakibara. **Texture Art**: Yuichi Suehiro. **Animation Production**: Madhouse Studios.

Piano: The Story of a Young Girl's Heart (2002–2003)

Original Title: *Piano: The Story of a Young Girl's Heart*. **Status**: TV series (10 episodes). **Episode Length**: 24 minutes. **Director**: Norihiko Sudo. **Script**: Mami Watanabe, Ryunosuke Kingetsu. **Music**: Hiroyuki Kouzu. **Original Creator**: Kousuke Fujishima. **Character Designer**: Kosuke Fujishima. **Art Director**: Junichi Higashi. **Sound Director**: Toru Watanabe. **Executive Producers**: Hiroyuki Soeda, Yoshiki Kumazawa, Yutaka Takahashi. **Producers**: Koichi Kikuchi, Shyukichi Kanda, Tomoko Takayama, Toshiaki Okuno, Yuuko Yamada. **Animation Production**: Oriental Light and Magic. **Production**: ANIMATE, KIDS STATION, Marine Entertainment, PIONEER LDC. **Recording Studio**: Sanpunzaka Studio. **Sound Effects**: Suwara Production. **Sound Production**: Half H.P Studio.

Princess Tutu (2002)

Original Title: *Purinsesu Chuchu*. **Status**: TV series (38 episodes). **Episode Length**: 23 minutes. **Chief Director**: Junichi Sato. **Series Director**: Shougo Kawamoto. **Directors**: Kiyoko Sayama, Shougo Kohmoto. **Series Composition**: Michiko Yokote. **Music**: Kaoru Wada. **Original Creator**: Ikuko Ito. **Original Manga**: Mizuo Shinonome. **Character Designer**: Ikuko Ito. **Art Director**: Kenichi Tajiri. **Chief Animation Director**: Ikuko Ito. **Sound Director**: Satoshi Motoyama. **Director of Photography**: Takeo Ogiwara. **Color Designer**: Yoshimi Kawakami **Editing**: Megumi Uchida, Mutsumi Takemiya, Takeshi Seyama. **Animation Production**: Hal Film Maker. **Production**: GANSIS. **Sound Production**: Omnibus Promotion.

Swan Lake (movie; 1981)

Original Title: *Sekai Meisaku Douwa Hakuchou no Mizuumi*. **Status**: movie. **Director**: Koro Yabuki. **Length**: 75 minutes. **Script**: Hirokazu Fuse. **Music**: Peter Tchaikovsky. **Art Director**: Tadanao Tsuji. **Animation Director**: Takuo Noda. **Director of Photography**: Hiroshi Mekuro. **Audio Director**: Yasuo Ida. **Production**: Toei Animation.

Touka Gettan (2007)

Original Title: *Touka Gettan*. **Status**: TV series (26 episodes). **Episode Length**: 30 minutes. **Director**: Yuji Yamaguchi. **Original Creator**: Root. **Series Composition**: Tomomi Mochizuki. **Scenario**: Ai Shimizu, Mamiko Noto. **Music**: Akifumi Tada. **Original Character Designer**: Carnelian. **Character Designer**: Asako Nishida. **Art Director**: Toshihisa Koyama. **Chief Animation Director**: Asako Nishida. **3D Animation**: Akira Inaba, Naoyuki Ikeno. **Background Art**: Katsuhiro Yamada, Masami Oishi, Megumi Ogawa, Naoki Aoyama, Yukiko Nakayama, Yukiko Ogawa. **Sound Director**: Kouji Tsujitani. **Color Designer**: Eiko Kitazume. **Animation Production**: Studio Deen. **Sound Production**: Darks Production.

Yakitate!! Japan (2004–2006)

Original Title: *Yakitate!! Japan*. **Status**: TV series (69 episodes). **Episode Length**: 25 minutes. **Director**: Yasunao Aoki. **Series Composition**: Katsuyuki Sumisawa. **Script**:

Akatsuki Yamatoya, Katsuyuki Sumisawa, Tetsuko Takahashi, Toshifumi Kawase. **Episode Director**: Shin'ichi Masaki. **Music**: Taku Iwasaki. **Original Creator**: Takashi Hashiguchi. **Character Designers**: Atsuo Tobe, Hiromi Maezawa, Yoshihito Hishinuma. **Art Director**: Shigemi Ikeda. **Animation Directors**: Ken Sakuma, Yasushi Shingou. **Sound Director**: Eriko Kimura. **Producers**: Hideyuki Tomioka, Norio Yamakawa. **Color Coordination**: Miyuki Sato. **Color Setting**: Kenji Chiba. **Editing**: Tomoaki Tsurubuchi. **Photography**: Emi Inoue, Kumiko Ito, Yoshio Sugizawa, Youhei Sakurai, **Sound Effects**: Masakazu Yokoyama. **Sound Production**: Takashi Hayashi, Takuya Ono. **Special Effects**: Toshio Hasegawa. **Animation Production**: Sunrise. **Digital Effect**: Sunrise D.I.D. **Production**: Aniplex. **Sound Production**: Tohokushinsha Film Corporation.

Secondary Titles

Antique Bakery (TV series; dir. Yoshiaki Okumura, 2008)
Bartender (TV series; dir. Masaki Watanabe, 2006)
Ef—A Tale of Memories (TV series; dir. Shin Oonuma, 2007)
Ef—A Tale of Melodies (TV series; dir. Shin Oonuma, 2008)
Evangelion Shin Gekijouban: Ha—Evangelion: 2:0—You Can (Not) Advance (movie; dirs. Hideaki Anno, Masayuki, Kazuya Tsurumaki, 2009)
Evangelion Shin Gekijouban: Jo—Evangelion: 1.0—You Are (Not) Alone (movie; dirs. Hideaki Anno, Masayuki, Kazuya Tsurumaki, 2007)
GA: Geijutsuka Art Design Class (TV series; dir. Hiroaki Sakurai, 2009)
Gilgamesh (TV series; dir. Masahiko Murata, 2003–2004)
Kanon (TV series; dir. Tatsuya Ishihara, 2006)
The Melody of Oblivion (TV series; dir. Hiroshi Nishikiori, 2004)
Moyashimon (TV series; dir. Yuichiro Yano, 2007)
Mushi-Shi (TV series; dir. Hiroshi Nagahama, 2005)
Myself; Yourself (TV series; dir. Testuaki Matsuda, 2007)
NANA (TV series; dirs. Morio Asaka and Norimitsu Suzuki, 2006–2007)
Neon Genesis Evangelion (TV series; dir. Hideaki Anno, 1995–1996)
Neon Genesis Evangelion: Death & Rebirth (movie; dirs. Hideaki Anno, Masayuki, Kazuya Tsurumaki, 1997)
Neon Genesis Evangelion: End of Evangelion (movie; dirs. Hideaki Anno and Kazuya Tsurumaki, 1997)
Shinkyoku Soukai Polyphonica (TV series; dir. Junichi Watanabe, 2007)
Shinkyoku Soukai Polyphonica Crimson S (TV series; dir. Toshimasa Suzuki, 2009)
Skip Beat! (TV series; dir. Kiyoko Sayama, 2008–2009)
Sola (TV series; dir. Tomoki Kobayashi, 2007)
Speed Grapher (TV series; dirs. Kunihisa Sugishima and Masashi Ishihama, 2005)
The Tale of Genji (TV series; dir. Osamu Dezaki, 2009)
Tenpou Ibun Ayashi Ayakashi (TV series; dir. Hiroshi Nishikiori, 2006–2007)
True Tears (TV series; dir. Junji Nishimura, 2008)
Yumeiro Pâtissière (TV series; dir. Iku Suzuki, 2009)

Additional Titles

Chance Pop Session (TV series; dir. Susumu Kudu, 2001)
Chocolate Underground (ONA series; Takayuki Hamana; dir. 2008)
Clannad (movie; dir. Osamu Dezaki, 2007–2008)
Clannad (TV series; dir. Tatsuya Ishihara, 2007–2008)
Comic Party (TV series; Norihiko Sudo, 2001)
The Complete Works of Yuri Norstein (movie compilation; dir. Yuri Norstein, 2006)
Cosplay Complex (OVA series; dir. Shinichiro Kimura, 2002)
Exquisite Short Films of Kihachiro Kawamoto (movie compilation; dir. Kihachiro Kawamoto, 2008)
Full Moon O Sagashite (TV series; dir. Toshiyuki Kato, 2002–2003)
Gauche the Cellist (movie; dir. Isao Takahata, 1982)
Gokinjo Monogatari (TV series; dir. Atsutoshi Umezawa, 1995–1996)
Gravitation (TV series; dir. Bob Shirohata, 2000–2001)
The Illusionist (movie; dir. Sylvain Chomet, 2010)
Kaleido Star (TV series; dir. Junichi Sato, 2003–2004)
Kujibiki Unbalance (OVA series; dir. Takashi Ikehata, 2004)
Kujibiki Unbalance (TV series; dir. Tsutomu Mizushima, 2006)
Lotte Reiniger — Fairy Tales (movie compilation; dir. Lotte Reiniger; 2008)
Only Yesterday (movie; dir. Isao Takahata, 1991)
Otaku no Video (OVA series; dir. Takeshi Mori, 1991)
The Piano Forest (movie; dir. Masayuki Kojima, 2007)
Puppet Films of Jiří Trnka (movie compilation; dir. Jiří Trnka, 2000)
Sailor Moon (TV series; dir. Junichi Sato, 1992–1993)
Tsuyokiss — Cool x Sweet (TV series; dir. Shinichiro Kimura, 2006)
Whisper of the Heart (movie; dir. Yoshifumi Kondou, 1995)

Appendix

Japanese Art Periods Timeline

Paleolithic	35,000–14,000 BC
Jōmon period	14,000–300 BC
Yayoi period	300 BC–AD 250
Yamato period	250–710
Kofun period	250–538
Asuka period	538–710
Nara period	710–794
Heian period	794–1185
Kamakura period	1185–1333
Muromachi period	1336–1573
Nanboku-chō period	1336–1392
Sengoku period	1467–1573
Azuchi Momoyama period	1573–1603
Edo period	1603–1868
Meiji period	1868–1912
Taishō period	1912–1926
Shōwa period	1926–1989
Heisei period	1989–present

BIBLIOGRAPHY

The websites cited in this bibliography were active at the time of writing. Their long-term existence cannot be assured because of the volatile nature of the world wide web.

Albright, D. 2000. *Untwisting the Serpent: Modernism in Music, Literature, and Other Arts.* Chicago and London: University of Chicago Press.
Ausoni, A. 2008. *Music in Art.* Trans. S. Sartarelli. Los Angeles: J. Paul Getty Museum.
Avella, N. 2004. *Graphic Japan: From Woodblock and Zen to Manga and Kawaii.* Hove, East Sussex, England: RotoVision.
Barker, C. 2002. *Making Sense of Cultural Studies—Central Problems and Critical Debates.* London: Sage.
Bashou, M. 1994. *Anthology of Japanese Literature*, ed. D. Keene. New York: Grove.
Baudelaire, C. 1961. [1857]. *Les fleurs du mal.* Paris: Garnier.
Baudelaire, C. 1965a. "The Salon of 1846." In *Art in Paris, 1845–1862: Salons and Other Exhibitions.* Trans. J. Mayne. Oxford: Oxford University Press.
Baudelaire, C. 1965b. "The Salon of 1851." In *Art in Paris, 1845–1862: Salons and Other Exhibitions.* Trans. J. Mayne. Oxford: Oxford University Press.
Bordwell, D. 1985. *Narration in the Fiction Film.* Madison: University of Wisconsin Press.
Bowring, R. 2004, *Murasaki Shikibu: The Tale of Genji*, 2d ed. Cambridge: Cambridge University Press.
Butler, C. 2004. *Pleasure and the Arts: Enjoying Literature, Painting, and Music.* Oxford: Oxford University Press.
Butler, J. 1990. *Gender Trouble.* London and New York: Routledge.
Butler, J. 1993. *Bodies that Matter.* London and New York: Routledge.
Butler, J. 1994. "Gender as Performance." *Radical Philosophy* 67. http://www.theory.org.uk/but-int1.htm.
Caillois, R. 1973. *La Dyssymmétrie.* Paris: Gallimard.
Calvino, I. 1993. [1981.] *If On a Winter's Night a Traveler.* Trans. W. Weaver. London: David Campbell.
Calza, G. C. 2007. *Japan Style.* London and New York: Phaidon.
Canetti, E. 1984. *Crowds and Power.* New York: Farrar, Straus and Giroux.
Cardozo, K. H. 2003. "The Power of a Name." *Suite 101.* http://www.suite101.com/article.cfm/baby_names/100021.

Certeau, M. de. 1984. *The Practice of Everyday Life*. Trans. S. Rendall. Berkeley: University of California Press.
Clements, J., and H. McCarthy. 2006. *The Anime Encyclopaedia: A Guide to Japanese Animation Since 1917*. Rev. and expanded Ed. Berkeley, CA: Stone Bridge.
Darling, M. 2001. *Art Journal*. Vol. 60, No. 3 (August).
Dawson, C. 1901. "Japan and its Colour Prints." In *The Process Yearbook*. Bradford, England: Percy, Lund and Humphries.
Debussy, C. 2005. *Correspondence 1872–1918*, ed. F. Lesure and D. Herlin. Paris: Éditions Gallimard.
Derrida, J. 1981. [1972.] *Positions*. Trans. A. Bass. Chicago: University of Chicago Press.
Derrida, J. 1998. [1967.] *Of Grammatology*. Trans. G. C. Spivak. Baltimore: Johns Hopkins University Press.
Di Silvio, R. "Peter Tchaikovsky." http://www.d-vista.com/OTHER/tchai.html.
Dorment, R. 1994. *Whistler*, ed. R. Dorment and M. F. MacDonald. London: Tate Gallery.
Dütching, H. 1997. *Paul Klee — Painting Music*. Trans. P. Crowe. Munich, Berlin, London and New York: Prestel.
Ekuan, K. 2000. *The Aesthetics of the Japanese Lunchbox*. Trans. D. Kenny. Cambridge, MA: MIT Press.
Eliot, T. S. 1944. "Little Gidding." *Four Quartets*. http://www.tristan.icom43.net/quartets/gidding.html.
Emerson, R. W. "Hue Quotes." *ThinkExist*. http://thinkexist.com/quotes/with/keyword/hue/.
Eng, L. 2001. "The Politics of Otaku." http://www.cjas.org/~leng/otaku-p.htm.
Faulkner, R. 2009. "Folk Art." In *Japanese Art and Design*, ed. J. Earle. London: V & A.
Fénéon, F. 1966. *Au-deláde l'impressionisme*, ed. F. Cachin. Paris: Hermann.
Ferrell, R. 1991. "Life Threatening Life: Angela Carter and the Uncanny." In *The Illusion of Life*, ed. A. Chodolenko. Sydney: Power.
Frampton, K. 1995. "Essay — Thoughts on Tadao Ando." *The Pritzer Architecture Prize*. http://www.pritzkerprize.com/laureates/1995/essay.html.
Frankel, S. 2010a. "In Praise of Shadows." In *Future Beauty: 30 Years of Japanese Fashion*, ed. A. Fukai, B. Vinken, S. Frankel, H. Kurino. London and New York: Merrell.
Frankel, S. 2010b. "Tradition and Innovation." In *Future Beauty: 30 Years of Japanese Fashion*, ed. A. Fukai, B. Vinken, S. Frankel, H. Kurino. London and New York: Merrell.
Fukai, A. 2010a. "Preface." In *Future Beauty: 30 Years of Japanese Fashion*, ed. A. Fukai, B. Vinken, S. Frankel, H. Kurino. London and New York: Merrell.
Fukai, A. 2010b. "Future Beauty: 30 Years of Japanese Fashion." In *Future Beauty: 30 Years of Japanese Fashion*, ed. A. Fukai, B. Vinken, S. Frankel, H. Kurino. London and New York: Merrell.
Furniss, M. 2007. *Art in Motion — Animation Aesthetics*. Rev. ed. New Barnet, Herts: John Libbey.
Gage, J. 1993. *Colour and Culture*. London: Thames and Hudson.
Gatten, A. 1977. "A Wisp of Smoke: Scent and Character in *The Tale of Genji*." *Monumenta Nipponica*, vol. 32, no. 1 (Spring), pp. 35–48. Sophia University.
Girard, R. 1976. *Deceit, Desire, and the Novel: Self and Other in Literary Structure*. Baltimore: Johns Hopkins University Press.

von Goethe, J. W. 1978. *Theory of Colours*. Trans. by C. L. Eastlake. Boston: Bulfinch.
Grassmuck, V. 1990. "'I'm Alone, but Not Lonely': Japanese Otaku-Kids colonize the Realm of Information and Media. A Tale of Sex and Crime from a Faraway Place." http://www.cjas.org/~leng/otaku-e.htm.
Haga, T. 1982. "Color and Design in Tokugawa Japan." In *Japan Color*, ed. I. Tanaka and K. Koike (unnumbered pages). San Francisco: Chronicle.
"Hikikomori." Wikipedia. http://en.wikipedia.org/wiki/Hikikomori.
Hume, N. G. 1995. *Japanese Aesthetics and Culture: A Reader*. Albany: State University of New York Press.
"The Jackson Symphony." 2010. "Understanding Relationships between Art and Music: A Teaching Unit for Art, Music and Classroom Teachers." http://thejacksonsymphony.org/assets/downloadables/Understanding%20Relationships%20Between%20Art%20and%20Music%202010-11.pdf.
"Japan Smitten by Love of Cute." 2006. http://www.theage.com.au/news/people/cool-or-infantile/2006/06/18/1150569208424.html.
"Japanese Aesthetics." 2005. *Stanford Encyclopedia of Philosophy*. http://plato.stanford.edu/entries/japanese-aesthetics/.
"Japanese Traditional and Ceremonial Colors." *TemariKai.com*. http://www.temarikai.com/meaningoftraditionalcolors.htm.
Juniper, A. 2003. *Wabi Sabi: The Japanese Art of Impermanence*. Tokyo, Rutland, and Singapore: Tuttle.
Junod, P. 2000. "The New *Paragone*: Paradoxes and Contradictions of Pictorial Musicalism." In *The Arts Entwined: Music and Painting in the Nineteenth Century*, ed. M. L. Morton and P. L. Schmunk. New York and London: Routledge.
Kandinsky, W. 1955. *Rückblicke*. Baden-Baden: Woldemar Klein Verlag.
Kandinsky, W. 1977. [1910.] *Concerning the Spiritual in Art*. Trans. M. T. H. Sadler. New York: Dover.
Kandinsky, W. 1979. [1926; 1928.] *Point and Line to Plane*. Trans. H. Dearstyne and H. Rebay. New York: Dover.
Kassner, R. 1942. *Gli elementi dell'umana grandezza*. Milan: Bompiani.
Katzumie, M. 1980. "Japan Style: Yesterday, Today and Tomorrow." In *Japan Style*. Tokyo: Kodansha International.
Kawai, H. 1988. *The Japanese Psyche, Major Motifs in the Fairy Tales of Japan*. Dallas: Spring.
Keehn, L. F. [a]. "Hungry Ghosting for More." *Swindle*. Issue 12. http://swindlemagazine.com/issue12/heisuke-kitazawa/.
Keehn, L. F. [b]. "Takashi Murakami." *Swindle*. Issue Icons 2. http://swindlemagazine.com/issueicons2/takashi-murakami/.
"Kimono History: The Heian Era." http://www.bookmice.net/darkchilde/japan/khist4.html.
Kinsella, S. 1996. "Cuties in Japan." In *Women, Media and Consumption in Japan*, edited by L. Skov and B. Moeran. Honolulu: University of Hawaii Press.
Klee, P. 1974. *The Diaries of Paul Klee: 1898–1918*, ed. F. Klee. Berkeley: University of California Press.
Kondo, S. 2007. "Logo of the Agency of Cultural Affairs." www.bunka.go.jp/english/pdf/h21_logo.pdf.

Koyama-Richard, B. 2010. *Japanese Animation From Painted Scrolls to Pokémon*. Paris: Flammarion.
Lamarre, T. 2004–2005. "An Introduction to Otaku Movement." *EnterText* 4.1.
Lee, D. 2005. "Inside Look at Japanese Cute Culture." *Uniorb*. http://uniorb.com/ATREND/Japanwatch/cute.htm.
Lim, S. 2007. *Japanese Style — Designing with Nature's Beauty*. Layton, UT: Gibbs Smith.
Lippit, Y. 2008. "Figure and Facture in the *Genji* Scrolls — Text, Calligraphy, Paper, and Painting." In *Envisioning The Tale of Genji: Media, Gender, and Cultural Production*, ed. H. Shirane. New York: Columbia University Press.
Lockspeiser, E. 1978. *Debussy: His Life and Mind*. Vol. 2. Cambridge: Cambridge University Press.
Lonsdale, S. 2008. *Japanese Style*. London: Carlton Books.
MacWilliams, M. W. 2008. "Introduction." In *Japanese Visual Culture: Explorations in the World of Manga and Anime*, ed. M. W. Williams. Armonk, NY, and London: M. E. Sharpe.
Mahnke, F. H. 1978. *Color, Environment, and Response*. New York: Van Nostrand Reinhold.
McWilliams, D. 1991. *Norman McLaren on the Creative Process*. Montreal: National Film Board of Canada.
Mizuno, K. 2005. *Styles and Motifs of Japanese Gardens*. Tokyo: Japan Publications Trading.
MOFA (Ministry of Foreign Affairs, Japan). 2007. "Introduction." *Creative Japan*. http://www.uk.emb-japan.go.jp/en/creativejapan/introduction.html.
Morris, I. 1994. *The World of the Shining Prince: Court Life in Ancient Japan*. New York, Tokyo and London: Kodansha International.
Nagatomo, S. 2010. "Japanese Zen Buddhist Philosophy." In *The Stanford Encyclopedia of Philosophy* (Winter 2010 Edition), edited by E. N. Zalta. http://plato.stanford.edu/archives/win2010/entries/japanese-zen/.
Nakashima, M. 2003. *Nature Form and Spirit: The Life and Legacy of George Nakashima*. New York: Harry N. Abrahams.
Natsume, S. 1984. *The Three Cornered World*. Trans. E. McClellen. London: Arrow.
Okakura, K. [1906.] 1964. *The Book of Tea*. Tokyo: Charles E. Tuttle.
Ota, H. 1966. *Japanese Architecture and Gardens*. Tokyo: Kokusai Bunka Shinkokai.
Pascal, D. "Japanese Aesthetics and the Nature of Anime." *Unreal City: Literature of the Twenty-First Century*. http://www.davidpascal.com/unrealcity/reviews/anime.html.
Peacock, K. 1985. "Synaesthetic Perception: Alexander Scriabin's Color Hearing." *Music Perception* 2, no. 4 (Summer).
Poitras, G. 2006. "The Word 'Otaku' Today." *Newtype USA*, vol. 05, no. 12.
Pound, E. 1936. "The Chinese Written Character as a Medium For Poetry." Adapted from Ernest Fenollosa. Extracts from: http://www.levity.com/digaland/celestial/fenollosa/fenollosa.html.
Pound, E. 1980. *Ezra Pound and the Visual Arts*, ed. H. Zinnes. New York: New Directions.
"Rebuild of *Evangelion*." Wikipedia. http://en.wikipedia.org/wiki/Rebuild_of_Evangelion.
Reeve, J. 2006. *Japanese Art in Detail*. London: British Museum.

Richie, D. 2007. *A Tractate on Japanese Aesthetics*. Berkeley, CA: Stone Bridge Press.
Sadao, T. S., and S. Wada. 2009. *Discovering the Arts of Japan*. New York: Abbeville.
Sagan, C. "Carl Sagan Quotes." *Brainy Quote*. http://www.brainyquote.com/quotes/authors/c/carl_sagan.html.
Saito, Y. 2007. "The Moral Dimension of Japanese Aesthetics." *Journal of Aesthetics and Art Criticism* 65 (1), 85–97.
Samuels, D. 2007. "Let's Die Together: Why Is Anonymous Group Suicide So Popular in Japan?" *The Atlantic Monthly*. May.
Santos, C. 2005. "*Honey and Clover*." Anime News Network. http://www.animenewsnetwork.co.uk/review/honey-and-clover.
Shaw-Miller, S. 2002. *Visible Deeds of Music: Art and Music from Wagner to Cage*. New Haven and London: Yale University Press.
"The Shinto Tradition." http://www.shadowrun4.com/resources/downloads/catalyst_streetmagic_preview2.pdf.
Shirane, H. 2005. "Performance, Visuality, and Textuality: The Case of Japanese Poetry." *Oral Tradition*, 20/2, pp. 217–232.
Signac, P. 1978. [1899.] *D'Eugène Delacroix au néo-impressionnisme*. Paris: Hermann.
Slade, T. 2009. *Japanese Fashion: A Cultural History*. Oxford and New York: Berg.
Snyder, M. 2008. "The Swan Maiden's Feathered Robe." *The Endicott Studio Journal of Mythic Arts: Farewell Issue*. http://www.endicott-studio.com/rdrm/rrSwan.html.
Sontag, Susan. 2003. "The Image World." In *Visual Culture: The Reader*, ed. J. Evans and S. Hall. London: Sage.
"The Spirit of Sumi-e: An Introduction to East Asian Brush Painting." 2009. *Prairiewoods*. http://prairiewoods.org/the-spirit-of-sumi-e-an-introduction-to-east-asian-brush-painting-091911.
Stanley-Baker, J. 2000. *Japanese Art*. London and New York: Thames and Hudson.
Stelzer, O. 1964. *Die Vorgeschichte der abstrakten Kunst: Denkmodelle und Vorbilder*. Munich: Piper.
Suzuki, D. T. 1970. *Zen and Japanese Culture*. Princeton, NJ: Princeton University Press, Bollingen Foundation.
Tanizaki, J. 2001. [1933.] *In Praise of Shadows*. Trans. T. J. Harper and E. G. Seidensticker. London: Vintage.
Taruskin, R. 1996. *Stravinsky and the Russian Tradition: A Biography of the Works through Mavra*. Berkeley and Los Angeles: University of California Press.
"Temari (toy)." *Wikipedia*. http://en.wikipedia.org/wiki/Temari_(toy).
Ueda, M. 1967. *Literary and Art Theories in Japan*. Cleveland, OH: Case Western Reserve University Press.
Vergo, P. 2010. *The Music of Painting: Music, Modernism and the Visual Arts from the Romantics to John Cage*. London: Phaidon.
Vinken, B. 2010. "The Empire Designs Back." In *Future Beauty: 30 Years of Japanese Fashion*, ed. A. Fukai, B. Vinken, S. Frankel, H. Kurino. London and New York: Merrell.
Vodvarka, F. 1999. "Aspects of Color." *Midwest Facilitation Network*. http://www.midwest-facilitators.net/downloads/mfn_19991025_frank_vodvarka.pdf.
Warner, M. 2000. *No Go the Bogeyman*. London: Vintage.
Whistler, J. A. M. 1967. [1892.] *The Gentle Art of Making Enemies*. New York: Dover.

Williams, R. 2001. *The Animator's Survival Kit*. London: Faber and Faber.
Woodson, Y. 2006. "On Idleness." In *Traditional Japanese Arts and Culture*. Honolulu: University of Hawaii Press.
Wordsworth, W. 1994. *The Collected Poems of William Wordsworth*. Ware, Herts.: Wordsworth Editions.
Yagi, K. 1982. *A Japanese Touch for Your Home*. Tokyo: Kodansha.
Yanagi, Soetsu. 1989. *The Unknown Craftsman: A Japanese Insight into Beauty*. Tokyo: Kodansha International.
Yanagi, Sori. 1991. "The Discovery of Beauty: Soetsu Yanagi and Folkcrafts." In *Mingei: Masterpieces of Japanese Folkcraft*. Japan Folk Craft Museum. Tokyo: Kodansha International.
Yeats, W. B. 1996. *The Collected Poems of W. B. Yeats*, ed. R. J. Finneran. New York: Scribner.
Yoshida, M. 1980. "Japanese Aesthetic Ideals." In *Japan Style*. Tokyo: Kodansha International.
Yoshida, M. 1982. *The Compact Culture*. Tokyo: Toyo Kogyo.
Yoshida, M. 1984. *The Hybrid Culture: What Happened When East and West Met*. Hiroshima: Mazda.
Yoshida, M. 1985. *The Culture of Anima: Supernature in Japanese Life*. Hiroshima: Mazda.

INDEX

Adam, A. 7
Alberti, L.B. 201
Albright, D. 141, 164
Alciato, A. 132
Ando, T. 26, 51
Antique Bakery 32, 170, 171, 172
Aristotle 9
Ausoni, A. 132
Avella, N. 21, 23, 28

Bach, J.S. 7, 210
Bakuman 105–109, 172–173
Barker, C. 19, 26
Bartender 171–2
Bashou, M. 42
Baudelaire, C. 9, 35–36, 97
Beck: Mongolian Chop Squad 128, 142–146, 209
Beer, U. 96
Beethoven, L. van 7, 183, 190, 202, 209, 212
Berlioz, H. 7
Bizet, G. 183
Böcklin, A. 7
Boethius 125
Bonnard, P. 21
Bootleg 121
Bordwell, D. 109
Bowring, R. 114
Brahms, J. 7, 194
Braque, G. 7
Burty, P. 22
Butler, C. 109
Butler, J. 182

Cage, J. 214, 215
Caillois, R. 53
Calvino, I. 45
Calza, G.C. 21, 30–31, 44, 58, 60, 87, 160
Canetti, E. 161

Cardozo, H.K. 72
de Certeau, M. 156
Cézanne, P. 28, 145
Chagall, M. 7
Chance Pop Session 141, 209
Chéret, J. 23
Chocolate Underground 121
Chomet, S. 176–7
Chopin, F. 22, 142, 183
Clements, J. 149
The Comedy of Errors 64
Comic Party 150
The Complete Works of Yuri Norstein 176
La Corda d'Oro 122, 130–141, 142, 143
Cosplay Complex 149

Darling, M. 27
Dawson, C. 29
Debussy, C. 7, 192–193, 203–204
Degas, E. 26
Delacroix, E. 187
Derrida, J. 5
Di Silvio, R. 99
Dorment, R. 22
Dütching, H. 14

Ef—A Tale of Melodies 161–162
Ef—A Tale of Memories 67–68
Ekuan, K. 31–2
Eliot, T.S. 42
Eng, L. 146
Escher, M.C. 49
Exquisite Short Film of Kihachiro Kawamoto 112
Eyes Wide Shut 123

Fantin-Latour, H. 7
Faulkner, R. 6
Fénéon, F. 145
Ferrell, R. 29–30
Frampton, K. 52

Frankel, S. 38, 54
Freud, S. 30
Friedrich, C.D. 104
Fukai, A. 32, 43, 46, 52
Furniss, M. 30

GA: Geijutsuka Art Design Class 89
Gage, J. 9, 214
Gatten, A. 17
Gaugin, P. 28, 187
Gershwin, G. 194
Ghost Slayers Ayashi see *Tenpou Ibun Ayashi Ayakashi*
Gilgamesh 212–214
Girard, R. 175
Glass Mask 162–165
Goethe, J.W. von 9, 10–11
Gokinjo Monogatari 166
Gossec, F.J. 140
Goya, F. 7
Granados, E. 7
Grassmuck, V. 146–147
Gravitation 145–146, 209
Gropius, W. 21

Haga, T. 89, 92
Handel, G.F. 209
Hartmann, V. 7
Hedgehog in the Fog 176
Hendrix, J. 190
Hoffmann, E.T.A. 177
Hokusai, K. 192
Honey and Clover 77–89, 98–106
Hume, N.G. 43–44

The Illusionist 176–177
Ingres, J.A.D. 192

J.C. STAFF 203
La Joie de Vivre 140
Juniper, A. 42

Kaleido Star 65
Kamo no Choumei 44
Kandinsky, W. 10, 11, 12, 102, 103, 213–4
Kanon 120, 210, 212
Kasai, K. 105, 106, 172, 173, 188, 203, 204, 205
Kassner, R. 161
Katzumie, M. 54, 56
Kawai, H. 40
Kawakubo, R. 38, 43, 53
Kawamoto, K. 112
Keehn, L.F. 26, 27
Kimikiss Pure Rouge 12, 106, 173–5
Kinsella, S. 47

Kitakawa, H. (a.k.a. PCP) 26
Klee, P. 11, 12–14
Klimt, G. 7
Kobayashi, O. 166
Kondo, S. 18–19, 24
Koyama-Richard, B. 24–25, 29
Kubrick, S. 123
Kujibiki Unbalance 152, 153, 154
Kuki, S. 61
Kuma, K. 51
Kupka, F. 204
Kyoto Animation (KyoAni) 212

Lamarre, T. 151–152
Lasso, O. di 193
Le Corbusier 21
Lee, D. 47
Leonardo da Vinci 202
Lim, S. 51
Lippit, Y. 77
Liszt, F. 7
Lockspeiser, E. 193
Lonsdale, S. 23, 32, 33, 57
Lotte Reiniger — Fairy Tales 75
Lowry, R. 212

MacWilliams, M.W. 156
Mahnke, F.H. 96
Mallarmé, S. 203
Manet, E. 21, 203
Marc, F. 11
The Matrix 66
Mauclair, C. 193
McCarthy, H. 149
McLaren, N. 12
The Melody of Oblivion 66–67
Mendelssohn, F. 183, 193
Mendelssohn, M. 193
Miuchi, S. 162
Miyake, I. 53
Mizuno, K. 25
Monet, C. 21, 203
Morris, I. 16
Morris, W. 6
Moyashimon 122
Mozart, W.A. 7, 183, 189, 190, 194, 201, 208
Murakami, T. 26–27
Mushi-Shi 76
Mussorgsky, M. 7
Myself; Yourself 69–70, 209

Nagatomo, S. 60–61
Nakashima, G. 113
NANA 63–64, 65, 66, 209
Natsume, S. 60

Neon Genesis Evangelion 209–211
Neon Genesis Evangelion: Death & Rebirth 209, 210
Neon Genesis Evangelion: End of Evangelion 210, 211
Neutra, R. 21
Newton, I. 10, 11
Nietzsche, F. 140
Nodame Cantabile 9, 12, 13, 184–208, 209
Nolde, E. 98–99
Norstein, Y. 176

Okada, T. 149
Okakura, K. 50–51
Only Yesterday 65–66
Ota, H. 129
Otaku no Video 149

Pachelbel, J. 210, 212
Palestrina, G.P. da 193
Palladio, A. 202
Paradise Kiss 166–170
Pascal, D. 41, 42
PCP (Kitakawa, H.) 26
Peacock, K. 98
The Piano Forest 142, 209
Piano: The Story of a Young Girl's Heart 61–63, 92–93
Picasso, P. 28, 87, 140
Plato 9, 125
Poitras, G. 147, 149
Pound, E. 34, 163
Princess Tutu 98, 106, 176, 177–184, 209
Prokofiev, S. 183
Puppet Films of Ji_i Trnka 112
Pythagoras 202

Rachmaninov, S. 7, 194, 196
RahXephon 215
Raphael 7
Ravel, M. 7, 183, 186, 203, 204
Rebuild of Evangelion 211
Reeve, J. 14–15, 20, 36, 50
Reiniger, L. 75
Rich, R. 70
Richie, D. 36
Rimsky-Korsakov, N. 183
Rohe, M. van der 21
Runge, O.P. 104

Sadao, T.S. 20
Sailor Moon 183
St. Augustine 125
St. John of the Cross 95
Saint-Saens, C. 183
Saito, Y. 31

Samuels, D. 148
Santos, C. 105
Satie, E. 183
Sato, J. 183
Schubert, F. 137
Schumann, R. 7, 183
Scriabin, A. 97–98
Sejima, K. 26
Shakespeare, W. 64, 73
Shaw-Miller, S. 8, 215
Shearer, A. 121
Shikao, S. 105
Shimoku, K. 153
Shinkyoku Soukai Polyphonica 66, 209
Shinkyoku Soukai Polyphonica Crimson S 66
Shirane, H. 31, 157–158
Shounagon, S. 46
Signac, P. 192
Skip Beat! 65, 66, 106, 209
Slade, T. 53–54, 136–137
Snyder, M. 72–74
Sola 123–124
Speed Grapher 122–123
SPITZ 105
Stanley-Baker, J. 56, 77
Stelzer, O. 193
Strauss, J. 183
Stravinsky, I. 7, 34–35, 188
Studio Gainax 149, 151
Sugiyama, T. 46
Svankmajer, J. 100
Swan Lake 70–74, 75, 97–98
The Swan Princess 70

The Tale of Genji 20, 76–77, 128, 129, 130, 161, 162
Tanizaki, J. 24, 37–39
Taruskin, R. 34–35
Taut, B. 21
Tchaikovsky, P.I. 7, 70, 74, 98, 177, 183, 184
Tenpou Ibun Ayashi Ayakashi (a.k.a. *Ghost Slayers Ayashi*) 75–76
Touka Gettan 9, 29, 124–128, 137, 207, 209
Toulouse-Lautrec, H. de 21, 23
Trnka, J. 112
True Tears 69–70
Tsuyokiss—Cool x Sweet 65
Turner, J.M.W. 192
Tylor, E.B. 142

Ueda, M. 47
Umino, C. 101–104

Van Gogh, V. 21

Varèse, E. 193
Verlaine, P. 203
Vergo, P. 10, 36, 104, 186–187, 214
Vinken, B. 52–53
Vodvarka, F. 96, 99

Wada, K. 184
Wada, S. 20
Wagner, R. 7, 12, 104, 145, 183, 214
Warner, M. 95–96
Whisper of the Heart 65
Whistler, J. A. M. 21, 22, 187
Wilhelmj, A. 210
Williams, R. 12
Woodson, Y. 40

Wordsworth, W. 86, 145
Wright, F. L. 21

Yagi, K. 129
Yakitate!! Japan 32, 115–121, 122, 128
Yamamoto, Y. 32, 38, 43
Yanagi, Muneyoshi 6
Yanagi, Soetsu 43, 158
Yanagi, Sori 33
Yazawa, A. 166
Yeats, W.B. 80
Yoshida, M. 14, 15–16, 28, 42, 75, 91, 111–112, 113, 117, 118, 129, 158, 159
YUKI 105
Yumeiro Pâtissière 32, 121–122